Customer-Centric Organisation

Dr. V. Nagajothi
B. Sc., MBA., PhD.
Assistant Professor Selection Grade
SRM B School, SRM University
Vadapalani,
Chennai - 600 026.

FIRST EDITION : 2010

Himalaya Publishing House

MUMBAI • NEW DELHI • NAGPUR • BENGALURU • HYDERABAD • CHENNAI • PUNE • LUCKNOW • AHMEDABAD • ERNAKULAM • BHUBANESWAR • INDORE • KOLKATA

First Edition : 2010

Published by : Mrs. Meena Pandey for **Himalaya Publishing House Pvt. Ltd.,** "Ramdoot", Dr. Bhalerao Marg, Girgaon, **Mumbai - 400 004.** Phone: 2386 01 70/2386 38 63, Fax: 022-2387 71 78 **Email: himpub@vsnl.com Website: www.himpub.com**

Branch Offices

New Delhi : "Pooja Apartments", 4-B, Murari Lal Street, Ansari Road, Darya Ganj, **New Delhi - 110 002.** Phone:23270392, 23278631 Fax: 011-23256286

Nagpur : Kundanlal Chandak Industrial Estate, Ghat Road, **Nagpur - 440 018.** Phone: 2738731, 3296733 Telefax : 0712-2721215

Bengaluru : No. 16/1 (Old 12/1), 1st Floor, Next to Hotel Highlands, Madhava Nagar, Race Course Road, **Bengaluru - 560 001.** Phone : 22281541, 22385461, Telefax: 080-22286611

Hyderabad : No. 3-4-184, Lingampally, Besides Raghavendra Swamy Matham, Kachiguda, **Hyderabad - 500 027.** Phone: 040-27560041, 27550139, Mobile:- 09848130433

Chennai : No. 85/50, Bazullah Road, T. Nagar, **Chennai - 600 017.** Phone: 044-28144004/28144005

Pune : First Floor, "Laksha" Apartment, No. 527, Mehunpura, Shaniwarpeth (Near Prabhat Theatre), **Pune - 411 030.** Phone: 020-24496323/24496333

Lucknow : C-43, Sector - C, Ali Gunj, **Lucknow - 226 024.** Phone: 0522-2339329

Ahmedabad : 114, "SHAIL", 1st Floor, Opp. Madhu Sudan House, C.G.Road, Navrang Pura, **Ahmedabad– 380 009.** Phone: 079-26560126, Mobiles:- 09327324149,09314679413

Ernakulam : 39/104 A, Lakshmi Apartment, Karikkamuri Cross Rd., Ernakulam, **Cochin – 622011**, Kerala. Phone: 0484-2378012, 2378016, Mob.: 09344199799

Bhubaneswar : 5 Station Square, **Bhubaneswar (Orissa) - 751 001.** Mobile:- 9861046007

Indore : Kesardeep Avenue Extension, 73, Narayan Bagh, Flat No. 302, IIIrd Floor, Near Humpty Dumpty School, Narayan Bagh, **Indore 452 007(M.P.)** Mobile:- 09301386468

Kolkata : 108/4, Beliaghata Main Road, Near ID Hospital, Opp. SBI Bank, **Kolkata** - 700 010, Mobile :- 09910440956

DTP by : HPH Editorial Office, Bhandup (Shobha).

Printed by : Heramb Printer, Bhandup, Mumbai-78.

PREFACE

This book represents an extended and thoroughly revised version of a collection of information on customer-focused organizations of the globe and few examples of Indian organizations as well. The key idea is to deal with a wide range of complex problems that the organizations are facing today related to the customers and retaining them.

Most of the material in this book was developed for lecture notes for teaching MBA classes in India on the most promising subject-matter related to customer centric organizations. A substantial proportion of the material is prepared specifically for this book; part is taken from published articles. With respect to the original collection of lecture notes, this new version contains several improvements, and several new customer problems and related solutions are also discussed.

About the Contents

Chapter 1 contains an introduction to general aspects and principles concerning the customer-centric organization, the objectives of customer centric organization, need and importance.

The main emphasis is on principles of customer focus. Relationships between the organizations and their customers. This chapter also dealt with the benefits of customer-centric organizations and the functions of customer-centric organizations.

Chapter 2 focuses on the key to customer retention in India is good customer service. Regardless of whichever industry one is a part of, customer care is of utmost importance. An increasing number of organizations are realizing that with growing competition, new technological innovations and constantly improving services and products, consumers are being pulled in different directions. It is vital to ensure that customer loyalty programes are an integral part of an organization. Acquiring new customers is important, but holding on to existing customers is crucial. After all, if existing customers are satisfied they will help in acquiring new ones by spreading the news of an organizations outstanding customer services.

Chapter 3 formally presents of the service mix of the modern organizations. A service is a product that is purely or mostly intangible. The size and growth of the service sector makes marketing important, but in the service sector marketing has been slowly taken up. This is because of competition. Consumers are changing the way they buy products and services.

Chapter 4 contains a review of the most common communications, advertising and promotions will also be in line with the receptivity of the customer rather than bombarding the customer as dictated by the demands of selling a prerequisite number of products. Co-creating value along with customer becomes possible as a customer-centric culture of an organization would establish systems that would enable a constant dialogue with customers.

Effectiveness of marketing can be shifted from the traditional market share and sales figures to more comprehensive measures such as – the customer lifetime value, satisfaction scores, and strength of customer loyalty.

Given the emphasis on relationship building in a customer centric culture, it allows companies to do a more long-term perspective rather than a short-term perspective with focus purely on quarterly results.

The customer centric philosophy will increasingly be adapted by businesses in their quest to master the new requirements and role of marketing-customer loyalty.

Chapter 5 is devoted to the formal theory of customer centricity refers to the orientation of a company to the needs and behaviours of its customers, rather than internal drivers.

Customer centric is defined as a comprehensive customer orientation – i.e., gearing actions to customers and their various needs when designing products and developing services.

The key to customer retention is relationship marketing. The service company should develop overtime the means of monitoring and evaluating the quality of relationship. There are two basic approaches that can be pursed to monitor the relationship: relationship survey and customer database.

Chapter 6 concerns on the customer centricity is an approach to doing business in which a company focuses on creating a positive consumer experience at the point of sale and post-sale.

Customers are an extension of the organization and act as raving fans, having a stake in the organization's success. Both the rational and emotional needs of the customers are considered and met.

Organizations often promote at the level of customer centric but deliver at customer focus, resulting in disappointment and unmet expectations. Customer-centric design is design centred on what the customer wants (as opposed to what the company wants). To do this, the organization always keep in mind why the customer came to the organization's site and make it as easy as possible for them to accomplish their goals. The customer focus is the essence of the organization. The organization changes the dynamics of the relationship between the organization and the customer. The customer is more empowered, more in control. To keep in touch with the customers the organization should have a customer-centric website.

Customer focus is about hard-edged business. customers are hugely impatient on the web. They don't need to hang around a website that is not directly focused on them. Customer focus is the beginning, middle and end of a successful web-strategy.

Chapter 7 examines the Customer experience is the sum of all experiences a customer has with a supplier of goods or services, over the duration of their relationship with that supplier. It can also be used to mean an individual experience over one transaction; the distinction is usually clear in context.

Background and Readership

In writing this book, I have assumed that readers are well acquainted with the very basic concepts of marketing concepts and understanding of customers.

I wish to thank our Chairman R. Pachamuthu, VC, R. Sathya Narayanan, Registrar Dr.Sethuraman, Director Dr. Muneeswaran, Our Dean Dr. Duraivelu, Professor T.P. Nagesh, for their valuable publishing suggestions.

Author

ACKNOWLEDGEMENT

In presenting this book on customer-centricorganization, I would first like to acknowledge my master and friend Professor K. Durai Pandian, whose intellectual stimuli introduced me to the fascinating world of marketing and to several of the problems which gave rise to part of the work-related to this book. I would also like to express my thanks to the many colleagues who read parts of the written material or gave me constructive criticism, useful suggestions.

I especially wish to express my thanks to Krishna Kumar, Lalitha, Shanthi, Karthikeyan, Nithya Maheswari and Mohanapriya for their continuous collaboration and help in: suggesting new aspects to be analysed, finding new problems, providing proof of some Theorems, revising most of the book, finding references etc.,

The responsibility for any mistakes and for the ideas expressed herein is mine alone.

Author

CONTENTS

1. Customer-Centric Approach 1 - 25
2. The Importance of Customer Satisfaction 26 - 57
3. Customer Service in India 58 - 75
4. Understanding the Market 76 - 159
5. Customer-Centricity 160 - 199
6. Designing a Customer-Centric Organisation 200 - 238
7. Customer-Centric Organisational Model 239 - 270

Chapter 1

CUSTOMER-CENTRIC APPROACH

Objectives

After going through this chapter, you will be able to understand:

1. To identify about the customer focus
2. To familiarize about the customer-centric approach of the present day organizations.
3. To identify the need for customer-centric approach
4. To distinguish between the product-centric approach and customer-centric approach
5. To learn about the objectives of the customer-centric organizations
6. To identify the key insights of a customer-centricorganizations.
7. To analyze the benefits of customer-centricorganizations
8. To identify the functions of customer-centric organizations
9. To identify the customer-centric models of organizations

Structure:

1.1 Introduction

1.2 Need for Customer-Centric Approach

1.3 Objectives of the Customer-Centric Organizations

1.4 Benefits of Customer-Centric Organizations

1.5 Functions of Customer-Centric Organizations

1.6 Case Studies

1.7 Summary

1.8 Self Assessment Questions

1.1 INTRODUCTION

It is today a real challenge to find the appropriate path to foster **a great consumer experience** across the different marketing channels. Being customer focused is not some 'nice thing to do.' Customer focus is about hard-edged business. Customer focus is the beginning, middle and end of a successful organization's strategy.

A customer, also client, buyer or purchaser is usually used to refer to a current or potential buyer or user of the products of an individual or organization, mostly called the supplier or seller. This is typically through purchasing or renting goods or services. However, in certain contexts the term customer also includes by extension anyone who uses or experiences the services of another. A customer may also be a viewer of the product or goods in which are being sold. In this case, a customer can walk into a building intending to buy a product but are not satisfied with what he or she may find in the store, resulting in them leaving without a purchase.

The word derives from "custom," meaning "habit"; a customer was someone who frequented a particular shop, who made it a habit to purchase goods of the sort the shop sold there rather than elsewhere, and with whom the shopkeeper had to maintain a relationship to keep his or her "custom," meaning expected purchases in the future.

The slogan "customer is king" or "customer is god" or "the customer is always right" indicate the importance of customers to businesses.

However, customer also has a more generalised meaning as in customer service and a less commercialised meaning in not-for-profit areas. To avoid unwanted implications, in some areas such as government services, community services and education, the term customer is sometimes substituted by words such as "constituent" or "stakeholder" to address concerns that the word "customer" implies a narrowly commercial relationship involving the purchase of products and services. Some managers in this environment, however, comfortably use the word customer in the sense used in talking about customer service to both internal and external customers where the emphasis is on being helpful to the people one is dealing with rather than commercial sales.

The modern organizations believe in achieving customer-centricity and developing customer relationships, therefore making world-class customer experience happen. The world-class customer experience cannot be managed or done in parts. It needs to have a road map, implement one step at a time but with a clear execution plan across important touch points. It must include all the people, processes and systems to make it seamless across various functions and departments.

The customer-centric approach focuses on understanding the organizations detailed customer demographic, behavioural, transaction related information combined with environmental (market, channels, competition) discovery and analysis. This is used to design broad, detailed, integrated experience strategies that address the customer needs and market opportunity.

The best customers of an organization are put in the centre of universe, and they'll show where to focus. Anywhere from new product development, marketing, research and development, sales and operations. That's the beauty of customer-centric business performance.

The customer-centric business performance helps to identify and prioritize opportunities for revenue growth and improved margins. Then we apply the strategies, ideas and tactics to get it done.

According to Craig Bailey and Kurt Jensen, **(2006)** "Aligning the resources of [your organization] to effectively respond to the ever-changing needs of the customer, while building mutually profitable relationships."

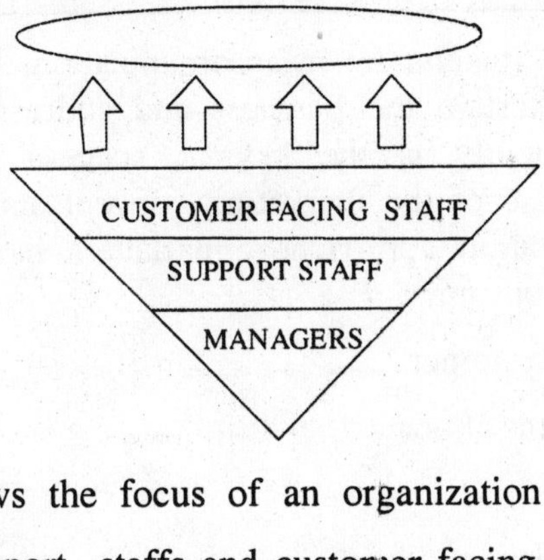

The diagram shows the focus of an organization towards the customers.

The managers, support staffs and customer facing staffs are focusing more on the customers.

The customer always comes first for any business. All organizations take customers' satisfaction on top to provide them the best services. The customer delight is the new mantra of all the modern organizations. Earlier when organizations were not focusing so much for their customers at that time loss was too high. This approach was detrimental to the growth of organizations. Companies are learning from their mistakes. In recent time, the difference and the distance between both organization and potential customers is declining with the help of the new technology medium of the customer's choice like– telephone, e-mail or web chat support and sales force automation. The CRM initiatives are responsible for bringing in more insight about the customers.

Today the customer has various options to get in touch with customer care executive, depending on the nature of the query and the required speed of response. The modern customer has variety of tools through which he or she keeps in touch with the customer care executive. Customer relationship management helps call centres to deals with the customers and clients and make best use of developments such as IP telephony, routing and screen popping - company-wide contact centres are designed to consolidate these interactions.

Customer orientation refers to the organizational culture, processes and systems aimed at strategically understanding customer needs and developing products and services that provide satisfaction to consumers in ways that yields profitability to the business.

Customer orientation or the customer is king is a key word of the management, which focuses on the dependence of the enterprises on customer points out.

1.2 NEED FOR CUSTOMER-CENTRIC APPROACH

Customer is the key stakeholder in an organization. We cannot exist without our customers. How to sustain the business and address the Wants and Needs of the customer consistently is the key to success in a Customer-Centric Organization. With the rise of the marketing concept and the institutionalization of various market orientation approaches, marketers have increasingly focused on understanding the consumer.

Who are today's customer?

- Increasingly Time Poor
- More Savvy
- More Demanding

- Declining Loyalty
- Speed is Evitable

The Organization need to notice the above facts and the key to increasing the loyalty is to build the brand of an organization.

An organization dedicates its energy to inculcate the culture of understanding the internal and external customer's concept. The organization associates the activities being performed by individuals and teams to prevent the problems recurring, to ensure better customer satisfaction.

Customer focus is, at best, only one element of the relationship between a company and its customers.

A customer focus puts the customers high on list of priorities of an organization.

When the organization put their customers into the heart of their business, make customers part of the culture, then the organization become customer-centric. Research conducted by Bain and Harvard Business School shows that the longer a customer is with the organization, the greater the annual profit generated from that customer. These increased profits come from a combination of increased purchases, cost savings, referrals and a price premium. Customer-centric communications will increase customer loyalty and, as a result, customers will buy more from the organization over a longer period of time.

The organization's marketing investment will be better aligned with customer profit potential so the organization's marketing will become more cost-efficient.

Product-Focused		Customer-Centric
• Discrete transaction at a point in time • Event- oriented marketing • Narrow focus	Customer Orlentation	• Customer life-cyde Organisation • Work with customer to solve both immediate and long-term issues • Build customer understanding at each interaction
• Narrow definition of the customer value proposition • off - the Shell Products • Top-down design	Solutions Mindset	• Broad definition of the customer value proposition Bundes that combine products, services, and knowledge • Bottom-up be signed other front lines.
• Perceived as outsider selling in • Push Product • Transactional relationship • Incentives to Individual	Adobe Orientation	• Working as an insider • Solution Focus • Advisory relationship • Team-based selling
• Centrally driven • Limited decision making power in the feld • Individual based on product economics and individual to Performance	Customer Interface	• Innovation and authority at the Front line with the customer • Incentives based on customer economics and team performace
• "One size its all' Processes • Customization adds complexity (e.g, one-off Workaround)	Businesses Processes	• Tallored Business streams • Balance between customization end complexiely • Complexlty isolated within the system
• Read Organization boundaies • Organizational Sllos Control resources • Limited trust across organizational boundaries	Organizations Linkages and Metrics	• Cross-organizational learning • Joint Credit • High degree of organization trust

Source: Booz Allen Hamintan

"A product-*centric* company tries to find as many uses and *customers* as possible for its product. In contrast, a *customer-centric* company tries to find as many products as possible for its *customer*, and it has to integrate those products," according to Jay R. Galbraith.

The commercial transaction seems simple enough. Seller has product, wants money. *Customer* has money, wants product. But it turns out that complications abound. For one thing, all customers are not created equal. Some yield more profit, some offer more loyalty, some are less demanding, some are more open to expanded offerings. There are, says Jay Galbraith in this book, two main types of selling organizations:

A product-*centric* company tries to find as many uses and *customers* as possible for its product.

In contrast, a *customer-centric* company tries to find as many products as possible for its *customer*, and it has to integrate those products.

Jay R. Galbraith argued that to progress toward customer-centricity, one must create a team in the *organization* dedicated to each important customer (or category of *customers*). This team (or it could be an individual) assumes the (or category of *customers*). This team (or it could be an individual) assumes the *customer's* point of view and coordinates all relations with the *customer*. So there's a boss-*centric* through whom all *customer* contacts are coordinated. The company must reorganize to make that happen, and there are degrees of reorganization.

Just about everyone who has ever sat through a board meeting agrees with Peter Drucker's statement that "the purpose of a business is to create a customer." And yet it is remarkable how few companies can be described as "customer-centric," In fact, writes Barbara Bund, a senior lecturer at the MIT Sloan School of Management, "Many people in business have fallen into the habit of thinking from the inside out, strongly emphasizing the capabilities, people and processes within their companies, instead of concentrating on the customers and the marketplace outside." The need for customer-centric approach gains further importance as the focus should be more on the customers.

1.3 OBJECTIVES OF THE CUSTOMER-CENTRIC ORGANIZATIONS

The objectives of the customer-centric organization are as follows:

(i) To meet the need, want and demand for products or services of the customers.

(ii) To meet high customer expectations is making organizations rethink its customer service strategies.

(iii) To find the unique balance between delivery of a service, the cost of the delivery and customer expectations.

(iv) To identify the corporate qualities (core competencies) and the guiding principles (specific behaviours) that foster a quality service culture within the organization.

(v) To identify the present customer satisfaction level with respect to the product or service offerings of an organization.

(vi) To identify the attitudes and behaviours within the organization that support the long-term success of the organization by committing to excellent customer service.

(vii) To look for future aspirations of the customers of an organization.

(viii) To Gain insight into the level of commitment to customer service; identify current practices as they relate to customer service; identify customer service areas that are a challenge and may require improvements; and determine where any changes could be made to strengthen customer service.

(ix) To determine the level of commitment to support a customer-centric strategy; gather feedback on how they perceived customer service was provided today by the organization.

(x) To identify customer service areas that are a challenge and may require improvements; and determine where any changes could be made to strengthen customer service.

(xi) To gather information on use of technology and identify opportunities for service delivery improvements, review channels of communication, i.e., telephone, e-mail and face-to-face services and provide alternative service delivery methods; and observe general customer service practices and identify areas that may require improvements.

(xii) To understand the current state of customer service and how it is delivered today. To provide a framework or set of guiding principles within which decisions about customer service can be made.

(xiii) To identify opportunities for customer service improvements and deliver a Customer Service Strategy that provides a roadmap for the organization.

(xiv) To evaluate key customer service activities within the organization to be measured and reported against customer service standards, report on results and identify areas or improvement, decide on public feedback mechanisms regarding customer service, improve service delivery and accountability, continuous mechanism for quality improvements, mechanism to help determine if sufficient resources are available to do the job effectively.

1.4 BENEFITS OF CUSTOMER-CENTRIC ORGANIZATIONS

Increase customer focus

- Single point of contact for multiple services
- Increase accountability for service delivery
- Improve quality of customer experience
- Ease of access for citizens
- Advocates for the customer
- Service standards and performance measures
- Gain efficiencies within the organizations
- Cost effective means for providing customer service
- Customer-centric by bundling multiple services to the public

- Reporting capabilities
- Change in corporate culture

Increase profitability

Improve customer satisfaction and retention

Increase operational efficiencies

Improve employee satisfaction

1.5 FUNCTIONS OF CUSTOMER-CENTRIC ORGANIZATIONS

Customer Centricity optimizes the interaction between people, process and technology in several ways:

- Comprehensive assessment methodology to identify the actions that will yield the organization's clients the greatest return
- Skills training to enable customer-facing personnel to deliver exceptional levels of customer service
- Design and implementation of business processes to serve the customer and manage corporate resources in efficient, effective and consistent manners
- Identification of the appropriate business processes to automate, enabling companies to get the most from their investments in technology

In a customer-centric organization, managers are leaders, and their primary roles are to

(1) assist the executive team in communicating the direction;

(2) walk the talk by coaching and facilitating their operations to constantly improve business processes;

(3) Delegate responsibility, while supporting wherever possible; and

(4) Work closely with managers across the organization to ensure that horizontal integration becomes a reality.

Customer-Centric Organization is an organization that encourages Customer Service to permeate the decisions and attitudes of the entire company.

Repeatedly, studies show that companies focused on their customers' needs, desires, and attitudes demonstrate higher financial success and greater safety during economic turbulence. After all, as the adage goes, it's the customer who really signs your paycheck, not your boss. Steady, dependable customers who are treated fairly and become advocates for your company will sell you better than you can ever sell yourself. Many companies overlook the power of a customer-focused mentality, and as a result they continue to spend more and more attracting new customers because existing customers don't stay.

A customer-centric organization is one where the customer is at the heart of everything the company does; not just a marketing slogan or a culture programme. One definition is: A company organized to develop and maintain long-term mutually, trusting and profitable relationships with customers. It's the way the whole organization relates to customers at every customer touch point, decision point and influencing point. It's about aligning the business to be consistent and cost effective. The customer experience is at the heart of the business and is fully reflected in the metrics used to drive operational performance. The acid test is seeing customer service people measured and rewarded. If it is purely on customer satisfaction, then there is a good change that the company is customer-centric. Another tell-tale sign is how improvements to products, processes and policies are initiated. If it's from customers or those who serve them, the company is probably customer-centric.

There are 5 key enablers that have to be consistent or aligned:

- Business leadership (company vision, brand values, goals etc.)
- Customer strategy—managing the customer through the life cycle and aligning marketing, sales, customer service and collections
- Organization design—how the company is organized and its culture (including the reward and recognition, decision-making authority)
- Information architecture—the technology that underpins the customer experience and
- Performance measures—how people are measured across the business and at all levels.

"Customer-centric" has become the new buzz phrase thrown about at most executive planning sessions, and has replaced "innovative" as the new, mandatory strategic language. The truth is, it takes a lot more to become customer-centric than changing the company vision—it requires a departure from years of tradition, a clear look at who and what type of organization is, and a deeper understanding of what motivates the customers to buy from the organization, or from the competitors present in the industry.

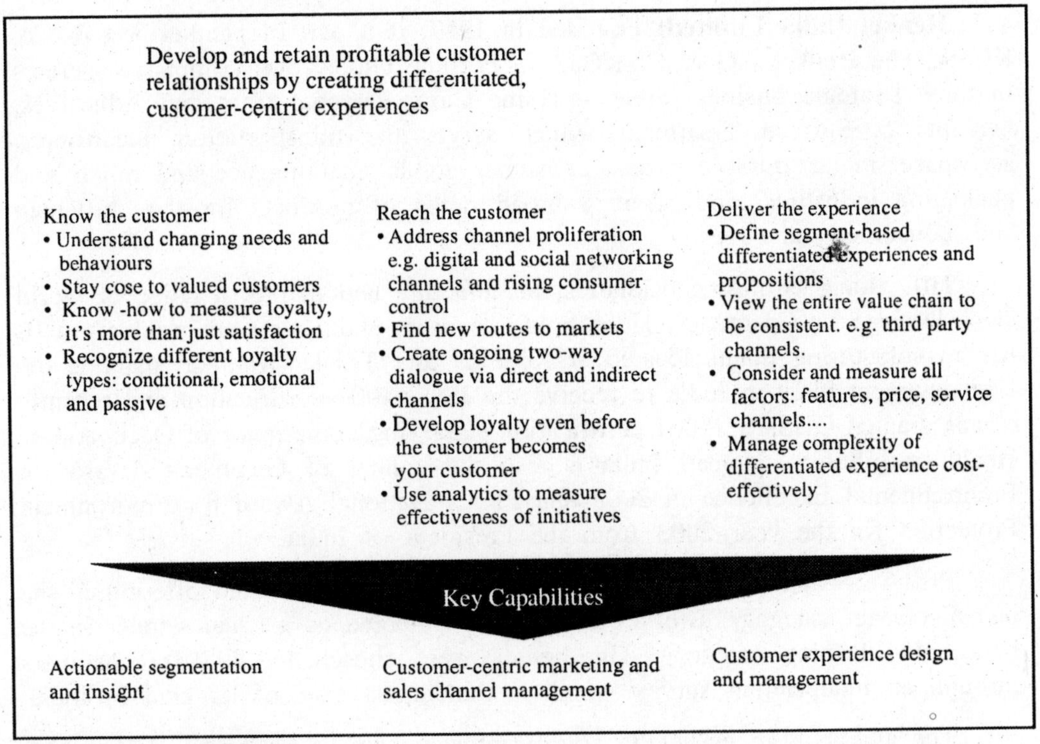

Source: www.accenture.com

Henkel India Limited's customer-centric approach.

Henkel, headquartered in Düsseldorf/Germany, has about 52,000 employees worldwide and counts among the most internationally aligned German-based companies in the global marketplace. People in approximately 125 countries around the world are using the brands of Henkel.

In India, Henkel India Ltd., established in 1987, is a subsidiary of Henkel AG & Co. KGaA, Germany. Headquartered at Chennai in India, Henkel India Ltd:, operates in business areas of Laundry, Home Care, Cosmetics, Toiletries and Hair Care. It comprises of national and international brands such as Pril, Henko, Fa, Margo, Mr. White, Chek, Bref, Igora Royal, BC Bonacure, Strait Therapy, Glatt & Natural Styling and Osis. Laundry and Home Care has always played an important role for Henkel. The Company's success story started with a product from this business sector. Henkel India has got a whole lot of international as well as national products under its arm. Product portfolio includes international brands like Henko, Mr White, Pril and Fa, besides domestic brands like Margo, Neem Toothpaste, Aramusk, Tuhina and Chek.

Henkel India Limited: Founded in 1987, is a part of Henkel AG & Co. KGaA. The Henkel AG & Co.KGaA, a Fortune Global 500 company, operates in three strategic business areas – Home Care, Personal Care and Adhesives, Sealants & Surface Treatment, which serves the transportation, electronics, aerospace, metal, durable goods, consumer goods, maintenance and repair and packaging industries, and offers a broad range of products for the craftsman and consumer adhesives.

HIL along with its subsidiaries, manufacture and market a range of world class Detergents, Cosmetics, Household Cleansers and Hair Care products. HIL has manufacturing plants located at Karaikal and Tiljala. Karaikal plant is the first detergent plant in India to receive the ISO 14001 certification and recently it was granted OHSAS 18001 certification signifying compliance of Occupational Health and Safety. Henkel India is also the winner of Greentech Award for Environmental Excellence in 2003 and FICCI National Award for Environment Protection for the year 2003 from the President of India.

Pril Anti-bacterial received the honour for its differentiated offering in the utensil cleaner category; Bref Power Cleaner emerged as a Clear winner in the household cleaning category. The brands were chosen by 40,000 consumers through an independent survey which is the largest ever of its kind in India.

The award is an especially significant achievement for brand Bref, which is just a year old in India, having been launched in the country only in March 2008. Bref power cleaner is the first multi surface cleaner in the country which comes in foam. The foam sticks to the dirt and reacts with it long enough to dissolve the toughest stains. Just Spray, keep it for a minute and wipe away the toughest stains effortlessly. The power foam becomes extremely effective when cleaning vertical surfaces and ceilings as normal liquid cleaners would fall down and a lot would be required. This recognition goes to show that Bref is all set to redefine the dynamics of household cleaning in India with its household and toilet cleaning range.

Pril Anti-bacterial Liquid that won the award for its innovation in utensil cleaner category has unique anti-bacterial properties of Neem which kills 99.9% germs making dishes clean beyond visibly clean. The award reinforced Pril's image as a true innovator and the preferred choice of consumers across the country. Pril has pioneered many innovations in the category and made a task of dishwashing a joyful experience for the consumer. Pril was also the first to bring in the concept of Odour neutralization in dishwashing by the addition of Vinegar. Only Pril has the double power of Lime and Vinegar, while lime does the basic degreasing like any other washing aid, Vinegar removes the residual food odour from the dishes. Now with the addition of 3rd element Pril reinforces the Claim of Pril Clean=Full clean.

'Product of the Year' is a globally known consumers' recognition forum which champions and rewards product innovation in the retail sector. It is the first ever recognition in India where consumers judge products in 27 different categories. This year the research was carried out by one of the largest independent agencies, AC Nielsen who conducted face to face interviews with the consumers.

The Group's principal activities are to manufacture and market household detergents and soaps under the trade names of Henko, White Giant and Zeolite and also cosmetics and toiletries.

It operates through three business segments:

Detergents and Cleansers products comprising of zeolites such as Henko and Mr White Detergent Powder.

Body Care comprising of soaps, cosmetics, hair oil, deodorant, toothpaste and others provide products and services of bona cure hair care therapy, home care, personal care, adhesives, sealants and surface treatment. Product Portfolio Heavy-duty detergents

Fabric softeners

Laundry conditioning products

Dishwashing products

All-purpose cleaners

Scouring agents floor and

Carpet care products

Bath and WC cleaners

Glass cleaners

Kitchen cleaners

Specialty cleaning products

Air fresheners and insecticides for household applications

"Water is the gold of the 21st century." This statement expresses the growing worldwide concern regarding water resources and their conservation. This topic has long been of vital importance to Henkel. As long ago as 1958 – 50 years ago - Henkel started to analyze the water in the Rhine and its tributaries systematically to determine the levels of washing active substances. Beginning in 1959, Henkel introduced regular ecological quality checks for all their laundry detergents and household cleaners. Henkel innovative pioneering spirit was also demonstrated by the launch of phosphate-free Persil in 1986, after Henkel researchers had discovered that phosphate in laundry detergents can result in nutrient-rich surface waters. This encourages excessive growth of algae, which may seriously disrupt aquatic ecosystems. A research programme was started, which eventually resulted in the development a phosphate substitute. This was a milestone in the history of laundry detergents. Henkel used the knowledge gained to develop high-performance and more environmentally compatible laundry detergents. Today, the accumulated data tell the story of how Henkel innovations have contributed to keeping the surface waters clean. Henkel also use these data internationally, to enable computer programmes to simulate the pollution of surface waters in Europe.

Energy and Climate

Everyone who opens a newspaper or watches the news on television knows that ensuring the provision of adequate energy supplies will be a major challenge in the future. Closely connected with this are emissions of carbon dioxide (CO_2) and the threat of climate change. Henkel has always been aware of the relevance of these issues – not least in the context of production costs and the electricity bills of customers and consumers. One major contribution to reducing energy consumption in the household is the pioneering work in enzyme research that Energy and climate Henkel has carried out since the 1970s. In fact, the high performance of modern laundry detergents at low washing temperatures would be unthinkable without the help of highly effective enzymes: Laundry used to be washed at 90 degrees Celsius. Henkel laundry detergent Persil for example now achieves the same level of cleanliness and removes stains better than ever at just 20 degrees Celsius. Overall, lower washing temperatures have helped to halve electricity consumption per machine load since the 1970, thereby decreasing carbon dioxide emissions by 1.5 million metric tons in Germany alone.

In line with its worldwide endeavour of innovating with brands and technologies to make people's lives easier, better and more beautiful, Henkel India Limited launched new Henko Stain Champion with anti-bacterial neem in the Indian market. Henkel has been winning many awards internationally for its environment friendly and sustainability practices. With its launch, Henko will be the first detergent powder brand in India to offer anti-bacterial and disinfection benefits.

Henko Stain Champion, the flagship brand of Henkel in India, is a premium detergent powder and bar promising superior stain removal. With the re-launch, Henko Stain Champion is packed with strong oxygen power formula + the ancient goodness of neem. The active oxygen power + neem penetrates deep into the layers of fabric and directly attacks stains to break them down, and kill 99.9% germs. In addition Henko also comes with a new refreshing European scent which tested strong with Indian housewives. A wash with new Henko results in stain free, clean, hygienic clothes and cleanliness that one can see, feel and smell.

Announcing the launch, Mr. Jayant Singh, Managing Director, Henkel India Limited, said, "At Henkel, we believe strongly in understanding our consumers better and reflecting on their needs and wants through innovative products. Consumers tell us that with all the threat of new diseases and infections, hygiene is becoming a big concern for them and their families. The quality of water that people use has a strong impact on the issue of hygiene. People go at great lengths to ensure they get good quality water for drinking purpose but there continue to be issues around the water they use for their other daily needs like laundry. The quality of water used for laundry has an impact on how clean and germfree their laundry is.

That's why, Henkel decided to add proven anti-bacterial Neem in the trusted Henko Stain Champion. Neem is used widely in India and has proven anti-bacterial properties. New Henko Stain Champion with antibacterial Neem, kills 99.9% of germs in the laundry thereby ensuring hygienically clean clothes. So now with new Henko Stain Champion, our consumers not only get superior cleaning performance but they also get their laundry 99.9% germ free.

Through an extensive research conducted in India and consumer feedback, Henkel India found that bacteria and germs protection for all clothes is a high priority for consumers. This led to the innovation of Henko's anti-bacterial qualities which not only cleans laundry perfectly but also kills 99.9% germs and bacteria. The new Henko Stain Champion with anti-bacterial neem comes with the promise of delivering stain free and germ free laundry.

Discussion

1. What are the customer-centric approaches of Henkel India Limited?
2. Discuss the corporate social responsibility of Henkel India Limited.

Getting back to "customer-centric," Harvard Management Update Newsletter (August 2001) offers these seven key insights:

1. It goes beyond handling customer calls efficiently. It means addressing all customer issues fully and resolving them completely.
2. It's not just ensuring that your support departments regard frontline workers as their internal customers. It's ensuring that everyone adopts an external focus.
3. It involves more than telling your employees how to treat customers right. You've got to give employees the authority and tools to decide the right way to treat customers.
4. It's not a matter of steering customers through your Website or store just the way you envisioned. Customer-centrism means letting customers interact with your locations just the way they want.
5. It's not just giving customers what they want, it's giving them what they will want.
6. It's not organizing the company to serve customers. It's letting customers determine how you organize.
7. Customer-centrism isn't just about winning new customers from recommendations of current customers. It's about having customers say you should raise your prices.

According to Akram Raffoul, Executive Board Director, Jacobsons Direct Marketing Services,"In tomorrow's business environment the need to engage with the customer in order to strengthen dialogue and generate loyalty is an absolute priority. Companies have to strategize in terms of delivering a happy customer experience that guarantees long term business stability when dealing with existing and potential customers".

The business environment in India is undergoing tremendous changes after the implementation of the New Economic Policy in 1991. The business scenario has witnessed the proliferation of MNCs and host of their new offerings. The Indian consumers started exposing themselves for the new products and services offered by these organizations. By the mid-1990s, the number of sectors reserved for public ownership was slashed, and private-sector investment was encouraged in areas such as energy, steel, oil refining and exploration, road building, air transportation, and telecommunications. An area still closed to the private sector in the mid-1990s was defense industry. Foreign-exchange regulations in India were liberalized, foreign investment was encouraged, and import regulations were simplified.

Former President of the Royal Scandinavian Airlines Jan Carlzon wrote in his book *Moments of Truth*: "Anytime a customer comes into contact with any aspect of a business, however remote, is an opportunity to form an impression." It is at these moments that a company either causes customer delight or customer dismay or in most cases of successful companies what is known as "customer comfort."

When performance equals expectation there is comfort; when performance exceeds expectation delight is experienced and when it grossly falls short, it results in customer dismay.

Timothy Keiningham and Terry Vavra unveil a customer delight principle based not on wishful thinking and outdated research but instead on current real-world findings that include:

- Perceived costs of negative outcomes to a customer, and how they far outweigh the perceived benefit from expected outcomes
- The nonlinear relationship between perceived performance and customer satisfaction, in which customer attitude changes follow a classic diminishing-returns model.

1.6 CASE STUDY– A

"Our agents take complex orders, verify available resources, coordinate directly with drivers, offer the best option, assign a truck, secure an aircraft and even give back money under certain circumstances."

Fedex Custom Critical is North America's largest, time-specific expedited carrier. Part of the $29 billion FedEx family of companies, FedEx Custom Critical offers 24/7 service throughout the U.S. and internationally, providing nonstop door-to-door delivery. FedEx Custom Critical specializes in same-day and next-day delivery, utilizing more than 1,400 exclusive-use vehicles, ranging in size from minivans to tractor-trailers. Most shipments are business to business, and have to be implemented urgently (inventory shortages, new product rollout, disaster recovery and the like). Most business is on an *ad hoc* basis, and the majority of customer interactions take place over the phone, via the company's contact centre.

FedEx Custom Critical agents work together with customers, doing whatever is necessary to meet customers' needs. If a truck breaks down, the company transfers the freight to another unit or maybe uses air transportation to make the deadline. These complex processes can take two or more work shifts to complete, so it is essential for agents to be able to listen to calls and verify that information was noted correctly, and transferred accurately between teams and across shifts.

The Challenge

Fedex Custom Critical wanted to be able to effectively service all customers, by identifying – immediately – the potential need for routing a call to a different division that is better positioned to provide the required service.

Another challenge was to maximize driver satisfaction and retention. Since FedEx Custom Critical utilizes a fleet comprised of independent contractors, it is critical to ensure their satisfaction, since increased retention rates result in lower recruiting costs. FedEx Custom Critical needed a solution for identifying contractors who may be unhappy in order to solve related issues before the drivers leave.

The Solution

FedEx Custom Critical implemented NICE Perform, for extracting insights from interactions. Through its advanced content analytics with emotion detection and word spotting, the goals of improving customer satisfaction and driver retention were met with success.

FedEx Custom Critical specializes in same-day and next-day delivery, but sometimes receives calls from customers requiring different shipping services. Since the FedEx family of companies offers a broad spectrum of services, there are ample opportunities to field a range of shipping requests from customers. And to ensure that no opportunities are lost, FedEx Custom Critical is using NICE Perform's advanced speech analytics to flag and route calls to the relevant division. Being able to spot these calls and take immediate action allows FedEx Custom Critical to take corrective action, resulting in increased customer satisfaction, as well as maximized revenue.

Word spotting and emotion detection is also being used to identify contractors (drivers) who are unhappy (maybe they thought something else was going to happen in a specific situation, or concerns have built up along an axis of time) and is helping solve these issues, resulting in significant savings.

Once NICE Perform was implemented, FedEx Custom Critical quickly realized that the solution can benefit the entire enterprise. For example, Human Resources is using it to identify new skill requirements to improve recruiting; the Operations department for uncovering need for new services (e.g. acting on a critical mass of requests for shipment services to a new geography with revenue potential); Finance for improving Days Sales Outstanding (DSO) by ensuring

Accounts Receivable agents are offering the right payment options; IT to aid in the creation of a new order-entry system; and Training for improving their focused quality training of new hires.

"We're just at the beginning of what we're going to do with NICE Perform. This is the most exciting and the most usable technology that we've implemented in the last few years, because we've gone outside the operations arena and seen what you can do with this tool. If you open your eyes, the possibilities are endless."

About NICE Perform

NICE Perform is a fully integrated suite of solutions that extracts critical business insight from customer interactions. It applies advanced interaction and speech analytics to locate, tie in and help understand information that is normally dispersed and difficult to decipher. NICE Perform brings meaning and value to the information contained in the thousands of customer interactions that come into a contact centre everyday. With capabilities such as speech recognition, emotion detection, customer feedback, and call flow analysis, it enables decision makers in the contact centre and throughout the enterprise better understand and anticipate market and customer dynamics, make more informed business decisions, take immediate action to implement change, reduce risk and drive business performance.

About NICE Systems

NICE Systems (NASDAQ: NICE) is the leading provider of Insight from Interactions™, based on advanced content analytics of telephony, web, radio and video communications. NICE's solutions improve business and operational performance, as well as security. NICE has over 23,000 customers in 100 countries, including the world's top 10 banks and 75% of the Fortune 100.

Case discussion: Discuss the customer-centric approach of **FedEx Custom Critical.**

CASE STUDY – B

Brand Parle-G Case Study

Born: 1939

History: Flagship brand of Parle Products Pvt. Ltd. **Status:** Has a market share of 60% in the glucose biscuits category, worth about Rs. 2,000 crore.

Brand story: In the hit Bollywood movie Welcome, actor Nana Patekar, in a passing reference to Parle-G, notes that even biscuits command respect and have to be addressed with a *ji* (a term of respect in Hindi). His remark, while made in jest, is not far off the mark.

"It is a heritage brand. We sell over 25 crore packets every month. That should reflect the stature of the brand," says Praveen Kulkarni, marketing head at Parle Products Pvt. Ltd.

Parle's mantra has always been about repositioning the brand without tweaking the look and feel of the product. "The brand is clearly an Indian brand and it straddles all economic strata. The fact that it is a staple for everyone in the house keeps it going," says Nirvik Singh, chairman and president, Grey Global Group, South and South-East Asia, the agency that handles the Parle-G account.

There was a time when Parle-G's dominance was threatened by rival brands, especially the Tiger brand from Britannia. "We found out that Tiger was getting stronger in the kids segment, and we decided to change our positioning," says Kulkarni.Later, when the company sponsored the television show Shaktimaan on Doordarshan, it literally rescued Parle-G.

The brand also had some innovative commercials involving young children with a new punchline, G means Genius, which was an instant hit. While rivals have signed on celebrities, Parle-G has managed to retain its leadership position with just a simple white-and-yellow striped wrapper with a picture of a baby on it. "We don't need celebrities as the brand equity is so strong," says Kulkarni.

The biggest concern is that the brand shouldn't become outdated as it is a historic brand. The brand has managed to retain its leadership position because it has evolved its campaign with every consumption trend," says Singh.

The last campaign, Hindustan ki Takat, (the strength of India) is a huge position which no other brand can take so effortlessly."

Case discussion: Discuss the customer-centric approach of Parle-G.

1.7 SUMMARY

The modern organizations believe in achieving customer-centricity and developing customer relationships, therefore making world-class customer experience happen. The customer-centric approach focuses on understanding the organizations detailed customer demographic, behavioural, transaction related information combined with environmental (market, channels, competition) discovery and analysis. This is used to design broad, detailed, integrated experience strategies that address the customer needs and market opportunity. Customer-Centric Organization is an organization that encourages Customer Service to permeate the decisions and attitudes of the entire company.

Anytime a customer comes into contact with any aspect of a business, however remote, is an opportunity to form an impression. It is at these moments that a company either causes customer delight or customer dismay or in most cases of successful companies what is known as "customer comfort."

1.8 SELF ASSESSMENT QUESTIONS

Part – A

1. Define 'customer.'
2. What do you understand from the term customer-centric and product centric?
3. What are the differences between the customer-centric approach and product-centric approach?
4. Define customer-centric experience.
5. What is customer orientation?
6. What is the need for customer-centric organization?
7. What are the key insights of customer-centric approaches of an organization?

Part – B

1. Expalin the functions of customer-centric organization in India.
2. Discuss the emerging trends in CRM initiatives of the organization.
3. Discuss the role of the manager in customer-centric organization.
4. Explain the functions of customer-centric organization.
5. Discuss the need, scope and importance of customer-centric organization. Elaborate the Indian corporate customer-centric approaches.

OBJECTIVE TYPE QUESTIONS

1. Which is not a part of Business leadership
   (a) Company vision
   (b) Brand values
   (c) Goals
   (d) Production
2. A product-centric company tries to find
   (a) As many uses and customers as possible for its product.
   (b) As many uses and products as possible for its customers.
   (c) As many uses and services as possible for its customers.
   (d) As many uses and customers as possible for its services.
3. A customer-centric company tries to find
   (a) As many products as possible for its customer, and it has to integrate those products.
   (b) As many services as possible for its customer, and it has to integrate those services.
   (c) As many customers as possible for its products, and it has to integrate those customers.
   (d) As many offerings as possible for its products, and it has to integrate those offerings.
4. The customer-centric approach not focuses on
   (a) Understanding the organizations detailed customer demographic related information
   (b) Understanding the organizations detailed customer behavioural related information
   (c) Understanding the organizations detailed customer transaction related information
   (d) Understanding the organizations detailed customer satisfaction related information
5. Who are not today's customer?
   (a) Increasingly Time Poor
   (b) More Savvy

(c) More Demanding

(d) Declining interest.

6. Which is not a part of customer-centric organization?

(a) A company organized to develop and maintain long-term mutually, trusting and profitable relationships with customers.

(b) It's the way the whole organization relates to customers at every customer touch point, decision point and influencing point.

(c) It's about aligning the business to be consistent and cost effective.

(e) The product offerings are at the heart of the business and are fully reflected in the metrics used to drive operational performance.

7. Customer-Centric Organiation is an organization that encourages

(a) Customer Service to permeate the decisions and attitudes of the entire company.

(b) Customer focus to permeate the decisions and attitudes of the entire company.

(c) Customer interest to permeate the decisions and attitudes of the entire company.

(d) Customer needs and wants to permeate the decisions and attitudes of the entire company.

8. Customer-Centricity optimizes

(a) The interaction between people, process and technology

(b) The interaction between product, process and technology

(c) The interaction between service, process and technology

(d) The interaction between organization, process and technology

9. Customer-centric communications will

(a) increase customer loyalty

(b) increase customer attrition

(c) increase customer satisfaction

(d) increase customer focus

10. Which is not the objective of the customer-centric organization?
    (a) To meet the need, want and demand for products or services of the customers.
    (b) To meet high customer expectations is making organizations rethink its customer service strategies.
    (c) To find the unique balance between delivery of a service, the cost of the delivery and customer expectations.
    (d) To analyze the market for the product or services and offer the same for the consumption of the customers.
11. Customer relationship management helps
    (a) company-wide contact centres are designed to consolidate these interactions.
    (b) product-wide contact centres are designed to consolidate these interactions.
    (c) service-wide contact centres are designed to consolidate these interactions.
    (d) internet-wide contact centres are designed to consolidate these interactions.
12. Customer Delight means
    (a) more than just feeling great about a product or service.
    (b) more than just feeling great about an organization or service.
    (c) more than just feeling great about a technology or service.
    (d) more than just feeling great about a strategy or service.
13. A customer-centric business means
    (a) A customer-centric business defines its mission as creating meaningful value for customers, leading to sustained competitive advantage and both short-term and long-term organizational success.
    (b) A customer-centric business defines its vision as creating meaningful value for customers, leading to sustained competitive advantage and both short-term and long-term organizational success.
    (c) A customer-centric business defines its mission as creating meaningful value for organizations, leading to sustained competitive advantage and both short-term and long-term organizational success.

(d) A customer-centric business defines its mission as creating meaningful value for products, leading to sustained competitive advantage and both short-term and long-term organizational success.

14. Which is not a benefit of customer-centric organizations?

(a) Increase customer focus

(b) Single point of contact for multiple services

(c) Increase accountability for service delivery

(d) Customer attrition

□□□

2 Chapter
THE IMPORTANCE OF CUSTOMER SATISFACTION

Objectives

After going through this chapter, you will be able to understand:

1. To identify the importance of customer satisfaction
2. To customer services are important
3. To understand customer satisfaction in the market
4. To analyze how customer service initiatives play a crucial role in maintaining customer loyalty
5. To learn how to measure customer satisfaction structure of the lesson

Structure:

2.1 Introduction

2.2 Why Customer Service Matters

2.3 Understanding Customer Satisfaction in the Market

2.4 Customer Service Initiatives Play a Crucial Role in Maintaining Customer Loyalty

2.5 Measuring Customer Satisfaction

2.6 Summary

2.7 Self Assessment Questions

2.1 INTRODUCTION

The key to customer retention in India is good customer service. Regardless of whichever industry one is a part of, customer care is of utmost importance. An increasing number of organizations are realizing that with growing competition, new technological innovations and constantly improving services and products, consumers are being pulled in different directions. It is vital to ensure that customer loyalty programmes are an integral part of an organization. Acquiring new customers is important, but holding on to existing customers is crucial. After all if existing customers are satisfied they will help in acquiring new ones by spreading the news of an organization's outstanding customer services.

Take a look at these statistics:

Repeat customers spend 33% more than new customers. Referrals among repeat customers are 107% greater than new customers.

It costs 6% more to sell something to a prospect than to sell that same thing to a customer.

Source: www.outsource2india.com

Therefore we can see the need for a consistent and committed customer support service that will nurture and strengthen this bond. Some of the main problems customers have are of unresolved complaints, pricing issues, competitors having better offers, or they just feel that the organization do not care enough. One has to be constantly tuned in to a customer's needs. Determining what they want is an important factor in organizational success. Since the market is in constant flux, one needs a consistent and committed approach in order to gauge and be in touch with the changing whims of a consumer.

2.2 WHY CUSTOMER SERVICE MATTERS

Business in India loses up to Rs 11,640 crore (Rs 116.4 billion) in revenue every year because of poor service as customers abandon transactions or end relationships when companies do not meet their expectations, a survey says.

"India loses Rs 11,640 crore ($2.46 billion) because of poor customer service every year in revenue because of inability to meet customer expectations," a survey conducted by Greenfield Online said.

"Businesses in India, Australia and New Zealand suffer significant losses every year because of poor customer service over the web, in the contact centre, or via mobile devices as consumers abandon transactions or end relationships when companies do not meet their expectations," it added.

Of the over 1,500 people surveyed, the biggest complaint was about trying to reach through to the call centre, the survey found.

In India, 56 per cent consumers admitted to having ended a relationship because of poor customer service, while 50 per cent had an experience that made them more likely to do so in the past year, the survey said.

No. of multi-millionaire families	
2001-02	20,000
2005-06	*53,000
2010	*1,40,000
No. of households with annual income of more than Rs 1 core. Between 2001-2 and 2005-6, the increase is two and a half times. *estimated	

Figure 1: number of multi–millionaire families in India

The above figure shows the number of households in India with annual income of more than Rs 1 crore has gone up almost two and half times during the period between 2001-02 to 2005-06. Further the number of households in India with annual income of more than Rs 1 crore is expected to reach 1,40,000 by the end of 2010.This clearly shows the affordability of the Indian customers falling under the high income group. The higher the income level the service expectations are equally higher.

Customer service is as much a part of building the brand as is advertising, or positioning, or any form of communication — and needs to be treated as an integral part of the marketing mix. How many organizations today can truly claim that their service apparatus, whatever it may be — contact centre, channel partners, extended enterprise — is truly integrated with the way the brand is positioned?

Example:

In India, like everywhere else in the world, American Express has taken the lead in innovating products and services. American Express have set customer service standards for others to follow. For instance, several years ago, American Express set 24-hour customer service centres for their card business across the world. This is now being offered by others as a "new" benefit. For American Express, this is "given" in the card business.

LG India has decided to put in operation at least 24 company-owned Direct Service Centres (DSCs) across the country. LG India launched the 2-1-1 customer service concept in 2008. The idea is to provide fast and reliable service to the customer of the organization. For the customer it means an engineer will call a customer within two hours of a complaint registered at the call centre. He will give a specific time to attend within one hour and once the complaint is understood, the service or rectification would be completed in one day. The novel customer service is now available in select centres in the country where LG has a strong presence, including in Hyderabad. Another customer service effort launched by the company to bolster customer care is tie-ups with ITIs (Industrial Training Institutes) to train technicians. With an agreement from 22 ITIs (including 3 in Andhra Pradesh), about 2,000 such professionals are being hired by LG India Limited.

2.3 UNDERSTANDING CUSTOMER SATISFACTION IN THE MARKET

Customer Satisfaction is defined as "The provision of goods or services which fulfil the customer's expectations in terms of quality and service, in relation to price paid." Customer satisfaction is essential to the survival of a business. The best way to determine customers' level of satisfaction is to ask them. The degree to which there is match between the customer's expectations of the product and the actual performance of the product is known as customer satisfaction. An organization can measure the customer satisfaction through the following ways:

An organisation must continue to satisfy customers, but lets be honest, it is very difficult to keep 100% of the customers satisfied all the time, one reason is because needs and wants of the customers change. So we have to monitor what is happening in our customer environment.

Methods used to monitor customer satisfaction include:

Focus groups
Personal interviews
Questionnaires
Mystery shoppers
Customer complaints
Suggestion boxes
Online surveys
General comments

In order to retain customers the organization must keep up-to-date with the needs of its customers. Customer needs do not remain static and always change. Adapting and changing along with these needs will help the organization develop the relationship it wants with the customer. The benefit, well increased profit, market share and brand awareness.

Example:

The French luxury goods conglomerate LVMH which owns several famous brands in various product categories: wines and spirits (Dom Pérignon, Moët & Chandon, Veuve Clicquot and Hennessy), perfumes (Christian Dior, Guerlain and Givenchy), cosmetics (Bliss, Fresh and BeneFit), fashion and leather goods (Christian Lacroix, Donna Karan, Givenchy, Kenzo and Louis Vuitton), watches and jewellery (TAG Heuer, Ebel, Chaumet and Fred).

At the heart of LVMH's business model is a well-thought-out process for creating and growing star brands. According to Bernard Arnault, the CEO, star brands must be timeless, modern, fast growing and highly profitable.

A star brand has to be built for eternity. It must have been around for a long time. It should have become an institution. For example, Dom Perignon was created 250 years ago, but LVMH is confident it will be relevant and desired for another 100 years and beyond.

Timelessness takes years, even decades to develop. Such a brand must have come to stand for something in the eyes of the world. A star brand has to remain current and fashionable. It needs sex appeal and has to be modern. It has to be so new that people would want to buy it. A star brand has to keep growing. Growth is a clear signal that the brand has consumer appeal. Last but not the least, a star brand has to be profitable. Profitability depends on both the price and the costs incurred. So even in case of star brands, operational excellence is important. That means sourcing of raw materials, manufacturing and distribution must be efficient.

LVMH realises that in the case of luxury brands, the innovation supporting the creative process and the advertising are very expensive. High profitability can only come with discipline in the manufacturing process. This discipline includes a tremendous emphasis on quality and productivity. For example, Vuitton's manufacturing is labour-intensive, with a team of 24 workers producing about 120 handbags a day. The manufacturing process is carefully planned and executed with modern technology. LVMH analyses how to make each part of the product, and from where to buy each part. It finds the best leather at the best price and gives it the treatment it needs. A single purse can have up to 1,000 manufacturing tasks. LVMH plans each of these steps carefully.

The Boulogne Multicolor, a shoulder bag that went on sale in 2004 in Vuitton stores worldwide for about $1,500, illustrates how LVMH coordinates its operations. With the success of the Murakami line in 2003, Vuitton's marketing executives quickly began looking for a way to capitalise on it. They learnt from store managers that there was latent customer demand for a shoulder bag. In a workshop attached to the marketing department, technicians took a classic bag, the Boulogne, reworked it in multicoloured toile, added metal studs and other touches, and named it the Boulogne Multicolor. The prototype went directly from the marketing department to top executives, who approved the bag without any involvement by the design team. In June, the prototype reached Vuitton's factory in Ducey.

When LVMH opened its first store in Delhi last year, it found strong demand for its premium, aspirational products. According to LVMH sources, the major reason for the success was the simultaneous launch of products and services in flagship stores in Paris and India. This earned LVMH the trust of discerning Indian consumers.

LVMH's experience is clear evidence that the super rich of the world, irrespective of which country they belong to, have similar lifestyles, tastes and aspirations. They want the best and the latest in fashion. At many big social functions today in the country, it is not uncommon to see women carrying Vuitton's Theda or Monogram Ambre handbags.

LVMH planned its entry carefully after spending sufficient time trying to understand the Indian market. The company closely monitored Indians who were buying abroad. This gave the company a good feel for how the market worked. Now LVMH has plans to launch other brands like Fendi, Dior and Celine for Indian customers. The company has also started introducing products from the spirits division ranging from Moët & Chandon champagne to Hennessy cognac and the recently launched luxury vodka Belvedere that retails for Rs. 2,000 a bottle.

Customer service initiatives of MFHC

Recently, alumni of American Express and the Monitor founded Micro Finance Housing Corp (MFHC), India's first housing loan company that combines the advantages of a bank and MFI in one entity. MFHC gives loans of about Rs. 5 lakhs (US$10,000) for a tenure of 15 years at a prime-lending rate of 12% using the home mortgage as security. It has tied up with low-cost developers including Shubhgriha by Tata Housing, Global City (a Rustomjee/

Evershine joint venture), Shree Vaishnavi Constructions and Tanaji Malusare City. All these projects are in Maharashtra — in Virar and Karjat.

The attraction for MFIs is that some of them who remain connected to their customer base understand the urban poor consumer psyche better than the regular mainstream bankers. For instance, most poor households can afford to pay regular small sums everyday over a long period to the MFI loan collector. But ask them to provide up-front advances and large monthly payments, and chances are they will default. Some MFIs understand this better than others and are willing to structure arrangements that involve daily collections against the house purchase.

Critics of the MFI model highlight its inherent fallacies. As Aneel Karnani, a professor of strategy at Michigan's Ross School of Business writes, "Beneath these beliefs in the market-readiness of poor people lies a more basic assumption: People in dire straits are well-informed and rational economic actors. Yet this view denies the fact that poor people often act against their own self-interest. Of course, wealthier people sometimes do so, too. But poor people face far worse consequences for their bad choices than do more affluent people. And so romanticized views of Bottom of Pyramid (BOP) people as value-conscious consumers and resilient entrepreneurs are not only false, but also harmful. These views lead states to build too few legal, regulatory, and social mechanisms to protect the poor, as well as to rely too heavily on market solutions to poverty."

Customer service is considered a necessity by most service and retail businesses. Supporting customers through the process of selecting, purchasing, and maintaining a product or service can be done by hiring knowledgeable employees, providing online or telephone support, offering generous return policies, or including warranties that guarantee customer satisfaction.

2.4 CUSTOMER SERVICE INITIATIVES PLAY A CRUCIAL ROLE IN MAINTAINING CUSTOMER LOYALTY

The organization should make customer satisfaction everyone's responsibility. If the organisation is customer-driven, then everyone in the organisation is committed to satisfying customers which includes the CEO. When Lou Gerstner took the top job at IBM, he made it clear that he would be the sales representative for five customers and sent a very clear message to all those in the organisation regarding the importance of customers to IBM.

For many years, ARA-MARK has had what they called the 20/20 rule—that every manager at every level of the company had to know the top 20 customers in their area and the top 20 potential customers in their area. Top executives in some banks and airlines are required each year to spend time in positions that bring them into contact with customers.

British Air has gone to enormous lengths to provide their customer servers with power to solve customers' problems such as lost baggage or mishandled reservations. They can provide customers with gifts, upgrades, and other favours to help preserve their relationship. United Airlines allows flights attendants to recommend that passengers receive flight certificates or frequent flyer miles in reparation for problems encountered during flights such as videos or headphones that do not work.

In a service initiative aimed at providing seamless after-sales service to owners of its high-end consumer electronics products, Philips India has launched Star Service Centre in Delhi. This is part of its strategy to improve service and customer satisfaction.

The Star Service Centre (SSC) in fact marks the regional roll-out of Philips' global strategy on service. These centres will essentially work as confidence centres and support base for Philips high-end products. The centres, manned by well-trained service engineers and with advanced fault detection diagnostic tools like Compair and Searchman, will offer high quality and speed of service and repair. Compair helps to make alignments and software upgrades, while Searchman is an electronic service manual that helps in trouble shooting tips.The SSCs would also be linked online with the Philips Service headquarters at Amsterdam/Singapore.

J. D. Power Asia Pacific

2006 India Customer Satisfaction Index (CSI) Study

Customer Satisfaction Index Ranking

(Based on a 1,000- point Scale)

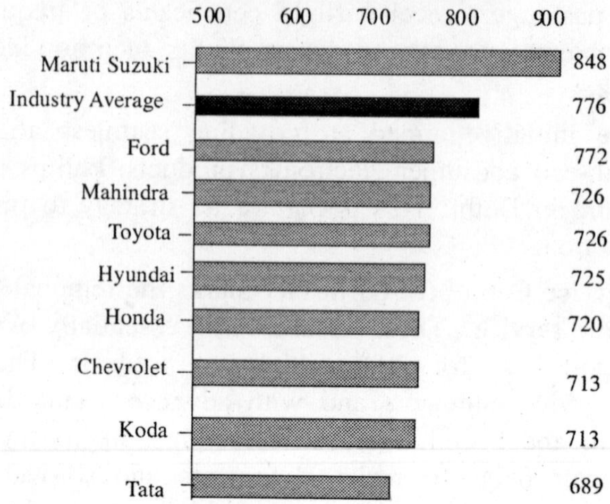

Sources: J. D Power Asia Pacific 2009 India Original The customer Satisfaction Index Study SM

Charts and graphs extracted from this press reface must be accompanied by a statement identifying J. D. Power Asia Pacific as the publisher and the J. D power Asia Power Pacific 2009 India Orginised the customer satisfaction index (CSI) Study SM as the source No advertising of other promotional use can be made of the information in this refuse of J.D. Power Asia Pacific study results without the express prior written consent of J. D Power Asia Pacific

The above figure on J.D. Power Asia Pacific 2006 customer satisfaction index ranking shows that Maruti Suzuki secured 848 as the customer satisfaction index above the industrial average of 776 followed by the Ford and Mahindra.

J. D. Power Asia Pacific
2006 India Customer Satisfaction
Index (CSI) Study[SM]

Factors Contributing to Overall Satisfaction

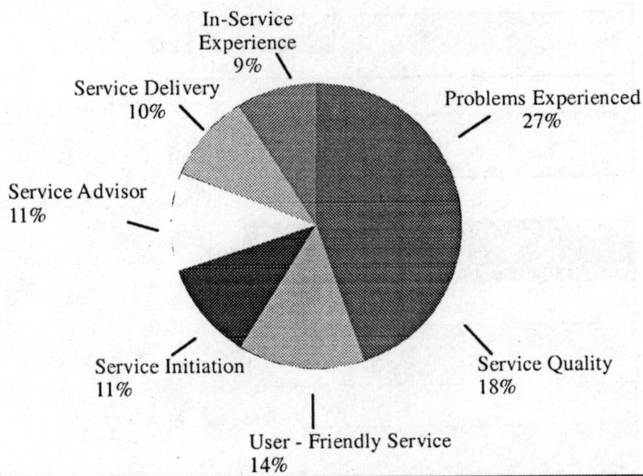

Source: J D Power Asia Pacific 2006 India Customer Satisfaction Index (CSI) Study.

Chart and graphs extracted from this Press refease must be accompanied by a statement identifying J. D. Power Asia Pacific as the Publisher and the J.D.Power Asia Pacific 2006 India Customer Satisfaction Index (CSI) Study[SM] as the source. No adverting of Other Promotional use can be made of the information this release of J. D. Power Asia Pacific Study results without the express prior written consent of J. D. Power Asia Pacific

Figure 3: Factors contributing to overall satisfaction shows that the top three factors are problems experienced, service quality and user friendly service.

J. D. Power Asia Pacific
2009 India Original Tire
Customer Satisfaction Index Study SM

Tire Customer Satisfaction Index Ranking
(Based on a 1,000-point scale)

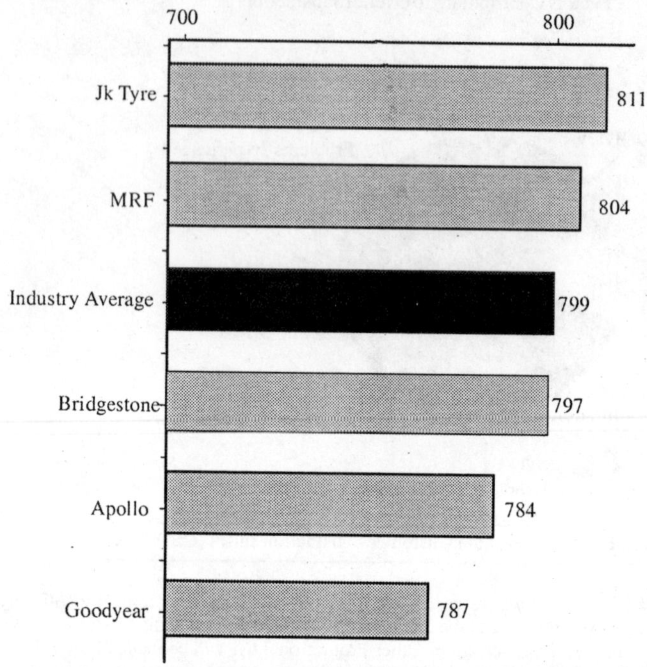

Source: J. D Power Asia Pacific 2009 India Original The Customer Satisfaction Index Study SM

Charts and graphs extracted from this press refease must be accompanied by a statement identifying J. D. Power Asia Pacific as the publisher and the J. D Power Asia Pacific 2009 India Original The Costomer Satisfaction Index Syudy SM as the Rankings are based on numerical Scores and not necessary on statistical Significance No advertising of other promotional use can be made of the information in this refuse of J.D. Power Asia Pacific study results without the express prior written consent of J. D Power and Associates.

J.D. Power Asia Pacific 2009 original tire customer satisfaction study shows that the first position was owned by the J.K.Tyre, secured 804 as rating by the completely satisfied customers against the industry average of 798. The second and third position were owned by the Bridgestone and Apollo Tyres respectively.

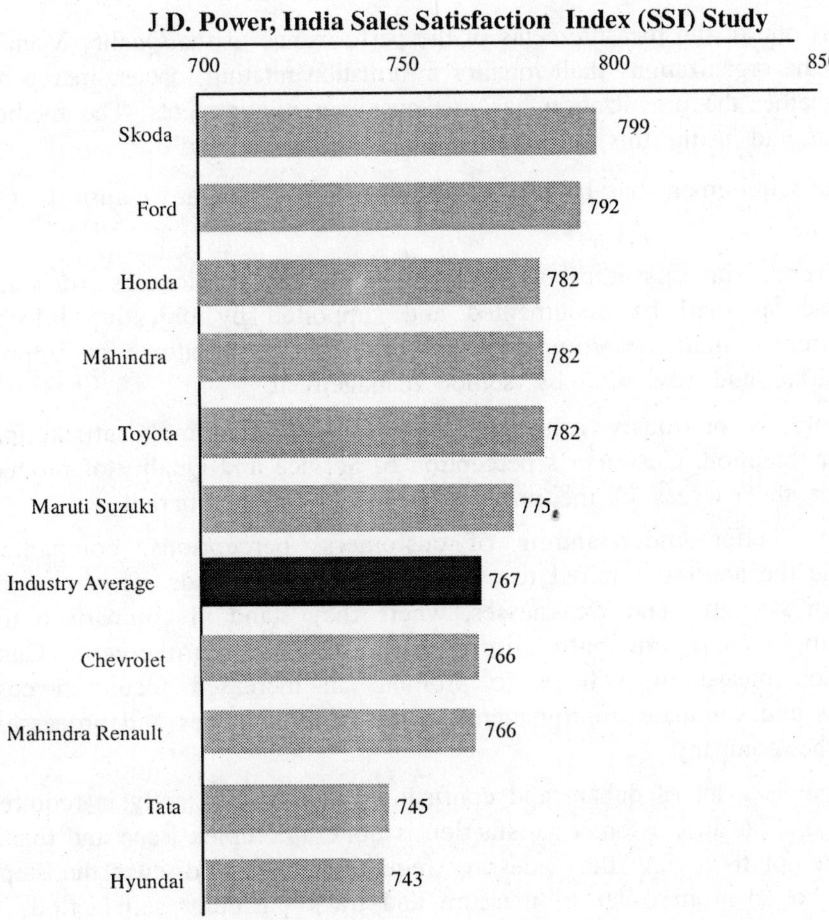

The above figure shows that the India sales satisfaction index of automobiles The first three positions were secured by the Skoda, Ford and Honda.

2.5 MEASURING CUSTOMER SATISFACTION

Measurement of Customer Satisfaction is a new significant addition to the new ISO9000: 2000 standard. Organizations certified to this standard are now required to identify parameters that cause customer satisfaction or dissatisfaction and consciously measure them.

Clause 8.2.1 in ISO9000: 2000 states:

"As one of the measurements of the performance of the Quality Management System, the organizations shall monitor information relating to customer perception as to whether the organization has met customer requirements. The methods for obtaining and using this information shall be determined".

The requirement has been there in the QS9000 standard clause 4.1.6 which says:

"Trends in customer satisfaction and key indicators of customer dissatisfaction shall be documented and supported by objective information. These trends shall be compared to those of competitors, or appropriate benchmarks, and reviewed by senior management."

There is obviously a strong link between customer satisfaction and customer retention. Customer's perception of Service and Quality of product will determine the success of the product or service in the market.

With better understanding of customers' perceptions, companies can determine the actions required to meet the customers' needs. They can identify their own strengths and weaknesses, where they stand in comparison to their competitors, chart out path future progress and improvement. Customer satisfaction measurement helps to promote an increased focus on customer outcomes and stimulate improvements in the work practices and processes used within the company.

There is a lot of debate and confusion about what exactly is required and how to go about it. Customer satisfaction is quite a complex issue and this article is an attempt to review the necessary requirements, and discuss the steps that need to be taken in order to measure and track customer satisfaction.

What do Customers Want?

Before we begin to create tools to measure the level of satisfaction, it is important to develop a clear understanding of what exactly the customer wants. We need to know what our customers expect from the products and services we provide.

Customer expectations are the customer-defined attributes of the product or service the organization should meet or exceed to achieve customer satisfaction.

Customer expectations are of two types–Expressed and Implied.

Expressed Customer Expectations are those requirements that are written down in the contract and agreed upon by both parties, for example, product specifications and delivery requirements. Supplier's performance against these requirements is most of the times directly measurable.

Implied Customer Expectations are not written or spoken but are the ones the customer would 'expect' the supplier to meet nevertheless. For example, a customer would expect the service representative who calls on him to be knowledgeable and competent to solve a problem on the spot.

There are many reasons why customer expectations are likely to change over time. Process improvements, advent of new technology, changes in customer's priorities, improved quality of service provided by competitors are just a few examples.

The customer is always right. Supplier's job is to provide the customer what he wants, when he wants it. Customer satisfaction is customers' perception that a supplier has met or exceeded their expectations.

It is therefore important to periodically update our knowledge of customer expectations.

What Constitutes Satisfaction?

We cannot create customer satisfaction just by meeting customer's requirements fully because these have to be met in any case. However falling short is certain to create dissatisfaction.

Major attributes of customer satisfaction can be summarized as:

* Product Quality
* Product Packaging
* Keeping delivery commitments
* Price
* Responsiveness and ability to resolve complaints and reject reports
* Overall communication, accessibility and attitude

We cannot begin to address the customer satisfaction issue we define the parameters and measures clearly.

It may be easier to track supplier's performance against stated requirements of quality and timeliness because there is documentary evidence. Some indication of whether a supplier is meeting the requirements can also be obtained from data on scrap rates, PPM, complaints database, sales improvements, repeat orders, customer audit reports etc.

It is far more difficult to measure the level of performance and satisfaction when it comes to the intangible expectations.

What are the Tools?

Customer expectations can be identified using various methods such as

* Periodic Contract Reviews
* Market Research
* Telephonic Interviews
* Personal Visits
* Warranty Records
* Informal Discussions
* Satisfaction Surveys

Henkel India Limited has adopted a marketing strategy during the year 2008,"A day in the market".According to this strategy a top official from the headquarters of the company accompanied with the territory sales in charge to know the responses of the customers and retailers by the top officials towards the products of the organization.

Depending upon the customer base and available resources, we can choose a method that is most effective in measuring the customers' perceptions. The purpose of the exercise is to identify priorities for improvement. We must develop a method or combination of methods that helps to continually improve service.

Customer Satisfaction Surveys

Formal survey has emerged as by far the best method of periodically assessing the customer satisfaction. The surveys are not marketing tools but an information-gaining tool. Enough homework needs to be done before embarking on the actual survey. This includes:

* Defining Objectives of the survey
* Design Survey Approach
* Develop Questionnaires and forms
* Administer survey (e-mail, telephone, or post)
* Method of compiling data and analyzing the findings
* Format of the Report to present the findings

There is no point in asking irrelevant questions on a customer satisfaction questionnaire. The basic purpose is to find out what we are doing right or wrong, where is the scope for improvement, where do we stand vis-à-vis other suppliers, how can we serve the customer better?

A Customer satisfaction Measurement Survey should at least identify the following objectives-

* Importance to Customers (Customers' Priorities).
* Customers' perception of supplier's performance.
* Organization's performance relative to customers' priorities.
* Priorities for Improvement.

Survey forms should be easy to fill out with minimum amount of time and efforts on customer's part. They should be designed to actively encourage the customer to complete the questions. Yet they must provide accurate data to monitor improvements in the supplier's performance. The data should also be sufficiently reliable for management decision-making. This can be achieved by incorporating 'objective' type questions where customer has to 'rate' on scale of say, 1 to 10. For repeated surveys, you could provide the rating that was previously accorded by the customer. This works like a reference point for the customer.

Space should always be provided for the customer's own opinions. This enables them to state any additional requirements or report any shortcomings that are not covered by the objective questions.

Normally, we deal various personnel at various levels in the customer's organization– the buyer, user, receiving inspector, finance and purchase persons etc. Surveying a number of respondents for each customer gives a complete perspective of customer satisfaction. It may be necessary to device a different questionnaire for each of them.

Respondents must be provided a way to express the importance they attach to various survey parameters. Respondents should be asked to give a weighting factor, again on a rating scale of say, 1 to 10, for each requirement. This gives a better indication of relative importance of each parameter towards overall customer satisfaction and makes it easier for suppliers to prioritize their action plans by comparing the Performance Rating (Scores) with Importance Rating (Weighting).

The questions are grouped together in a common parameter such as Product Quality, Delivery Performance, or Field Sales Performance.

A typical examples can be:

Survey parameter – Product performance

Questions: Provide rating on a scale of 1-10 on the following:

- Quality of the product
- Consistency of product
- Technical performance of product.
- Suppliers quality systems.
- Overall performance of the product.
- Price of the product

  Delivery of the product

  Distribution of the product

Survey parameter – Competitor performance

Questions: Rate our performance on a scale of 1- 10, as compared to your best vendor

- Adherence to delivery schedule
- Quality of product
- Cost of product
- Technological advancements of the product
- Marketing strategies of the product

It is often found that there is a dismal response from the customers. A recent study showed that only 15% of the customers to whom customer satisfaction surveys were sent gave a feedback. One of the reasons for this could be a poorly conceived survey. Defining a simple survey having less number of descriptive questions and more of objective type can increase the feedback rate. Electronic mailing of survey questionnaire is a very good option as the customer can fill out the questionnaire quickly rather than sitting with the supplier's representative disturbing his busy schedule. This can – where necessary-be backed up by a gentle reminder or a personal visit.

Analysis

The customer's requirements must be translated and quantified into measurable targets. This provides an easy way to monitor improvements, and deciding upon the attributes that need to be concentrated on in order to improve customer satisfaction. We can recognize where we need to make changes to create improvements and determine if these changes, after implemented, have led to increased customer satisfaction.

Two major factors that can be determined from the survey data are:

1. Performance Matrix (Organization performance relative to customers priorities) and
2. Satisfaction Index (Customer's satisfaction over a period of time).

Performance Matrix:

The average of the weightings and the scores given by the customer for each parameter is plotted on a Scatter graph. This Graphical representation is easy to understand without any great knowledge of statistics.

With the data obtained, the average Weighting (importance) on x-axis Vs average Scores (performance) on y-axis can be plotted for each parameter.

From this Scatter Plot the supplier can find out at a glance, the areas where there is scope for improvement, highlighted, where possible by using the Traffic Signal analogy.

High Weighting, High Score On Target

High Weighting, Low Score Underperformance

Low Weighting, High Score Overkill

Low Weighting, Low Score Supplier can afford to score low in that area

Performance Matrix

Satisfaction Index (CSI)

The Customer Satisfaction Index represents the overall satisfaction level of that customer as one number, usually as a percentage. Plotting this Satisfaction Index of the customer against a time scale shows exactly how well the supplier is accomplishing the task of customer satisfaction over a period of time.

Since the survey feedback comes from many respondents in one organization, the bias due to individual perception needs to be accounted for.

This can be achieved by calculating the Satisfaction Index using an importance weighting based on an average of 1.

Calculate the average of all the weightings given by the customer. Divide the individual weightings by this average to arrive at the weighting on the basis of average of 1. Customer's higher priorities are weighted more than[1] and lower priorities less than[1]. The averages of the Customers Importance Scores are calculated and each individual score is expressed as a factor of that average. To understand the calculations consider following example:

The following table shows the Weightings & Scores assigned on a scale of 1 – 10 by the Customer.

Parameter

P Weighting

A Score

B Weighting (avg. of 1)

C Weighting (avg. of 1) * Score

D = B *C

P	A	B	C	D
P1	7	8	1.17	9.24
P2	5	4	0.83	3.33
P3	9	8	1.50	12.00
P4	3	3	0.50	1.50
P5	6	4	1.00	4.00

Average = 6.00 Average = 5.40 CSI = 6.01

A = Average Weighting assigned by all respondents for each parameter

B = Average Score assigned by all respondents for each parameter

Avg. Weighting = (7 + 5 + 9 + 3 + 6) / 5 = 6

C = Weighting based on avg. of 1 = Individual Weighting / avg. Weighting

D = Weighted Score = Score * Average Weighting = B * C Satisfaction Index CSI = Average of (Weighted Scores)

CSI = (9.24 + 3.33 + 12 + 1.5 + 4.0) / 5 = 6.01

Since the scale used was 1 - 10, CSI = 60.10%

Parameterwise Satisfaction Index plotted over Time Satisfaction Index Thus Customer Satisfaction can be expressed as a single number that tells the supplier where he stands today and an Improvement plan can be chalked out to further improve his performance so as to get a loyal customer.

It is far less costly to keep existing customers than to win new ones. Loyal customers buy more products and help bring in more business by recommending your product to others. So if customer loyalty is the goal, then the supplier's efforts should begin with the knowledge of what constitutes value to his customers and the market.

A supplier should always keep on improving so as to achieve a greater profitability. This can be achieved by knowing the market well, i.e. understanding exactly what the customer wants. By discovering what the customer wants, the supplier can begin to understand how his products and services provide value for his customers.

A simple tool is to take customer satisfaction surveys and analyze the customer feedback. This gives the supplier an insight on where he lacks in delivering his products or services and where is the scope of improvement.

Responsibilities of the organization

The organization is responsible for providing superior support in all aspects of purchasing products,

All pre-order entry qualifications,

Order-entry and post-order entry enquiries and

Support for Company's products, subscriptions and renewals.

Responsible for providing direction,

Coaching and development of regional order management teams.

Serve as the main escalation point for all issues related to order entry, inquiries and customer satisfaction.

Monitors team performance and ensures all performance metrics are met.

Key Responsibilities:

Key responsibilities pertaining to customer satisfaction are given below:

The organization should ensure that all orders are entered into the appropriate order management systems in accordance to processes, policies and approval matrixes, within the agreed global and regional level.The organization further ensure that customer inquiries are responded in a timely manner through e-mails, systems, fax and phone within the agreed global and regional level. It also ensure that all Investigations regarding orders, shipments, verifications, registration and complaints are handled appropriately. The customer support manager should ensure that issues are escalated to the appropriate authorities and seek closure in a timely manner and ensure high level of customer satisfaction by fairly resolving escalated issues and take appropriate corrective action.

The customer care department should focuses on building up and maintaining customer relationships specific to regions. Further the organization acts as the key operations escalation point for order management teams, end-users, channel partners and Company's internal functions for all matters related to the assigned region(s).

The frontline and middle order managers works closely with regional/local sales office to understand sales forecasting and ensure that inventory levels are appropriate to fulfil orders and execute all month-end and quarter-end activities flawlessly.

Ensure that all orders are entered into the appropriate order management systems in accordance to processes, policies and approval matrixes, within the agreed global and regional level.

Ensure that customer inquiries are responded in a timely manner through e-mails, systems, fax and phone within the agreed global and regional level.

Ensure that all Investigations regarding orders, shipments, verifications, registration and complaints are handled appropriately.

Ensure that issues are escalated to the appropriate authorities and seek closure in a timely manner.

Ensure high level of customer satisfaction by fairly resolving escalated issues and take appropriate corrective action.

Builds and maintains customer relationships specific to regions.

Acts as the key operations escalation point for order management teams, end-users, channel partners and Company's internal functions for all matters related to the assigned region(s).

Works closely with regional/local sales office to understand sales forecasting and ensure that inventory levels are appropriate to fulfil orders.

Execute all month-end and quarter-end activities flawlessly.

Documents policies and procedures based on expertise in specific job areas.

Works with other Regional Support Managers to document best practices and workflow.

Provide other services or perform activities specific to the assigned region(s).

Develop initiatives and work closely with Sales Teams and Channel Partners to ensure that all supporting documents received are compliant with Company's requirements for order processing.

Schedule and perform Quarterly Business Reviews onsite with Channel Partners to review and drive operations improvement plans.

Participate in all new business models planning with other functional teams to ensure that the models meet operations' processes, systems and policies requirements.

Work closely with other Regional Support Managers to discover best practices and drive global consistency.

Draw on other support resources to drive performance improvement for the assigned region (s).

Perform all people management duties including recruitment, staff development, team building and performance reviews.

Monitors team performance and takes appropriate corrective action. Monitors team capacity and optimally distribute workload. Manage absence requests and ensure that proper cover is in place.

Translates high level organizational goals into operational requirements and work processes for staff. Define work schedules and perform resource planning to meet operational requirements.

Set high quality services levels for teams and monitors performance against those levels. Promotes and maintain a positive, professional, service-oriented company image. Provide feedback to correct performance as required.

Defines and builds processes with other Regional Support Managers as well as "touch points" with other teams within the company.

Ensures that employees are trained and executing on defined and agreed processes.

Participate in all other projects and initiatives as determined by the organization.

Case study

HCL Infosystems, India's premier information enabling, ICT System Integrator and Distribution Company today announced a pioneering initiative in the Indian ICT sector to further strengthen its customer care services. In an unprecedented move, HCL today announced the launch of **'HCL TOUCH'** its 24X7 round the clock, service and support for its Leaptop customers.

'HCL Touch' sets a new benchmark for laptop service in the country, and offers the support that today's users will need. A laptop user of today uses his/

her machine both at work and at home, works at home and while travelling and looks for a round the clock support with the facility to service his laptop anywhere he travels in India or abroad.

This new service has been configured keeping today's customer requirement in mind. It has various customer features some of which are described below.

HCL Touch offers **round-the-clock service** to Leaptop users across India through a **universal customer care number. Support is offered** in 11 **regional languages,** in addition to Hindi and English making it a very customer centric service addressing the needs of consumer both in metros and the interiors of India.

HCL Touch delivers for the first time in India a number of value added services that today's laptop user looks for. Services such as "Network and E-mail support", Peripherals and Hardware Configuration Support", "Fortressing Support", "Preventive Health Care" support, "Tracking Services" etc.

This is also backed by several other initiatives such as SMS request for support, pick and drop facility, and "On Site" direct Company service anywhere in India at the customer's premises.

This landmark Laptop service, will be delivered through India's largest IT Service and support network. A network that, reaches out to over 4000 towns, the HCL touch network consists of 14 remote support centres, 505 Service offices, 390 Warehouses & 150 repair centres, all of which are company owned, making it India's largest direct IT service infrastructure.

Speaking on the occassion, **Mr. Ajai Chowdhry, Chairman and CEO, HCL Infosystems** said, "*Customer has always been at the core of HCL's business with customer care services as a top priority. This initiative has been designed to address the service needs of today's customer, and will take us closer to the customer. By further extending our reach and offering round the clock service, HCL Touch will enable us to cement our stand in the industry as a customer-centric organization.*"

- First of its Kind initiative by an IT company in india
- HCL sets new benchmark for Laptop service and support
- 24×7 Round the clock anytime, anywhere service
- HCL Touch Service reaches out to over 4000 towns across India
- Support in 11 Regional languages in addition to Hindi and English
- Offers Lifetime telephonic support to Leaptop customers

1. Discuss the customer satisfaction initiatives of HCL.
2. Explain the customer care practices of HCL.

Case study

In a bid to enhance its customer services, Eureka Forbes Ltd. is planning to extend its recently-launched customer service initiative called 'Automatic Dust Tracker' (ADT) from Mumbai to other major cities across the country soon, informs Mr SK Palekar, senior vice-president (marketing), Eureka Forbes Ltd.

Says Mr Palekar: "Our new service initiative has been launched to educate our prospective customers on how to measure the exact amount of dust deposited in the nook and corner of their houses."

As for the rationale behind the launch of the company's new customer service initiative, Mr Palekar says that the main objective behind the move is to build and maintain an everlasting relationship with customers as their 'Friends for life' by meeting their health, hygiene and safety needs. Explaining the principle behind the new initiative on ADT, says Mr Palekar: "If the pollution levels outside 'suspended particulate matter (SPM)' is 476 kg/metre-cube, the amount of fine dust deposited in a 800 sq ft house would be 75.8 gm. This dust would contain close to 14 lakh dust mites causing allergic respiratory disorders in turn. Thus, each gm of dust has 19,000 dust mites."

Further, Mr Palekar informs that these results are based on research conducted at the company's laboratories.

At present, the Eureka Forbes Institute of Environment has 10 air monitoring labs across in Mumbai, Delhi, Kolkata, Hyderabad, Bangalore, Chennai, Ludhiana, Guwahati, Ahmedabad and Lucknow. On a daily basis, the institute monitors air pollution data at the above mentioned cities, adds Mr Palekar.

According to Mr Palekar, customers across the country can access Eureka's Customer Response Unit 24 hours of the day or register their complaints via 'Eurosmile', its virtual call centre. "Service call is guaranteed within 48 hours. Eureka Forbes has registered a Customer Satisfaction Index at 95 per cent. The total sales force of the company is over 4,000," adds Mr Palekar.

As regards new product launches, Mr Palekar informs that the company has recently unveiled a new compact electronic vacuum cleaner called 'Euroclean Bullet', in Mumbai in order to meet the evolving needs of Indian customers. After Mumbai, the company plans to roll out 'Euroclean' across the nation.

According to Mr Palekar, in the first phase, the company plans to market around 1.5 lakh pieces of Euroclean Bullet across the country, per annum.

"In addition, we also expect our sales to grow from Rs 388.80 crore (of which direct sales contribute Rs 291.90 crore and other divisions the balance) to touch Rs 450 crore by 2003-end," he adds.

With this move the company expects to spur the Rs 128-crore domestic vacuum cleaner market in India—which is currently growing at a rate of 10 per cent per annum—to grow by 15 to 20 per cent by 2003-end.

In order to promote the Euroclean Bullet range of dry vacuum cleaners and ADT service initiatives, the company plans to roll out mass media advertising campaign at an investment of Rs 16 to Rs 18 crore, informs Mr Palekar.

1. Discuss the customer care initiatives of Eureka Forbes.

1. CASE STUDY

Titan

Remember when the only Indian wristwatch brand you could buy came in a clutch of clunky models, one more ordinary than the other, when the craze for an imported watch never seemed to wane. That was before the time of Titan, a name which changed forever the way watches made in this country were seen by Indians and the world.

Launched in 1987, Titan is credited with transforming the face of India's watch industry. By offering consumers quality products that bended classy designs with superior technology, Titan became a byword for success stories. Outstanding service, a wide variety of models, and effective marketing has helped Titan consolidate its early gains, to the point where the company is a force to be reckoned with beyond Indian shores.

Understanding the Indian consumer's psyche has been vital to Titan reaching its current position of strength. The company today has a model for every price segment and every market, urban and rural, regional and international. Within the Titan mother brand are Nebula, which comes draped in 18-carat gold; the exclusive Insignia; PSI, for those turned on by technology; and Raga, which has been designed exclusively for women.

Titans focus has always been on India. Research reveals some interesting facts and figures about this heterogeneous market.

- The Indian market is estimated at 25 million watches a year, with 50 per cent being sold by the organised sector.

- Titan is the runaway market leader, with domestic sales of 6 million watches a year.
- There are 190 million watch-owning Indians; between them they own about 210 million watches.
- Urban India accounts for 120 million of these watches and 90 million are on rural wrists.
- More men than women own watches in India, and more working women than housewives own watches.

It is the rural segment within this diverse market that Titan is now looking to tap. "The key to success," says Bijou Kurien, vice-president (sales and marketing), "is getting into the rural market on a larger scale." The company's Sonata range is targeted at rural customers, and is part of a strategy where the alignment of price and reliability are crucial. The range costs between Rs 495 and Rs. 1,200, has showrooms exclusively for it, and is sold mainly in small towns in India.

Fast Track is a different kettle of fish. This range is broadly aimed at young Indians looking for watches that are fashionable and stylish. Then there is Dash, a range that Titan launched for children. Introduced in early 2000, Dash is priced low, but it hasn't sold too well. The company plans to change that with enhanced advertising and a different marketing strategy.

Titan's retail operations are a mix of company-owned and franchisee outlets, with the idea being to ensure a dominant presence in all market areas through different kinds of stores, and to assure the availability of every Titan product. Says Mr Kurien: "We have concentrated on customer perspective, and we have engineered the entire chain to suit different customers."

Manoj Chakravarti, general manager (retailing), has more to say on the customer theme. "Earlier there was no attempt in the retailing sector to entice customers to buy a watch," he says. "We have tried to bring the brand to the customer in an appropriate setting." The company does this through its World of Titan showrooms.

The franchisee is a critical cog in Titan's retail matrix. The company organises various programmes for franchisees, their managers and customer relationship officers. These include training workshops and seminars on market trends, visual merchandising, store operations and maintenance, and customer service initiatives.

According to Ajay Chawla, senior manager (retailing and supply chain), the real challenge in retailing is managing the franchisee network through processes and systems that ensure a superior brand experience for every customer. "Franchisee relationship management is important because of increasing competition, not only from the watch business but also from other businesses in the retail industry," he says. "The market is opening up and the franchisee is, after all, looking for what is most profitable."

Besides the franchisees and its own showrooms, Titan sells its products through other outlets as well. Among them are the Time Zone stores, which stock all the leading brands, and the Value Mart outlets, which operate in Bangalore and Chennai and sell surplus-to-export watches at a discount.

For its many customers Titan has Tata Signet, a 1,36,000-member club that looks to build relationships through rewards, regular discounts and special offers. Customers can also count on a service-centre network that is 550-strong and spread over 30-odd cities and towns across the country. The service centres have been deliberately kept apart from Titan's showrooms. "The business is different and the customer is in two different moods at the two places," says Mr Kurien.

Titan's blueprint for the future includes making watches for international heavyweights such as YSL, Christian Dior and Gucci. Mr Kurien believes there is huge potential at the designer end of the market. The marketing investment is lower because "the brand is doing the marketing for you". Also on the anvil are speciality stores for niche customers, and an expansion into product categories like sunglasses and leather goods.

However, it is staying ahead of the competition that is the overall priority. Says Mr Chakravarti: "We have to ensure that Titan has the best wristwatch store in any given city or town." You don't really have to watch this space for confirmation on that count.

1. Discuss the case and highlight the customer care services of Titan.

CUSTOMER SERVICE

In Indian Oil Corporation's pursuit to provide better services, IVSR based complaint tracking and redressal system for customers was launched in 33 Indane Area Offices. Further, in order to provide value added services to monitoring public, Indian Oil Corporation, in association with State Bank of India, launched the SBI-Indian Oil Co-branded pre-paid card called "Smart Gold" for customers to avail of products and services at Indian Oil retail outlets. Indian Oil Corporation introduced 35 ATMs at retail outlets during the year in various parts of the country, thereby bringing the total number of ATMs installed to 57. The Indian Oil-Citibank co-branded credit card has reached a membership of 1.48 lakh as on 31.03.2002.

Indian Oil Corporation, in association with Chennai based Sundaram Finance Ltd., also launched "Power Plus Fleet Card" for transport fleet operators.

The innovative customer service initiatives of three Oil Marketing Companies (OMCs) by sending an SMS on IOC's SMS booking number. He also unveiled the IVRS (Integrated Voice Response System) mechanism of HPCL. With this the consumers of domestic LPG have been provided a platform for quick and smooth booking of LPG Refills. They will not only get acknowledgement but also get information about cylinder delivery. The facility has been initially launched in Delhi and would be expanded in a phased manner to cover all towns of the country having population of over 5 lakhs.

The customer service initiative of IOCL is considered as one of the best from the public sector undertaking.

CASE STUDY

Management Solutions Software AG

Management Solutions, based at the village of Hall, near Canberra, is a small software company that has built its export markets with a sensible application of limited funds, rather than a scattergun approach to exports. Most muscle has been applied to market research, then to providing service before and after a sale, and finding credible locally-based partners.

Management Solutions produces FINEST software, which is tailored for the public sector. The company sought countries with either large governments or numerous federal and provincial governments. This led to Europe and the US, rather than Asia. The British market presented an opportunity in the early 1990s: Management Solutions seized it. Almost every British agency was being rationalised and needed a product such as FINEST. The rest of Europe was seen as having slower potential, while the US was too big for a new exporter.

The Australian marketing manager was seconded to Britain and a partnership was formed with a large European software company, Software AG, helping credibility. Management Solutions sent eight research and development staff to St Albans in Britain for 18 months to adapt the software to British needs. With them went 12 consultants for support work, convincing UK clients that the company was in for the long haul. The first sale was to the Commonwealth Secretariat in 1993, followed by large contracts with the Department of the Environment and the Scottish Prison Service.

In late 1994, Software AG began sales and support of FINEST, with Management Solutions taking a consulting and technical role. This soon led to major sales to the Inland Revenue, Devon County Council, Devon and Cornwall police and other Authorities. Management Solutions is transferring technology to Software AG to expand the business without putting unreasonable demands on Australian staff. New marketing is focused on Africa and Asia.

2.6 SUMMARY

The key to customer retention in India is good customer service. Regardless of whichever industry one is a part of, customer care is of utmost importance. An increasing number of organizations are realizing that with growing competition, new technological innovations and constantly improving services and products, consumers are being pulled in different directions. It is vital to ensure that customer loyalty programs are an integral part of an organization. Acquiring new customers is important, but holding on to existing customers is crucial. After all if existing customers are satisfied they will help in acquiring new ones by spreading the news of an organizations outstanding customer services.

Student exercises

1. What is the advantage of having a locally based partner to provide customer sales and service?
2. What 'niche' market did Management Solutions identify and how did they exploit it?
3. How did Management Solutions prioritise the markets for selection?
4. What strategies can smaller companies, new to exporting, employ to gain credibility in new markets?

2.7 SELF-ASSESSMENT EVALUATING QUESTIONS

Part – A

1. Define customer satisfaction
2. What do understand by the term customer value?
3. What is customer satisfaction survey?
4. Define Customer Satisfaction Index (CSI).
5. Name the two types of customer expectations.
6. How does the organization measure customer satisfaction?
7. Why do we give importanceto customer satisfaction?

Part – B

1. Customer service is as much a part of building the brand as is advertising, or Positioning, or any from of communication-and needs to be treated as an integral part of the marketing mix.–Discuss.
2. Explain the objectives of a Customer Satisfaction Measurement Survey.
3. Define customer service experience. How the corporate houses are adopting to their customer service experience? Explain.

OBJECTIVE TYPE QUESTIONS

1. "The provision of goods or services which fulfil the customer's expectations in terms of quality and service, in relation to price paid," is known as
   (a) Customer satisfaction
   (b) Customer centricity
   (c) Customer value
   (d) Customer focus
2. Which is not the part of the customer satisfaction survey?
   (a) Defining Objectives of the survey
   (b) Design Survey Approach
   (c) Develop Questionnaires and forms
   (d) Customer proposition

3. Organization performance relative to customer's priorities
   (a) Performance Matrix
   (b) Performance indicator
   (c) Performance monitor
   (d) Performance factor
4. Customers' Satisfaction over a period of time.
   (a) Satisfaction Matrix
   (b) Satisfaction indicator
   (c) Satisfaction monitor
   (d) Satisfaction Index
5. Customer service initiatives play a crucial role in maintaining
   (a) Customer loyalty
   (b) Customer loyalty indicator
   (c) Customer loyalty monitor
   (d) Customer loyalty Index
6. Which is not a method of measuring Customer expectations
   (a) Periodic Contract Reviews
   (b) Market research
   (c) Telephonic Interviews
   (d) Customer visits
7. Which is not a problem faced by the customers
   (a) Unresolved complaints
   (b) Pricing issues
   (c) Competitors having better offers
   (d) Satisfaction Index
8. Customer's perception of Service and Quality of product will
   (a) Determine the success of the customer satisfaction in the market.
   (b) Determine the success of the product or customers in the market.
   (c) Determine the success of the customer or service in the market.
   (d) Determine the success of the product or service in the market.

9. The customer care department should focuses on
   (a) Building up and maintaining customer relationships specific to regions.
   (b) Building up and maintaining customer reactions specific to regions.
   (c) Building up and maintaining customer satisfaction specific to regions
   (d) Building up and maintaining customer feedback specific to regions.
10. Customer expectations are the customer-defined attributes of the product or service the organization should meet or exceed to achieve
    (a) Customer satisfaction
    (b) Customer perception
    (c) Customer loyalty
    (d) Customer behaviour

□□□

3 Chapter CUSTOMER SERVICE IN INDIA

Objectives

After going through this chapter, you will be able to understand:

- To learn about the services component
- To identify how to develop and targeting the services
- To analyze the role of IT in improving customer service
- To learn about how poor customer support can affect the business
- To learn about the customer service experience

Structure:

3.1 Introduction

3.2 The Role of IT in Improving Customer Service

3.3 How Poor Customer Support Can Affect Your Business?

3.4 Summary

3.5 Self Assessment Questions

3.1 INTRODUCTION

Service Economy

A service is a product that is purely or mostly intangible. The size and growth of the service sector makes marketing important, but in the service sector marketing has been slowly taken up. This is because of:

Competition:

Many service industries have been regulated i.e. banking, public utilities etc. and thus they have faced little competition.

Lack of creative management:

Most service industry leaders have been accused of lacking creativity.

No obsolescence:

Many services are not subject to obsolence unlike goods. This reduces urgency to make changes.

Lack of innovation in the distribution service.

Characteristics of Services:

Intangibility

Inseparability

Since services are intangible, this leads to them being produced and marketed simultaneously. Inseparability means that customers not only want a particular type of service, they want it to be provided by particular people or group of people.

Involvement of the customer: This is caused by inseparability in that customers are involved to a relatively greater degree in the production and marketing of many kinds of services.

Variability of Quality

The quality of services varies due to the fact that they are produced and consumed at the same time.

Perishability

It's important to plan for fluctuation in demand of the service e.g., if no one makes an appointment to see a doctor at 6.00 pm then the service is perishable Categories of Service mix:

Developing and targeting the service: The organization must tailor these services to the needs of specific customers.

Pricing the service

Distribution channels for the service

Communication about the service

The service mix for the service industry is much like the product mix of the products.

Marketing mix for services

The characteristics of services give rise to special needs in preparing the market mix.

Developing and targeting the services through

1. Quality:

To provide quality service, organizations must tailor these products to the needs of specific customers. A marketer should ensure that the organization employees are providing quality service time after time. An org should include quality measures in the org performance standards.

The org should also have its employees practice focusing on quality by setting the standard that each employee must satisfy his or her internal customers.

Another approach to improving standards of service is empowering the employee to satisfy customers. This allows employees to make effective decisions thus providing quality service to employees.

Lack of patent protection

Marketers of service should continually innovate and improve so as to distinguish themselves from competition.

Managing fluctuating demand

When demand for a service is low, this leads to staff being idle so an organization should pay staff on commission so as to help to keep costs in line with sales.

Pricing the service

Prices influence a buyer to buy particular products thus an organization should make sure it understands the various costs also the org must understand which customers want.

Customers are usually happy when they look at an itemized bill and see the value for their money. Services are perishable thus marketers use price to limit idle time i.e. the organization might use off-peak pricing, this includes charging different prices during different times in order to stimulate demand during slow periods.

Distribution demands for the service

Since production and mixing a service are difficult to separate distribution emphasis finding convenient ways to provide the services to customers. Distribution strategy can help to attract more clients and help a service provider position itself. A common strategy for distribution of services to a broad consumer market is through franchising.

Communicating about the service

Communication tries to explain what the service is and how it will affect the buyer. Advertising is one of the strategies helps an organization can advertise its service to the consumer through the media.

Another strategy is personal selling i.e. a sales person can advertise its service to a buyer, he can reassure prospective buyers by providing customer testimonials e.g. real estates agents.

Consumers are changing the way they buy products and services. If the marketing hasn't changed in response, it should. Marketing's one goal is "to reach consumers at the moments that most influence their decisions." That's why Amazon.com began ten years ago to offer product recommendations to consumers who were already logged in. And Proctor and Gamble long ago started to sponsor soap operas "to reach the audiences most likely to buy its products."

People form impressions of products and services from many sources (touch points), and when they're ready to make a decision, these accumulated impressions become crucial because that's how they shape their "initial-consideration set"—what they consider buying.

The consumers' decision processes include four primary phases critical for marketing: initial consideration; active evaluation; closure; and post purchase.

Example of customer service

CUSTOMER SERVICE

In Indian Oil Corporation's pursuit to provide better services, IVSR based complaint tracking and redressal system for customers was launched in 33 Indane Area Offices. Further, in order to provide value added services to monitoring public, Indian Oil Corporation, in association with State Bank of India, launched the SBI-Indian Oil Co-branded pre-paid card called "Smart Gold" for customers to avail of products and services at IndianOil retail outlets. Indian Oil Corporation introduced 35 ATMs at retail outlets during the year in various parts of the country, thereby bringing the total number of ATMs installed to 57. The IndianOil-Citibank co-branded credit card has reached a membership of 1.48 lakh as on 31.03.2002.

Indian Oil Corporation, in association with Chennai based Sundaram Finance Ltd., also launched "Power Plus Fleet Card" for transport fleet operators.

The innovative customer service initiatives of three Oil Marketing Companies (OMCs) by sending an SMS on IOC's SMS booking number. He also unveiled the IVRS (Integrated Voice Response System) mechanism of HPCL. With this the consumers of domestic LPG have been provided a platform for quick and smooth booking of LPG Refills. They will not only get acknowledgement but also get information about cylinder delivery. The facility has been initially launched in Delhi and would be expanded in a phased manner to cover all towns of the country having population of over 5 lakhs.

The customer service initiative of IOCL is considered as one of the best from the public sector undertaking.

According to David Court, Dave Elzinga, Susan Mulder, and Ole Jørgen Vetvik, (2009) the consumer buying decision involves the following:

Brand consideration. Brands in the initial consideration set are those most likely to be purchased. But as consumers actively evaluate brands, more brands are now added to the mix. And newly considered brands can push others out of the running.

Empowered consumers. Consumer-driven marketing is now more important than company-driven marketing. A study found that two-thirds of the touch points during consumers' active-evaluation stage involve activities such as Internet reviews and word-of-mouth recommendations, plus in-store interactions and recollections of past experiences. Only one third of the touch points involve company marketing. This means that marketers must move beyond traditional "push-style" marketing and "learn to influence consumer-driven touch points, such as word-of-mouth and Internet information sites."

Two types of loyalty. Actively loyal customers stay with a product and recruit new customers. Passively loyal customers may stay with a brand, but they aren't necessarily committed to it and are open to messages from competitors.

Marketers need to prioritize expansion of their active loyalists and focus on the new touch points. This will require new marketing efforts to align marketing with the customer decision journey. "The increasing complexity of the consumer decision journey will force virtually all companies to adopt new ways of measuring consumer attitudes, brand performance, and the effectiveness of marketing expenditures across the whole process."

Activities that will help address these new realities include the following:

Prioritize objectives and spending. Be much more specific about the touch points that influence customers' behaviours as they make decisions.

Tailor messaging. Use new messages to address weaknesses or concerns. For example, Hyundai developed a provocative message built around letting consumers return their cars if they lost their jobs. This helped "Hyundai break into the initial-consideration set of many new consumers. In a poor automotive market, the company's market share is growing."

Invest in consumer-driven marketing. Find ways to have your marketers interact with your customers in each decision-making phase.

Integrate customer-facing activities. Identify your active loyalists; understand what drives that loyalty and how to harness it via word-of-mouth. You need an integrated, organization-wide "voice of the customer," developed with skills from throughout your organization.

"The shift in consumer decision making means that marketers need to adjust their spending and to view the change not as a loss of power over consumers but as an opportunity to be in the right place at the right time, giving them the information and support they need to make the right decisions."

3.2 THE ROLE OF IT IN IMPROVING CUSTOMER SERVICE

The numbers don't lie

Improving customers' satisfaction with your business translates directly to your bottom line. Still not sure you're ready to invest in improving service? Check out these statistics:

- It costs between five and six times more to attract a new customer than to keep an existing customer.
- Companies can boost profits from 25 per cent to 125 per cent by retaining 5 per cent more existing customers.

- Only one out of 25 dissatisfied customers will express dissatisfaction to you.
- Happy customers tell at least four others of a positive experience. Dissatisfied customers tell as many as 12 about a negative experience.
- Two-thirds of customers do not feel valued by those serving them.
- Acquiring new customers can cost five times more than satisfying and retaining current customers.
- A 2 per cent increase in customer retention has the same effect on profits as cutting costs by 10 per cent.
- The average company loses 10 per cent of its customers each year.
- The customer profitability rate tends to increase over the life of a retained customer.

Sources: Extreme Management, Mark Stevens, 2001; Leading on the Edge of Chaos, Emmett C. Murphy and Mark A. Murphy, 2003

It is observed that retention of existing customers is economical for an organization as it incurs less expense. The retention of customers is possible through the offering of superior quality of services. The services rendered by the organization should be extraordinary therefore the customers not only enjoy the same but also spread the superior services to other customer and pull them toward an organization. Recently when the Hindustan Unilever launched the Pure it water filter, it attracted a larger customer base at water starved Chennai in Tamilnadu.

It is observed that the profit of an organization likely to go up when retention of existing customer base increases. Similarly the organizations should markets. In less than a decade, Huawei has penetrated almost every market around the world, investing heavily in its business and technology product lines, which includes fixed networks, mobile networks, data communications, optical networks, software and services, and terminals.

It is observed that the profit of an organization likely to go up when retention of existing customer base increases. Similarly the organizations should focus on the happy customers rather than unhappy customers, because, unhappy customers likely to spoil the business of an organization.

Huawei Technologies – Case study

A walk into a bookstore in Beijing and one will find shelves filled with books about Huawei Technologies. As one of China's fledging multinational companies and a major force in the international telecommunications equipment industry, Huawei is rewriting the rules of competition in a global industry.

According to some observers, it is the first non-state owned Chinese company to successfully expand its operations internationally.

"Huawei is currently the number three global company in wireless networks and number two in fixed line and switches," says founder and CEO Ren Zhenfei. "But Huawei's goal is to become number one in all three segments." Its competitors include both well-known European and American companies, such as Alcatel-Lucent, Cisco Systems, Nokia Siemens Networks and Ericsson Telephone Co., as well as lower-cost Chinese competitors such as ZTE Corp.

Huawei currently serves 270 operators in about 100 countries, including 35 of the world's top 50 telecommunications companies. As of March 2007, Huawei had more than 83,000 employees worldwide, of whom 43% are engaged in R&D.

The company reports that it dedicates at least 10% of its revenues to R&D and is now the fourth largest patent applicant worldwide, with more than 20,000 applications filed by 2007. Last year, Huawei won 45% of all new Universal Mobile Telecommunications System and High Speed Packet Access contracts, making it the top supplier in this area. Huawei is also now one of the top three suppliers in the global GSM market; by the end of 2007, it had shipped base stations with total capacity of 700,000 carrier frequencies, serving more than 300 million GSM users worldwide. (GSM is currently the most popular second-generation standard for mobile phones.)

It is hard to understand Huawei's success without considering its humble origins and distinctive corporate culture. In 1988, Ren, a former People's Liberation Army (PLA) officer, founded the company as a third-party reseller of telecom devices in Shenzhen, China. Five years later, Huawei achieved its first breakthrough when it launched its C&C08 digital telephone switch, which had the largest switching capacity in China at the time. Despite the challenges facing the global economy and the telecommunications industry, Huawei achieved contract sales of $16 billion, representing a 45% year-over-year increase, with approximately 72% of its revenues coming from international markets. In less than a decade, Huawei has penetrated almost every market around the world, investing heavily in its business and technology product lines, which includes fixed networks, mobile networks, data communications, optical networks, software and services, and terminals.

According to an industry insider, Huawei segments the telecom equipment industry into three major categories: Internet switches, fixed line networks. From 1996 to 1998, Huawei experienced exponential growth, coinciding with the boom in China's telecommunications industry. After winning its first overseas contract in 1996 with Hong Kong's Hutchison-Whampoa, Huawei expanded to to Russia and Africa. In Africa, Huawei began operations in 1998, starting in Kenya, and has now become the largest CDMA product provider in the region. During the same year, Huawei hired IBM consultants to gain expertise in management strategies in a concerted effort to learn industry best practices. First, the Countryside as a follower of Mao's thought, Ren has drawn much inspiration from the PLA's military strategy — reflected in Huawei's business strategy, organization and corporate culture. For example, Huawei has relied on a well-known Maoist strategy of first focusing on seizing the countryside, then encircling and conquering cities. Huawei followed this strategy, achieving its first breakthrough in 1993 when it aggressively marketed its digital telephone switches in smaller towns before expanding all over China. Later, Huawei utilized this same strategy by first targeting the underserved markets of Russia and Africa before moving into Europe.

Military culture is also epitomized in Huawei's rigidly hierarchical organization, where emphasis is placed on hierarchical management rather than on individual employees, who are viewed as easily replaceable foot soldiers. Like that of many other East Asian firms, Huawei's corporate culture relies heavily on rhetoric and propaganda. The introductory article of Huawei's basic law reads: "Love for our homeland, fellow citizens, work and life is the source of our cohesion; responsibility, creativity, respect and solidarity represent our company's quintessential culture."

Other aspects of Huawei's culture are characteristically Chinese. Resilience and hard work, qualities valued in traditional Chinese culture, are emphasized at Huawei as a way to gain competitive advantage. Another classic East Asian trait, putting the group before the individual, can also be seen. Huawei expects its employees to place their personal lives second in order to serve their company loyally. Its approach to business, referred to as "the way of the wolf," is characterized by reliance on instinct, extreme resilience and employees' willingness to cooperate and sacrifice themselves for the sake of the pack.

Huawei's strong identity, however, has not prevented the company from adopting Western tactics. In the mid 1990s, most Huawei managers were sanguine about the prospects of the firm.

However, Ren was aware that Huawei had severe growth limitations, mainly due to the lack of organizational expertise and the absence of a viable long-term strategy. He set out to change the company into a solutions provider. By 2000, when the communications industry slow down was noticeable, Huawei was already in the midst of a restructuring process that gave the firm its competitive edge against local rivals.

According to an industry insider, "Ren recognized that the best way to overcome Huawei's limitations was to learn from leading Western companies." Thus, from 1998 to 2003, the company hired IBM for management consulting services, modelling itself after the American company. Under IBM's guidance, Huawei significantly transformed its management and product development structure.

Ren prioritized R&D and supply chain management by adopting IBM's Integrated Product Development (IPD) and Integrated Supply Chain (ISC). After discovering Huawei's return on investment in R&D was one-sixth that of IBM, Ren stipulated mastery of IBM's IPD methodology. Furthermore, Huawei adopted ISC since supply-chain performance was far below potential. According to The World of Huawei, Huawei's on-time delivery rate in 1999 was only 50%, compared with 94% for competitors; annual inventory turnover was 3.6%, Adopting ISC entailed winning over suppliers and partners, many of whom had little appetite for Western management practices.

While working with Huawei, IBM was completing its own strategic change from a hardware vendor to an IT solutions provider. Ren drew from IBM's experience, also realizing that the future of Huawei was not in manufacturing what others invented, but in creating excellence in both research and service.

This strategy, which may be conventional for leading Western firms, is unusual in China. Although Huawei management possessed vision before hiring IBM, it was through the experience, insight and methodologies gained from working with IBM that Huawei managed to adopt new management practices and become a global player.

Nowhere is Huawei's presence and strategy more evident than in Africa, a continent it entered for the first time in 1998, where it successfully dispelled the "made in China" image of low cost and low quality.

Beginning in the 1990s, Huawei shifted its role from a manufacturer to that a complete solutions provider. Today, Huawei creates some of the most sophisticated telecommunications equipment in the world and, according to the company, is "not making it cheaper — it's making it better."

Armed with its combination of a corporate culture marked by Communist roots and leading Western business practices, Huawei has executed a strategy composed of superior pricing, customer service and brand awareness to penetrate and dominate the African market, one in which few multinationals have been successful. Huawei has established a reputation as the preferred low-cost, yet high-quality mobile network builder. Its sales in Africa had topped $2 billion across 40 countries by 2006.

According to the former head of Huawei's operations in West Africa, Wilson Yang, Huawei's profit margins in Africa can be up to 10 times greater than those it realizes in China. Huawei manages to achieve tremendous margins while still pricing itself only 5%-15% lower than its major international competitors, Ericsson and Nokia. Furthermore, Huawei is cautious not to price itself too low so that it will not be seen as yet another low-cost Chinese provider. In contrast, Huawei's main Chinese competitor in Africa, ZTE, consistently prices 30%-40% below European competitors and, consequently, its products are perceived as being of inferior quality.

Huawei's pricing methodology can also be traced back to its experience with IBM, a company that helped Huawei learn the importance of turning R&D into cash and of approaching product development from both technical and business angles to ensure investment returns. This represented the transition for Huawei from a low-cost volume competitor to a value-added leading enterprise.

Learning from the Master another factor behind its African success is its attention to superior customer service. In 2000-2001, Huawei faced a confluence of challenges: IT investment dried up, profit margins shrank and the market faced oversupply, leading profit growth to evaporate. IBM consultants stressed increasing profits through better supply-chain management, stronger R&D and more integrated corporate structure. However, Huawei was also learning a key strength of IBM: unparalleled service. Ren appreciated the value of this concept under looming adversity. Unmatched attention and commitment to service eventually came to dominate the firm's global strategy.

Indeed, superior service was a distinguishing feature of Huawei's business model in Africa and its core competitive advantage. Yang explains how this aspect of Huawei's business model ultimately led to global growth: "Three years into its Africa experiment, Huawei still had only 20 employees on the ground and very few contracts. However, our existing clients noticed the unparalleled responsiveness of management and personnel. We brought a Chinese attitude to both work ethic and relationship building in Africa. The result was that clients soon realized they could rely on Huawei 24 hours a day, seven days a week. We emphasized close relationships to foster that reliability and soon began to realize collateral benefits. All of a sudden, our reputation for superior service and higher quality gained us introductions to decision makers in new markets, faster network building and advanced notification of competitive bids.

This enhanced Huawei's ability to price safely below the competition." Huawei is also using its business in Africa as a training ground for establishing itself as a global brand through three distinct channels: policy, local investment and marketing. Huawei leverages its resources and products to connect with developmental policy throughout Africa. In May 2007, at a forum held in conjunction with the 2007 annual meeting of the African Development Bank Group (ADBG), Huawei set out a vision for Africa that is centered on "'bridging the digital divide and enriching the lives of Africans." Huawei prides itself on giving back to the African community; one of the ways it does this is through donating educational communications equipment to schools.

Huawei has begun to establish regional training centres in African countries such as Nigeria, Kenya, Egypt, Tunisia, Angola and Guinea. By August 2004, Huawei had invested more than $10 million dollars into its Nigerian training centre. Recently, Huawei opened a new training facility in South Africa, its fifth training centre on the continent. There is a sixth center currently being built in Angola. The company now provides training for up to 2,000 people annually. Such local investments by Huawei help bolster the local economy with job creation and localized management while improving the company's image in the eyes of local consumers, businesses and potential partners.

Huawei is asserting its brand potential in Africa by means of smart marketing strategies and "going reen," including optional use or solar and wind energy. It actively promotes its GSM base stations as among the most eco-friendly in the business, claiming that it cuts energy usage by 47% compared to regular towers. By the end of 2007, Huawei reported that it had deployed more than 100,000 green base stations, which saved 570 million kilowatt- hours, or 170,000 tons of coal.

Huawei Technologies has built a world-class enterprise, reaped tremendous profits in Africa over the last 10 years and is contributing to growth in Africa. In China, domestic media have heralded Huawei's success as a model for other Chinese companies trying to transform themselves from domestic entities into global players. Huawei has already profitably penetrated the European market, winning major contracts and servicing prominent clients such as Vodafone and Telefónica. As Huawei leads the way for home-grown Chinese corporations, the challenges its leaders face going forward include maintaining its growth and transferring the lessons learned in Africa to Europe and North and South America, all of which represent both enormous profit potential and new strategic challenges.

Source: Knowledge@Wharton Lauder Global Business Insight Report 2009

Questions for discussion:

1. Explain the customer-centric approach of Huawei Technologies in the African market.
2. Discuss the CSR initiatives of Huawei Technologies.

3.3 HOW POOR CUSTOMER SUPPORT CAN AFFECT YOUR BUSINESS?

- ⇨ Your customer feels ignored when their complaints go unresolved
- ⇨ Your customer loses trust in your company when you don't answer them
- ⇨ Dissatisfied Customers share Complaints with other potential customers
- ⇨ You lose both existing and Prospective Customers

Figure 3.1

Source: www.outsource2india.com

The above figure shows that how poor customer support affect the organization. This is clearly visible that when customer feels that he or she has been ignored, such thing will result in leaving the organization's products or services and they started complaining that the poor service rendered by the organization to all potential and future customers thus affects the bottom-line of an organization.

Therefore, to overcome the drawbacks organizations started to focusing on the information technology in rendering best possible customer service to the customers.

Examples: In Reliance Communications, till three years ago, IT teams were siloed across different business units. The CIO, has consolidated these units into a single IT service provider that subsequently became a separate IT company called Reliance Tech Services (RTS). With this, the company has reduced the cost to serve and benchmarked themselves against the best in class in the industry. They have also progressively showcased improvement in productivity and have been very effective in transforming the processes.

According to Shaun Smith co-author of the book "Managing the Customer Experience: Turning Customers into Advocates:" more than $46 billion was spent on CRM systems to help institutions get closer to customers.

Yet, Gartner Research estimates that 55 per cent of CRM programmes drive customers away and dilute earnings.

Brand loyalty has declined overall by 25 per cent, but good brand experiences can increase customer loyalty by 33 per cent.

Why are satisfied customers leaving?

80 per cent of customers who switch suppliers express "satisfaction" with their previous supplier.

Why? Because "customer satisfaction" is just not enough.

However, companies that are able to create a customer experience that is consistent, intentional, differentiated, and valuable have truly loyal customers that can't imagine doing business with anyone else. In fact, these "advocates" can't stop telling their friends and colleagues about you.

Therefore the organization should focus on excellent customer service through the use of information technology.

Gartner is one of many analysts firms stressing the importance of the customer experience and becoming more "customer-centric." In their 2006 CRM study, they state that four of the top ten priorities are:

1. Building and managing customer loyalty
2. Creating a single view of the customer
3. Creating a customer-centric enterprise
4. Managing/improving the customer experience Tata Teleservices, the customer is king

CASE STUDY

Telco TTSL, believes in top-class customer services Tata Teleservices (TTSL) is part of the Tata Group.The company provides basic telephony services and complements and competes with Bharat Sanchar Nigam (BSNL) in the circles it operates in. With a significant presence across the telecom value chain and the synergies after the acquisition of VSNL by the Tata group, TTSL is planning to expand the range of its coverage and services; advanced communication solutions now include seamless integration of voice, video, data and IP systems. As a basic telephone services provider, TTSL provides the backbone for India's corporate leaders such as GE Capital, Wipro, Magnacom, Citicorp Overseas software (now called Orbitech), Dr Reddy's Labs, Standard Chartered Bank, Motorola India Electronics, TCS and Satyam, in addition to servicing the telecom needs of retail customers.

After putting in place the required equipment and infrastructure, TTIL was committed to setting up a CRM solution that would cater to the varied needs of its vast customer base. "Oracle E-Business Suite has played an important role in helping TTSL meet its customer service needs," says S Ramakrishnan, managing director, Tata Teleservices.

Catalyst for change

In order to build its customer base, the TTSL management understood the need to have robust infrastructure in place to ensure quality customer service. This was to be a key differentiator for TTSL in the competitive landscape it was operating in. This was also a compelling need for the private sector service provider, as customer expectations were very high.

The TTSL management had the foresight to realise the potential of leveraging customer interaction to attract, maintain and enhance the lifetime value of the customer. The growth and wide acceptance of the service presented TTSL with an excellent opportunity to use customer interaction to enhance customer relationships as well as leverage the opportunity to up sell and cross-sell new products and offerings. To meet the strategic objectives of the customer care experience there was a need to have integrated processes and systems in place to:

Ensure that customers could access and get information about various services easily.

Provide quick and accurate resolution of customer requests.

Meet all the commitments.

Get things right the first time, all the time.

Constantly find ways to reduce costs and increase productivity to generate and safeguard company revenues and profitability.

Ensure that every interaction with the customer results in delight, produces joy and enhances the customer's relationship with TTSL.

Translating the corporate mission was a challenging task. TTSL realised very early that a CRM strategy required robust and scaleable tools. There was also a need to align all processes towards customer-centricity ethics and also to ensure that this got translated into faster, quicker and better service levels.

The solution

The evaluation by TTSL included getting multiple vendors to respond to detailed functional requirements, solution presentations, demonstrations and site visits. After a thorough techno-commercial evaluation, TTSL chose Oracle CRM tools. "The evaluation teams found the Oracle solution to be most integrated and with a clear growth path. This, coupled with the significant local presence of Oracle and excellent support for Oracle technology already in use at TTSL gave us the confidence to implement the Oracle CRM solution," says Rajeev Nagpal, CIO, TTSL.

TTSL chose sister concern Tata Consultancy Services (TCS) to implement Oracle CRM.

The implementation

The project team from TTSL along with TCS identified the processes that needed to be integrated. The integrated CRM solution feeds information into the enterprise-wide deployment of Oracle Data Warehouse, which is used for all MIS reporting.

"The solution deployed was a complete CRM suite, integrating data warehousing and ERP," says Nagpal. A modular implementation was worked out wherein data warehousing was followed by applications to streamline customer service operations integrated into the system. This was capped by a state-of-the-art computer telephony integration (CTI) application. Alongside, extensive user training and orientation was carried out.

Fruits of the loom Call centre throughput has gone up by 15-20 per cent. The first-time resolution of complaints has risen and turnaround time for complaints has dropped to a maximum of 24 hours.

Says Kurivilla Markose, general manager, Customer Service, TTSL, "The solution has also contributed in lowering the costs of customer service, thus directly contributing to the bottom line of the company."

Case discussion

Discuss the Tata Teleservices (TTSL) customer service initiatives in India.

3.4 SUMMARY

A service is a product that is purely or mostly intangible. The size and growth of the service sector makes marketing important, but in the service sector marketing has been slowly taken up. This is because of Competition. Consumers are changing the way they buy products and services. If the marketing hasn't changed in response, it should. Marketing's one goal is "to reach consumers at the moments that most influence their decisions."

3.5 SELF ASSESSMENT EVALUATING QUESTIONS

Part – A

1. Define Service economy
2. Why "customer satisfaction" is just not enough?
3. Define customer service.
4. Name the characteristics of services give rise to special needs in preparing the market mix.
5. How do you categorize the service marketing mix?

Part – B

1. Improving customers' satisfaction with your business translates directly to your bottom line. – Discuss.
2. Explain how poor customer support can affect the business.
3. Define customer service. Explain the customer service initiatives of an Indian organization and compare with a Multinational corporation.
4. The 80 per cent of customers who switch suppliers express "satisfaction" with their previous supplier. – Explain.

OBJECTIVE TYPE QUESTIONS

1. Happy customers tell at least four others of a positive experience. Dissatisfied customers tell as many as 12 about a negative experience.
   (a) A negative experience.
   (b) A positive experience.
   (c) Neutral experience.
   (d) No experience.
2. The average customers lose of a company of its customer's base each year.
   (a) 10 per cent.
   (b) 20 per cent.
   (c) 15 per cent.
   (d) 20 per cent.

3. Involvement of the customer is caused by inseparability in that customers are involved to a relatively greater degree in the production and marketing of many kinds of services.
   - (a) a relatively greater degree in the production and marketing of many kinds of services.
   - (b) a relatively greater degree in the production and human resources of many kinds of services.
   - (c) a relatively greater degree in the operations and marketing of many kinds of services.
   - (d) a relatively greater degree in the production and marketing of many kinds of products.
4. The best approach to improving standards of service is
   - (a) Empowering the employee to satisfy customers.
   - (b) Empowering the products to satisfy customers.
   - (c) Empowering the services to satisfy customers.
   - (d) Empowering the managers to satisfy customers.
5. Consumer-driven marketing is now more important than
   - (a) company-driven marketing.
   - (b) customer-driven marketing
   - (c) product-driven marketing
   - (d) service-driven marketing
6. To provide quality service, organizations must tailor these products to the needs of
   - (a) specific customers.
   - (b) specific markets.
   - (c) specific products.
   - (d) specific services.

□□□

4 Chapter

UNDERSTANDING THE MARKET

Objectives

After going through this chapter, you will be able to understand:

- To understand about the market
- To familiarize with the managing and challenges in front of the market
- To identify the role of marketing department
- To understand about the target market
- To understand about the marketing strategic focus on the customer-centricity

Structure:

4.1 The market

4.2 Managing the Market

4.3 Challenges in Front of the Market

4.4 Role of Marketing Department

4.5 Identifying the Target Market

4.6 Marketing Strategic focus on the Customer-Centricity

4.7 Advantages and Disadvantages

4.8 Summary

4.9 Self Assessment Questions

4.1 THE MARKET

The market is the place where both buyer and seller present.

A market is the set of all actual and potential buyers of a product or service.

This definition suggests that a market is the total value and/or volume of products that satisfy the same customer need.

In defining a market, it is important not to focus only on products/services that currently meet the customer need. For example, the two-wheeler manufacturer who believed that their market was the "two-wheeler market" would have made some poor marketing decisions unless he had seen the arrival of products such as higher end models – which also satisfy the same need – "to provide convenient travel".

Thinking about customer needs first – and then identifying the products that meet those needs – is the best way to define a market.

However, it is also important not to define a market too broadly. For example, it is not particularly helpful for a marketing manager to define his or her market as the "food market" or the "transport market". The purpose of market definition is to provide a meaningful framework for analysis and decision-making.

For example; consider the "FMCG market". The customer need is to be "satisfied". There are many products and services that can claim to meet that need in different ways:

The FMCG brand should meet the individual consumer demand. Or the brand needs to fulfil his or her family members demand.

It is important to avoid too broad a definition of a market For example, it will be more manageable for marketing managers in the sporting events market to further refine their market definition into more detailed classes or segments.

To help with calculating market share, the following definitions are helpful:

Product class – e.g. computers, televisions, holidays

Product subclass – e.g. laptops, digital televisions, long-haul holidays

Product brands – e.g. Dell, Panasonic, Kuoni

Kuoni as a brand, for the purposes of measuring market share, is only concerned with the aggregate of all other travel brands that satisfy the same group of customers. However, Kuoni also needs to be aware of the trends in long haul holidays and the holiday market in general.

A market is any one of a variety of different systems, institutions, procedures, social relations and infrastructures whereby person's trade, and goods and services are exchanged, forming part of the economy. It is an arrangement that allows buyers and sellers to exchange things. Markets vary in size, range, geographic scale, location, types and variety of human communities, as well as the types of goods and services traded. Some examples include local farmers' markets held in town squares or parking lots, shopping centres and shopping malls, international currency and commodity markets, legally created markets such as for pollution permits, and illegal markets such as the market for illicit drugs.

In mainstream economics, the concept of a market is any structure that allows buyers and sellers to exchange any type of goods, services and information. The exchange of goods or services for money is a transaction. Market participants consist of all the buyers and sellers of a good who influence its price. This influence is a major study of economics and has given rise to several theories and models concerning the basic market forces of supply and demand. There are two roles in markets, buyers and sellers. The market facilitates trade and enables the distribution and allocation of resources in a society. Markets allow any tradable item to be evaluated and priced. A market emerges more or less spontaneously or is constructed deliberately by human interaction in order to enable the exchange of rights (cf. ownership) of services and goods.

Historically, markets originated in physical marketplaces which would often develop into — or from — small communities, towns and cities.

Market

Actual or conceptual place in commercial world where forces of demand and supply operate, and where buyers and sellers interact (directly or through intermediaries) to trade goods, services, or contracts or instruments, for money or barter.

Markets include mechanisms or means for

(1) Determining price of the traded item,

(2) Communicating the price information,

(3) Facilitating deals and transactions, and

(4) effecting distribution.

Market for a particular item is made up of existing and potential customers who need it and have the ability and willingness to pay for it. All markets, ultimately, consist of people.

A market is the "place" where price is determined.

In other words, a market is the collection of buyers and sellers that, through their actual or potential interactions, determine the price of a product or set of products.

Market definition is important for a number of reasons. From the point of view of a company, it is crucial to understand the actual and potential competitors are with respect to the various products the organization now sell or might sell in the future. It is likewise important to know the product characteristic boundaries and geographical boundaries of one's marketing order to be able to set price, determine advertising budgets, or make capital investment decisions.

4.2 MANAGING THE MARKET

Organizations continuously learn about their markets through the linked processes of market sensing and sense making. Firms that have mastered these two processes gain an advantage by anticipating market opportunities ahead of their rivals and more accurately forecasting how the market will respond to their moves. The market mechanism incorporate the following:

(i) to describe the primary mechanisms for acquiring market information and turning it into market knowledge;

(ii) to assess the marketing models used by organizations to filter, sort and simplify market information into coherent patterns; and then to prescribe some ways to improve a market learning capability.

If the organization's focus and marketing success are important then the following factors are need to be focused:

1. Establish a memorable and unmistakable brand identity:

The secret to business success is determined by the organization's ability to powerfully communicate the business with laser precision and the organization's ability to deliver a clearly-defined and consistent experience.

In a nutshell... it's called branding, and, when done right, it ensures a thriving business with all the customers and profits the organization need. The secret is to establish a powerful brand identity that sings distinction. And establish that identity before the organization launches any marketing activities.

The organization need to create a deep connection with the core target audience initially.

The better the organization define this group, the more effective the marketing can be.

2. Design Compelling Offerings that Pull Customers in Like a Magnet

80% of all purchase decisions are based on emotion. It's the organization's job as a marketer to know how the customers want to feel and to get them to visualize how the organization's services can meet their needs.

The customers want to know, "What's in it for them?" The organization should tap into the emotion and create offerings that touch the customers.

3. Craft a Personal, Workable Marketing Plan

Marketing is everything one does to make the product or service more visible, more desirable and more profitable. The marketing plan will clearly define the big picture and provide focus and direction based on the 4 'P's of Marketing – product, price, place/distribution and promotion.

Following these 4 criteria will transform any organization or business organization into a money-making machine guaranteed to grow the client list, sales and profits.

Definition: A marketing plan is a business document written for the purpose of describing the current market position of a business and its marketing strategy for the period covered by the marketing plan. Marketing plans usually have a life of from one to five years.

Purpose of a Marketing Plan

The purpose of creating a marketing plan is to clearly show what steps will be undertaken to achieve the business' marketing objectives.

What's in a Marketing Plan?

A typical marketing plan might include a description of its competitors, the demand for the product or service, and the strengths and weaknesses from a market standpoint of both the business and its competitors.

Other elements usually contained in a marketing plan include:

Description of the product or service, including special features,

Marketing budget, including the advertising and promotional plan,

Description of the business location, including advantages and disadvantages for marketing.

Pricing strategy

Market segmentation (specializing in specific niche markets or, if mass marketing, how marketing strategy might differ between different segments, such as age groups).

Keeping a Marketing Plan up to Date

Like a business plan, a marketing plan is an important document that needs to be updated on a regular basis. Even five-year marketing plans should be revisited periodically – at least once each year – to address changes in market conditions, demand, pricing issues, etc.

Examples:

In 2007, the Bajaj Auto domestic market share was pretty high in the 30s and the overall motorcycle share at 36% had put the organization very close to the market leaders. But, during the 2008, Bajaj Auto sales had slipped back. This is mainly due to the shift in the strategy of moving away from typically 100cc bikes. All that Bajaj Auto had done in the past 18 months, including the launch of the Discover, is true to that strategy.

Discover succeeded because it is perceived to be bigger and sportier than the average 100cc bikes. The main reason for the change in strategy was profitability. The April-June quarter of 2009 was the best ever in the history of Bajaj Auto, in terms of profitability at about Rs 455 crore and an EBITDA margin of 19.5%.

The move away from the small and cheap motorcycles to bigger bikes is to have this kind of profit structure going forward. The change of strategy has undoubtedly led to Bajaj Auto losing some ground.

The Bajaj Auto now aligning its portfolio to rest on only two products –

Discover for those who want bigger commuters and Pulsar for those who want sporty bikes.

The Bajaj Auto trying to have the best possible price at the front-end because it's either a Discover or a Pulsar that commands a good price in the marketplace.

The Bajaj Auto has consciously chosen Discover and Pulsar as the lead brands in the commuting and the sporty segments. Ideally, if Bajaj Auto sells two lakh motorcycles a month in the domestic market, about one lakh should come from both. In the transition period, the Bajaj Auto will continue to make Platina or XCD as long as there are some buyers for them. But in the future, in terms of product development, capacity expansion and all downstream action at the retail point, focus will be on the two big brands.

According to the 2004 Business Week/Interbrand survey, Coca-Cola tops the list of the 10 most valuable global brands ($67.4 billion), followed by Microsoft ($65 billion), IBM ($53.8 billion), General Electric ($44.1 billion), Intel ($33.5 billion), Disney ($27.1 billion), McDonald's ($25 billion), Nokia ($24 billion), Toyota ($22.7 billion) and Marlboro ($22.1 billion).

These brands and others share some common features:

They have a consistent name that is easy to pronounce: Corporate sales are globally balanced with no dominant market; the essence and positioning of the brand is the same the world over.

They address the same customer needs, or the same target segment, in every market; and there is great similarity in execution (pricing, packaging, and advertising) across cultures.

What kinds of products do not lend themselves to global brands?

Food is one category where, literally, differences in tastes from culture to culture compel global companies to adapt to local conditions.

At the other end of the spectrum is a company like Intel, whose products and markets make it easier for executives to establish a truly global brand with a memorable catch-phrase: "Intel inside."

It's much easier for a company like Intel to establish a global brand. Intel has a smaller number of buyers [than many other global companies] and all of those buyers are using computer chips for the same purpose. And all of Intel's competitors are global. Intel is a global brand without significant local adaptation. The same holds true for Disney, which stands for family entertainment in all cultures.

These organizations know how to manage the market, mange their customers and manage their brands in the global market.

In the 1990s, Unilever was struggling under the weight of some 1,600 brands in more than 50 countries. Revenues were lopsided — 3% of the brands provided 63% of revenues — and the company was not growing. In 2002, Unilever launched a programme to reduce its number of brands to 400 "core" brands so that it could concentrate its resources on fewer products. The company combined branding strategies by placing the 400 in three categories:

international brands (such as Dove and Lipton), regional brands (such as a spread called Flora in the United Kingdom and Becel in Germany), and local brands with strong positions in single countries (including Wishbone salad dressing in the United States and Persil detergent in England).

India is among the world's fastest-growing markets for mobile phones. The country has some 170 million subscribers and adds 6 million to 7 million more each month. (China, in contrast, adds 5 million subscribers, and the U.S. 2 million subscribers a month.) Recognizing this potential, several global telecom giants jumped into the fray when the Indian government first opened up the country's telecom market to private enterprise in 1994. Among them, one company — Finland-based Nokia — forged ahead of rivals and today commands a 58% market share for mobile phones (also called "handsets"). In specific segments, such as GSM telephony, Nokia's market share in India is as high as 70%. (GSM, which stands for Global System for Mobile, is the world's most popular standard for mobile communications.)

D. Shivakumar, Nokia India's vice president and country manager, believes that focus played a key role in the company's growth in India. "If you look at the [mobile phone] landscape in 1995, anybody could have succeeded if they had done the same things as Nokia did," he says. "But all the other companies had something else to focus on, some other business. Nokia was completely focused on mobile phones; others had consumer electronics, home appliances, etc." Nokia's focus was not just on handsets, of course. The mobile infrastructure business — then part of Nokia India — was equally important. But, as of April 1, 2007, Nokia's joint venture with Siemens for mobile infrastructure has become an independent entity. Thus, Nokia India has become even more sharply focused.

Being ahead of the curve was another component of Nokia's strategy. "We invested before everybody else — in the brand, in people, in distribution," says Shivakumar. Adds Pankaj Mahendroo, president of the Indian Cellular Association: "Nokia invested in each vertical of the handset ecosystem — manufacturing, distribution and design R&D."

Nokia has invested more than $1 billion in India so far, and company headquarters at Helsinki has repeatedly said that more funds will be made available if required. The Indian company had revenues of more than $3.5 billion in 2006, which means there is also money to be reinvested. (The company does not disclose its profit numbers.)

Bombay Dyeing

The Wadia group, which came into existence after Nusli Wadia's great grandfather Nowrosjee Wadia started Bombay Dyeing in a small red-brick shed in Mumbai in 1879, has businesses ranging from textiles to airlines. Bombay Burmah, National Peroxide and Go Air are the other companies in the group.

Bombay Dyeing's textile business reported a loss of Rs 10.41 crore during the quarter ended June 30, 2009. While the company still retains the numero uno position in the home textile market, cut-throat competition and inability to connect with young customers are posing a major threat, according to textile industry experts. To overcome the problems the company has appointed Ms.Vinitha Bali as the CEO. From soft-drink concentrate to chocolates to Coke to biscuits and now textiles, the 'turnaround expert' becomes the first Indian woman professional to hold a key position in an organisation run by a promoter family. Britannia's turnover more than doubled to Rs 3,436 crore ever since Ms Bali joined as CEO in January 2005.

FMCG industry experts believe Ms Bali, who used aggressive marketing strategies and differentiated brand launches in Britannia, will replicate similar initiatives in the textile business too. Ms Bali is known for successfully launching the Rasna brand at the beginning of her career when she worked for Voltas HUL Indian Operations.

There is a visible sense of urgency within the Unilever system that subsidiaries such as HUL deliver strong volume growth. India and China, among the developing markets, are expected to lead Unilever out of the downturn.

HUL is committed to competitive growth. It will be the full portfolio of brands, across all categories because that is what HUL believe is required to successfully deliver on their ambition and goal to get competitive growth.

Market penetration varies quite dramatically — from very high to extremely low. There are a large number of personal care categories where the penetration levels are very low like deodorants, hair conditioners, and fabric conditioner in laundry, where the penetration is insignificant. For example the dish wash segment, surface cleaners will become a very large market. Till now, parts of house cleaners that have been penetrating are really dish wash. HUL now introduced 'CiF' to build and grow the market with right penetration.

In certain categories, the differences across regions are very significant in terms of presence and nature of competition. HUL first recognize that any company which wishes to be delivering competitive growth must be just as tight-focused and ruthless on elimination of cost.

HUL focused on growth or cost?

The way HUL manage is by continuing to be really tough from the elimination of structural cost in their business, the cost across their supply chain. Because that is the only way which will give HUL head room which is required, i.e. to invest as required behind their brands. So if competition is going to be intensive — HUL want to be one step ahead and invest in product, quality and advertising. HUL also committed to profitable growth.

The only way the organization will achieve this is by creating such headroom by removing costs from the system that it will lead the organization enough to invest behind the product, and the topline and yet leave a surplus to deliver the product.

HUL's extensive focus on cost-cutting involves cutting cost overheads and under heads and not brand investments. HUL want to be outward looking, dealing with the consumer interest. That is the first shift which HUL want. All at HUL must be spending more time with consumers and customers because there is no substitute for the first hand feel of what is going on in the market place.

4.3 CHALLENGES IN FRONT OF THE MARKET

Challenge No. 1: How does the organization define the market?

Several large markets in India are as yet highly underdeveloped. The market in which the organization operate, the type of customers served by the organization, the services or products offered by the organization etc., play an important role in defining the market.

Challenge No. 2: How to target the market?

The target market consists of the customers.The exact identification of such market may help an organization to tap its potential. By 2025, India is expected to emerge as the world's fifth-biggest consumer market as incomes and living standards improve, according to a study by the McKinsey Global Institute. Nearly 300 million Indians are expected to escape poverty, and the middle class will leapfrog by a factor of 10—from 50 million today to roughly 583 million 18 years from now.

Challenge No. 3: How to understand the consumer?

India should be seen as one country, with many states of various demographic characteristics of the market. So consumer behaviour may vary from north to south, big town to village. The understanding of the consumer is the most important point an organization should focused upon.

Challenge No. 4: How to tailor the product?

The positioning a product as per the expectations of the consumer will help an organization to capture a large market share from the market. For example the south based organization Cavin Kare positioned its fairness cream in such a way, so that it has emerged as a number one brand in southern districts of Tamil Nadu.

Challenge No. 5: How to make the packaging work?

Indian consumers believe in packaging should appealing as well as help them in reusing and recycling. Unlike traditional outlets, where space and ambience are serious constraints, modern format stores also provide an ideal environment for FMCG companies to initiate product trials and launch premium or niche products. In mid-2006, for instance, Dabur India launched a 400 gram squeeze pack of Dabur Honey only through modern format stores.

Challenge No. 6: How to price it right?

There are many approaches to the pricing game but Indian consumers need to see value. A well thought out pricing strategy is critical, not just a pricing strategy for entry. Microsoft has announced the worldwide availability of its new Windows 7 operating system. Windows 7 offers a streamlined user interface and significant new features that make everyday tasks easier and allow people to get the most out of computers of all styles and sizes.

A basic home version of Windows 7, available only in emerging countries such as India, Windows 7 Home Basic is priced at Rs 5,899 excluding taxes. Windows 7 Home Premium is Rs 6799, Windows 7 Professional is Rs 11199 and Windows 7 Ultimate is Rs 11799.

Challenge No. 7: How to reach the product to the consumer?

The presence of the wholesale trade is yet another complexity. Marketers have to decide on how to use these various channels to reach the consumers effectively. Here again it is necessary to define the roles of the various channels, and define the organization's own rules. Few years back a salt brand launched by a financial services firm in Mumbai failed in the market due to non-availability in spite of spending Rs three crore towards the advertising of the salt brand all over India.

Hindustan Unilever is involving family grocers, chemists and wholesalers in custom-made programmes that offer them targeted promotions, value deals and also build relationships through training sessions, newsletters and meetings.

For its part, Cadbury India has changed the rules for all its customers (retailers). It has created a menu-based approach – issues covered include prompt payment, efficiency and business building initiatives – that is common to all retailers, big and small.

A couple of years ago, it also started the Purple Star programme for traditional retailers, where it tailors promotions and schemes for selected stores.

Challenge No. 8: How to communicate?

The task of communication in FMCG marketing is to make the consumer remember the brand, like the brand and try the brand. The Indian consumer has not changed over a period of last few years but has become elusive. The word of mouth, technology, common sense and dialogue with consumers are the simple elements of creating media attention. Focus to narrowcast consumers and insights to communication are also important factors in creating distinctive brand identity.

The television channels and print publications have grown considerably in last seven years but consumers spend less time on each of them.The 80% growth of advertisers, the increase from 4120 in 2003 to 7368 advertisers in 2006 shows the immense opportunity for media. Retail and in-shop advertising is also going to play a major role in near future.

Challenge No.9: How to track the brand?

Now the global brands also have a focused market. Every person in India has multiple identities. This underlies the Indian consumer. India being a strong family oriented society, for the youth boarding and lodging becomes free even when they earn, so they have a huge disposable income to spend as per their will. Typically, Traditionalism and Modernism co-exist here. There is a value consciousness in the Indian homes, which lately MNCs have also realised. There is now a movement towards value added products as people now do not necessarily go for the cheapest ones. Any truth about India can be equally contradicted by an equally valid truth.The marketers were using different varieties and brands of similar products for different group of Indians to validate his theory of 'multiple identities and several markets within India'.

Using market research intelligently is an important part in tracking the brand. The ideal way to measure the success of the marketing mix is to do a real market pressure text. Hindustan Unilever tested Close-up in Tamil Nadu (a media isolatable state) before taking on Colgate on the national playing field.

Challenge No. 10:How to use promotions better?

Promotion: It is not enough to have good products sold at attractive prices. To generate sales and profits, the benefits of products have to be communicated to customers. Promotion is, therefore, about companies communicating with customers Promotion has several possible objectives and many pieces of marketing promotion aim to achieve several of the following objectives at the same time:

Inform

Management may need to make their audience aware that their product exists, and to explain exactly what it does. This is a particularly important objective for new products.

Persuade

An important stage in creating favourable attitudes towards the business and its brands.Through persuasive promotion, management will seek to persuade customers and the trade that their brand has benefits that are superior to competitors.

Image creation

Sometimes, promoting a brand image is the only way to create differentiation in the mind of the consumer (e.g., lager advertising).

Reassurance

Much promotion (particularly advertising) is about reassuring customers that they have made the right choice and encouraging them to stay loyal to a brand.

There are a large and growing number of promotional methods that businesses can use. The main instruments – advertising, direct response mailing, sales promotion, public relations and direct selling, are often mixed together as part of the promotional mix. Each has different strengths. What is important is that the promotional mix is carefully planned and the results monitored to ensure that the total promotional cost is controlled.

'Promotion' includes all of the tools available to the marketer for 'marketing communication.' Marketing communications has its own 'promotions mix.' Think of it like a cake mix, the basic ingredients are always the same. However, if we vary the amounts of one of the ingredients, the final outcome is different. It is the same with promotions. We can 'integrate' different aspects of the promotions mix to deliver a unique campaign. The elements of the promotions mix are:

1. Personal Selling
2. Sales Promotion
3. Public Relations
4. Direct Mail
5. Trade Fairs and Exhibitions
6. Advertising
7. Sponsorship

The elements of the promotions mix are integrated to form a coherent campaign. As with all forms of communication. The message from the marketer follows the 'communications process' as illustrated above. For example, a radio advert is made for a car manufacturer. The car manufacturer (sender) pays for a specific advert with contains a message specific to a target audience (encoding). It is transmitted during a set of commercials from a radio station (Message / media). The message is decoded by a car radio (decoding) and the target consumer interprets the message (receiver). He or she might visit a dealership or seek further information from a website (Response). The consumer might buy a car or express an interest or dislike (feedback). This information will inform future elements of an integrated promotional campaign. Perhaps a direct mail campaign would push the consumer to the point of purchase. Noise represent the thousands of marketing communications that a consumer is exposed to everyday, all competing for attention.

The Promotions Mix

All of the elements promotional mix are 'integrated' to form a specific communications campaign.

1. Personal Selling

Personal Selling is an effective way to manage personal customer relationships. The sales person acts on behalf of the organization. They tend to be well trained in the approaches and techniques of personal selling. However, sales people are very expensive and should only be used where there is a genuine return on investment. For example salesmen are often used to sell cars or home improvements where the margin is high.

2. Sales Promotion

Sales promotion tend to be thought of as being all promotions apart from advertising, personal selling, and public relations. For example the BOGOF promotion, or Buy One Get One Free. Others include couponing, money-off promotions, competitions, free accessories (such as free blades with a new razor), introductory offers (such as buy digital TV and get free installation), and so on. Each sales promotion should be carefully costed and compared with the next best alternative.

3. Public Relations (PR)

Public Relations is defined as 'the deliberate, planned and sustained effort to establish and maintain mutual understanding between an organization and its publics.' It is relatively cheap, but certainly not cheap. Successful strategies tend to be long-term and plan for all eventualities. All airlines exploit PR; just watch what happens when there is a disaster. The pre-planned PR machine clicks in very quickly with a very effective rehearsed plan.

4. Direct Mail

Direct mail is very highly focussed upon targeting consumers based upon a database. As with all marketing, the potential consumer is 'defined' based upon a series of attributes and similarities. Creative agencies work with marketers to design a highly focussed communication in the form of a mailing. The mail is sent out to the potential consumers and responses are carefully monitored. For example, if we are marketing medical text books, we would use a database of doctors' surgeries as the basis of your mail shot.

5. Trade Fairs and Exhibitions

Such approaches are very good for making new contacts and renewing old ones. Companies will seldom sell much at such events. The purpose is to increase awareness and to encourage trial. They offer the opportunity for companies to meet with both the trade and the consumer. Expo has recently finish in Germany with the next one planned for Japan in 2005, despite a recent decline in interest in such events.

6. Advertising

Advertising is a 'paid for' communication. It is used to develop attitudes, create awareness, and transmit information in order to gain a response from the target market. There are many advertising 'media' such as newspapers (local, national, free, trade), magazines and journals, television (local, national, terrestrial, satellite) cinema, outdoor advertising (such as posters, bus sides).

7. Sponsorship

Sponsorship is where an organization pays to be associated with a particular event, cause or image. Companies will sponsor sports events such as the Olympics or Formula One. The attributes of the event are then associated with the sponsoring organization. The elements of the promotional mix are then integrated to form a unique, but coherent campaign.

Is the promotion brand led or discount led?

Rin gave away open soap dishes, it helped the product usage since it dried better on an open dish. Nescafe gave away shakers to popularize the coffee milk shake.

Indian FMCG market today has become a sales promotion mela. There are 2 for 1 offers, banded packs, 50% extra offers, 3 for 2 offers... all chasing the discount buying tendency of Indian consumers. Sales Promotions need to help in building the brand values, in addition to generating short-term results.

8. Modern trends in advertising

According to India knowledge at Wharton it hasn't caught on yet in the U.S., but a global ad campaign for Unilever's army of laundry detergents — sold in Asia as Omo, in France as Skip, and by other names around the planet — hailing that "Dirt is Good," is considered by experts to be a perfect example of a new path for marketing in the 21st century.

The marketing push merges memorable images of children splashing in mud with a customer-engaging social message — "every child has a right to play and explore." Some claim the ad helped push Singapore to increase recess time at its academics-heavy, stress-inducing schools.

The early success of Unilever's advertising strategy is exactly the type of information that company marketing executives and ad agencies need to discuss as they struggle to develop new ideas to handle the cataclysmic changes in technology and communications — from Tivo to Twitter — that have altered the ways companies interact with customers. But until now, there has been surprisingly little coordinated effort to re-invent the science of advertising or to rewrite the basic manual of what advertising strategies don't work and which ones do — and under what set of circumstances.

The organizations should focus upon the trends that taking place in the advertising of a product or services.

9. How to understand the new consumers

Global launches can be rocky, as Apple knows well. Last year, the company introduced its iPhone in India, but instead of the throngs of consumers seen at launch events in the U.S., the journalists assigned to cover the rollout reportedly outnumbered the customers. According to experts, the problems included a lack of marketing and a price tag set too high for Indian consumers.

The another example of understanding the consumer dealt with the Red Bull provided the initial rush of energy drinks into the worldwide beverage market. The drink originated in Thailand and is now marketed globally by an Austrian company. Introduced in the United States in 1997, Red Bull is the world's leading energy brand.

According to Wharton marketing professor David Reibstein, Red Bull was originally marketed to Thai truckers who needed to keep awake while driving through the night. When it was launched in the United States, he says, it was positioned as a product that allowed young people "to stay up late and be able to do better on exams and sports. But it quickly evolved into something people used in the late-night rave and partying scene."

Red Bull has been banned at one time or another in a number of countries. The primary concern is that it is heavily caffeinated and — when used as a sports drink — could raise cardiovascular stress to dangerous levels. In addition, once it came to be used as a mixer in alcoholic drinks — Red Bull with vodka being the most popular combination — additional alarm bells went off. "Red Bull had this club aura around it. It was viewed almost as something illicit," Reibstein says. "It raised health concerns and I actually think that helped" the product.

A Mintel report noted an influx of new players in the energy drink market, up from 169 in 2007 to 306 in 2008; most of the entrants were small start-ups. Red Bull dominates the market with a 36.9% share, according to Mintel, although that is down 3 percentage points from a year earlier. At the same time, market share is becoming increasingly concentrated. In November 2008, Coca-Cola began distributing Monster Energy, the number two brand behind Red Bull, with a 20.6% market share. In February, PepsiCo signed a distribution deal with Rockstar Energy, the number three brand, with 12.9% of sales. According to Lal, the Mintel analyst, Coca-Cola and PepsiCo maintain a low profile in this sector, choosing to distribute independent brands rather than buy them outright. "You don't see Pepsi anywhere on those brands. They separate them under a different identity," she says.

Wharton marketing professor Geeta Menon suggests that Coca-Cola and PepsiCo risk cannibalizing their well-established carbonated soft drink business if they choose to build on their global brand recognition to promote alternative drinks. In this consumer segment, Coca-Cola, for example, wants consumers to think they are choosing between Coke and Monster, not between Coke and another kind of Coke. "Coke is an old brand now, while Monster is exciting and a new brand name. There is no stigma of it being attached to your parents' generation."

According to Hutchinson, the marketing of Red Bull and its energy drink competitors is decidedly skewing towards young consumers, posing a different dilemma than that faced by companies that sell alcohol.

10. Emerging newer technologies and its impact on marketing

What makes emerging technologies a "different approach"?

Higher levels of uncertainty and complexity, accelerating speed and competency-destroying change are among the characteristics that make managing emerging technology businesses distinct from managing established technology firms.

Managers who want to succeed in this environment, therefore, need to take innovative approaches to issues such as technology assessment, strategy, marketing and organizational design.

A triangular relationship exists between communication channels, brands and the customer. The choice of communication technology is the key to building a successful brand relationship with any given consumer. Given new technology, channels of communications are evolving at a speed that no one can keep up with.

One of the significant trends in consumer marketing is the emergence of multi-channel marketing of products and services. Organisations are using direct channels such as the Internet and catalogue channels and other channels such as brick-and-mortar environments, either to seamlessly integrate their offerings across all channels or to use these different channels to segment consumers and implement differential marketing strategies.

Technology-e-mail, e-commerce, the Internet and websites, the cell phone and laptop-are opening up a new world of marketing communication. A fundamental change has occurred and marketers need to rethink their promotional strategies. Today the customer has the opportunity to come to an organization you or an organization's competitor, by accessing through the website of an organization or sending an e-mail. All relevant information must be accessible and user friendly. It should also be a two-way flow.

Ten years ago, the Internet did not even exist as a marketing communications medium, yet now it is arguably the most powerful communication medium available to business. However, the key question is, can the Internet succeed as a medium in isolation, or will its success depend on its integration and support of more traditional marketing communication mediums?

The Internet is now settling down to its reality after all the hyperbole of the late 90s. There is no doubt that in many areas, the Internet provides unique characteristics that other media cannot match. But, we should be conscious that the Internet is simply a content delivery system as is television, radio, and even word of mouth. As technology develops into more and more digital interactive platforms, the relevance of the net may well shift. In basic terms, the net is probably the first truly global content provider and as such, its characteristics, benefits and uses are also global.

The Internet will continue to grow as a powerful marketing communications medium; however it cannot exist in isolation as a stand-alone device. Its power can only be maximised if it is integrated into a company's total marketing communications strategy.

Interactive Voting is one of the most successful revenue generating Interactive TV applications. Voting can be used to encourage first time users to interact with programmes and advertising, thus helping viewers become familiar with Interactive TV. Sky News repeatedly drive their UK audience to interact, adding value to their news service by personalising news and ensuring viewer retention, while at the same time generating significant revenues from the dial-ups to register viewer's votes.

Voting changes the dynamics of the viewer experience from a passive, one-way communication to a two-way exchange that draws in the audience by allowing viewers to interact with and influence the programme. Interactive Voting is a proven first move for both viewers and broadcasters. Viewers are comfortable pressing a coloured button to register their vote and can see clearly what this will cost them.

Several market research companies are already using wireless devices to obtain instantaneous feedback from fans at live concerts and performances. The subsequent offerings, e.g., music, songs and volume, etc., are appropriately modified based on customer feedback. Such customer feedback is also very useful in other service settings such as restaurants, theme parks and spectator sports, etc., where attributes of service offerings can be dynamically fine-tuned to match customer expectations.

The wireless devices can be used for dynamic promotion and pricing–electronic coupons as consumers shop, quantity discounts, auction pricing for certain items or bidding against other shoppers.

The use of advanced technologies to complement the more traditional channels can lead to more efficient and effective market communication techniques at significantly reduced cost.

Benefits to Consumers

Helps provide information about a range of products or services so consumers have more choices at varying quality levels and prices.

Competition is real when people know their alternatives. The superior or more economical product that no one knows about will benefit few consumers.

Introduces consumers to new products and new uses for old products, without the necessity of the costly and time-consuming process of consumers' trying numerous products until they find one that meets their needs.

Encourages product improvement and innovation among competitors, which can lead to lower prices for consumers.

Once an innovative product becomes popular, other companies follow the lead and may offer price incentives to switch to their product.

Companies can interact with customers to learn more about their needs and to build customer databases.

What is the Marketing Department's Role?

The marketing department must act as a guide and lead the company's other departments in developing, producing, fulfilling, and servicing products or services for their customers. Communication is vital. The marketing department typically has a better understanding of the market and customer needs, but should not act independently of product development or customer service. Marketing is the main thrust area in an organization. Marketing should be involved, and there should be a meeting of the minds, whenever discussions are held regarding new product development or any customer-related function of the company.

Marketing should not make the plans and recommendations alone. It is very important that the marketing department get input from many people within the company. Not only does providing input help the rest of the company understand and support the marketing efforts, it also provides some invaluable insights into what customers want and new ideas that may have slipped past the rest of the company. For example, the service technicians and the customer service reps will have great insights into customer opinions and needs. The Marketing department should get everyone involved and the organization will have a more cohesive effort.

Because the goals and guidelines set by the marketing department should, by design, be in line with the vision and mission of the company, the top level management should be involved in and endorse cooperation by all departments in following and implementing the plan and integrating a consistent message into all communication channels.

Another important part played by the marketing department through the reinforcing the idea among the employees of an organization that marketing is a team effort. Individuals may have their own goals and priorities, but if they don't also consider the goals and greater need of the company, they may hinder efforts and make the carefully planned marketing efforts fail.

To illustrate this, let us assume a company has implemented a direct mail programme and has placed key codes on the mailing labels to track the source of the mailing lists from which customers who place orders are coming. If the employees who take the orders don't ask for and record those codes, then the marketing department has no way of knowing which lists are working and which lists are not working. Cooperation among departments and support of top level management to enforce necessary procedures is often critical.

So, the marketing department studies the market and the customers, determines the best way to reach those customers, and works with the rest of the company to help determine the new product needs of the market and represent the company in a consistent voice.

The marketing planning process involves four stages of action:

Researching and analyzing the business and the market

Planning and writing the plan

Implementing the plan

Evaluating the results

Market Research and Analysis

The research and analysis stage of the planning process is very important.

For example:

Research and analysis are critical because they lead the organization to identifying the product's target audience or services target audience, as well as its strengths, weaknesses, threats and, most importantly, opportunities.

Knowing the threats and opportunities the product or services faces helps the organization more realistically set the sales goals and objectives.

Knowing the opportunities, target audience, and sales goals will give the information the organization need to set the marketing goals to take advantage of the opportunities and meet the sales goals.

Knowing the current marketing objectives will give the information the organization need to set the positioning, pricing, distribution, and other marketing strategies.

Having the strategies set will give the road map to set up the tactical elements of the marketing plan, such as advertising, promotions, branding, packaging, etc. — all of those things that have to tailor to the market.

Once the tactical elements are determined, the organization can determine the creative element, budgets, and calendar.

The Business Review

What is the scope of organization's business?

In other words, what business is the organization is in?

What is the essence of what the organization business does or what the organization's product provides?

Is it helping people lower their stress levels by helping them organize their daily lives (as in Day-Timers, PDAs, reminder services)?

Is it helping businesses save money, improve working conditions and increase the safety of their employees (as in safety consulting and training services)?

Is it helping kids learn to read and so have a greater chance in succeeding in school and their careers (as in educational television, educational computer games, or personal tutoring)?

What is the business's philosophy and mission?

Revisit the organization's vision and mission statements.

In order to put together a good plan for marketing, one should have a thorough knowledge of the product or services.

The organization need to perform an exhaustive review of :

features

benefits

life cycle stage

safety

reliability

appearance and packaging

technology level (if applicable)

sales history

seasonality

pricing history

distribution history

promotion history

other areas specific to the product or services.

The Market Review focuses on the following:

the size of the market

the segments of the market

who are the primary competitors?

what are the competitors'strengths?

what are competitors' weaknesses?

who are the target audiences?

and

what their needs are?

what their desires are?

what their tastes are?

what their buying patterns are?

their preferred distribution method?

their opinion of the organization's competitors' product?

their opinion of the organization's product

features they would like to see in organization's product

the seasonality of the market

the market growth, shrinkage, or flattening

The next step is to pay close attention to market segments.

Markets have become increasingly fragmented. Market segments can be based on price, quality, product use, or even benefits consumers find through a product's use.

Now it's time to cover some important planning elements commonly referred to as

SWOT and PEST.

PEST

PEST stands for Political factors, Economic factors, Social factors, and Technology factors. These are all elements that may have an effect on the future business of an organization. The organization should make a list of all factors that may be either beneficial or detrimental to the success of the marketing efforts or business through the PEST analysis.

Political factors include regulatory issues that affect the product line (e.g. ergonomics issues and the current regulatory rulings), legal aspects such as patents and copyrights, or just the current political climate.

Economic factors include current financial forces on the target market. Is there currently a recession? Is the stock market falling or rising? The macro-economic factors such as GDP growth, per capita income and national income too are having more implications on organizations..

Social factors include changes in social trends, fads, or demographic groups as they affect your target market and its current opinions. Society is normally divided in three classes by sociologists, namely upper class, middle class and lower class. Some divide it in further sets like upper-middle or lower-lower classes. All of these classes have their own characteristics, social values, set of needs and spending patterns. Obviously, the buying behaviour is going to be different for people belonging to any of these classes, the organization need to address the right set of needs when marketing for a specific class of society.

The social factors include changes in shopping habits, such as the increase in online shopping or the super-mall trend and the aging of the current target market, or the population increase in the over-50 group.

Technology factors include everything that affects the product, its market, or information-gathering efforts of the market that come as a result of changes in technology. This would include the Internet, wireless communications, handheld electronic devices, and anything else technology-driven that is affecting the product or service.

All of the PEST factors will tie into and possibly have an effect on the strengths, weaknesses, opportunities, and threats the organization identify for their product and market.

SWOT

SWOT stands for Strengths, Weaknesses, Opportunities and Threats and is critical to an organization's marketing plan. As mentioned before, the organization's marketing plan builds upon itself, and one of the anchoring steps is the identification of SWOT. By completing the review of the business and the market, the organization should be armed with the information necessary to identify the SWOTs and PESTs.

The organization's strengths and weaknesses are determined by internal elements, while opportunities and threats (OT) are dictated by external forces.

Sometimes it is recommended to identify the opportunities and threats first in order to more quickly bring to light the product strengths or weaknesses that should be considered first. For example, if an organization discover that its competitor is losing an exclusive distribution contract in the next two months, the organization could use this information to quickly fill that gap in the market. However, many of the threats will be based on weaknesses the organization have discovered.

Were any problems or opportunities identified in the organization's:

Company's philosophy or mission?

Company's vision?

product features, benefits or quality?

product's competitive advantage? (Is there a competitive advantage?)

distribution methods or distributor satisfaction?

pricing structures? Is it priced much higher or lower than the competition?

target market's awareness of your product?

target market's attitudes toward the product (or its category)?

target market's brand loyalty?

competition's activities? (new product launches, price changes, new companies, etc.) overall market? (shifts in needs, trends, behaviours, etc.)

When coming up with the organization's opportunities list, we should think specifically in terms of these processes:

Problem solving –

What problems do customers currently have with the product that aren't necessarily bad enough to warrant not using it or even complaining, but could benefit from improvement?

For example, interviewing a customer might bring to light an answer. New packaging might just give the product or service an advantage in the market.

Product use cycle – What steps does the buyer go through to purchase, use, and dispose of the product? This method might bring to light new product ideas (or just enhancements or packaging ideas), services, or other value options.

Ideal scenarios – Sometimes customers' statements can lead to whole new spin on a product.

For example, someone at some point probably said "I wish I could check my e-mail from anywhere!" Enter the wireless communications addition to the PDA line.

Other areas may also need to be addressed depending on the company, product or market.

Now identify strengths and weaknesses. Strengths can be defined as any available company resource that one can use to improve the market share or financial performance.

Weaknesses are any company resource that may cause the organization to lose a competitive advantage, position or financial state.

Rate the product (or company) strengths in these categories on a scale of one to five. You can also rate each by importance. Remember, many of the weaknesses will be based on the threats the organization identified above.

External – Market-oriented

Company/product reputation

Market share

Company's/product's ability to meet the needs and trends of the market

Value the company brings to the market

Quality of the product

Quality of the customer service and support (or other area of service)

Quality/effectiveness of past promotions and other marketing efforts

Pricing

Distribution

Geographical advantages

Internal

Operational leadership

Financial strength

Manufacturing capabilities

Responsiveness of workforce

Expand on these categories as needed for the product or company.

We should also keep in mind that, often, a threat can also be an opportunity, and a strength can also be viewed as a weakness, all depending upon the viewer's perspective.

For example, the organization may see the large selection of products as a strength, while the customers may consider it confusing and see it as making it difficult to find what they need. Put the organization in the consumer's shoes and be objective when making the determinations.

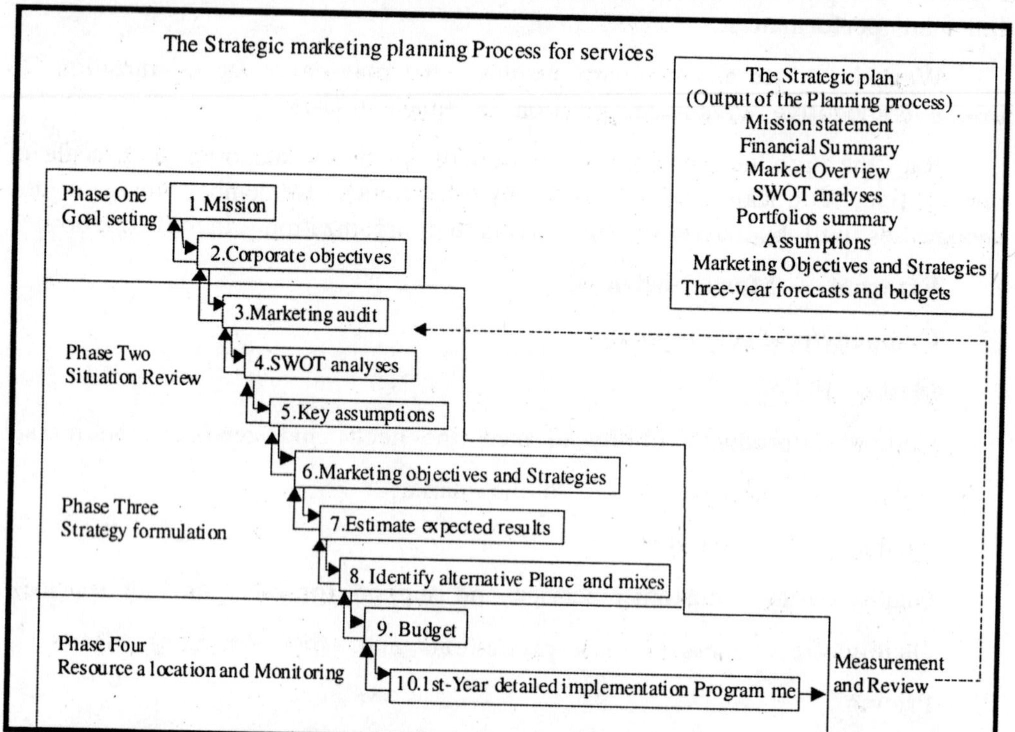

The Marketing Plan Outline

Marketing Plan overview:

It involves:

1 - Look at Objectives

2 - Conducting a Situation Analysis

3 - Conducting a Financial Analysis

4 - Setting objectives for Marketing Plan

5 - Formulating a Stratergy to achieve objectives

6 - Formulating tactics to implement the stratergy

7 - Establishing Controls (for monitoring procedures)

The marketing plan should include the following sections:

Executive Overview

Market Review

Trends Overview

Market Segments

Target Market

Primary

Secondary

Competitive Review

Product and Business Review

Strength, Weaknesses, Opportunities, Threats

Goals and Objectives

Sales Objectives

Marketing Objectives

Strategies

Positioning

Product

Pricing

Distribution

Communications/Promotion

Action Plan and Implementation

Media Plan

Budget

Schedule

Assignments

Evaluation

Lead Tracking Systems

Sales Reviews

We'll discuss all of these different parts in the following sections.

Executive Overview

Usually, the first section of a marketing plan is the Executive Overview. The executive overview summarizes the plan for a quick review by the executives of an organization. Although it comes first in the marketing plan, the executive summary is usually written last.

The executive summary should briefly cover:

Market Overview

Competitive Overview

Product Overview

SWOT (Strengths, Weaknesses, Opportunities and Threats)

Goals and Objectives

Strategies

Action Plan and Implementation Schedule

Evaluation Methods

Market Overview

In the research phase of this exercise, we did the legwork necessary for the first few sections of the business plan. Now we just need to get the information compiled in a clear and concise document so we can make use of it and others can read and understand (and support) it.

The following questions the organization need to answer in this overview are:

How big is the potential market?

Is the market growing, flat, or shrinking?

What changes do you see happening?

Is the market segmented by pricing, quality, age, income, or product usage?

Who is the organization's target audience?

Who are the organization's competitors?

The organization should organize the market overview section in the way that seems most logical and will best illustrate the product's market.

Market Segmentation

Because it is hard (and expensive) to be all things to all people (or markets), it is wise to target specific segments of your market, particularly if you are in a smaller business. Not only will this allow the organization to reach more of the people who will ultimately buy the product, but targeting segments may also reduce the competition the organization face. Finding the niche is often the key to success for small and medium and even large businesses.

The organization's market may naturally be segmented by price, quality, region, customer age, income, buying behaviour, industry or anything else. Typically, price and quality are the most evident, followed by product use and the benefits consumers get from using the product. Some segments will be very distinct, and some will be more subtle.

The best example of market segmenting is illustrated in the auto industry. They're all cars; but they come in all levels of luxury and utility, price and quality, etc. Some may even cross over into more than one segment, or move from one to the next.

Determine the segments of the organization's market and describe the ones the organization going to target. The organization should keep in mind that the product might cross into several market segments. Finally, the organization should address each of these segments when the organization is planning the marketing activities.

Target Audience

Determining the right target audience is probably the most important part of the organization's marketing efforts,. Describing in detail the audience (or audiences) for the organization is one of the critical factor. The organization want to reach and influence with their promotional messages — will help the organization to develop relevant messages and materials and identify the channels most likely to reach them. Few messages are appropriate for everyone, given the diverse interests, needs, concerns, and priorities of different segments of the public. Trying to reach everyone with one message or strategy may dilute the message so that it appeals to few rather than many people.

The following are the characteristics of the target audience include:

Physical — sex, age, health history of family, and type and degree of exposure to health risks, medical conditions, disorders, and illnesses.

behavioural — media exposure, membership in organizations, health-related activities, and other lifestyle characteristics demographic— occupation, income, educational attainment, family situation, places of residence and work, cultural characteristics

psychographic — attitudes, opinions, beliefs, values, self-appraisal and other personality traits

The more complete a profile or description the organization can develop of the target audience, the better it will be to develop a programme suited to them.

In this section of the marketing plan, the organization should go into as much detail as possible about who the target market is.

Describe the organization's typical customer in detail.

What is the age group, gender, education level, family size, income level, and geographic location?

For business-to-business markets, make sure the organization include the industry type, company size, job titles/departments, annual revenue, and geographic areas.

The organization should have a general picture of who the target market is, then back up that information with concrete numbers and statistics about the size of the market.

Determining the size of the market really requires that the organization already have a good profile of their typical customer.

Once the organization know "whom" you're looking for, the organization need to take into consideration things like the aging of the population, and regional variations in income levels and education levels.

The organization's product offering will also require that the organization consider not only income levels, but also disposable and discretionary income levels. The former refers to income after taxes that is used to pay for daily living expenses, and the latter refers to income that is left over after those necessities are paid for and can be earmarked for luxuries.

Psychographics

Even though the organization would have determined the demographic group, people within that group still have very different perceptions about the benefits or value of the organization's product and will be motivated for different reasons.

These differences are known as psychographics.

To further target efforts of an organization, it should determine not only who buys (or will buy) the product, but what makes them want to buy it. Include as much psychographic information as the organization can dig up, such as what their spending patterns are, whether they are brand conscious when it comes to the product type, what influences their buying behaviour, what promotional efforts they respond to most often, etc.

The organization also want to know how they go about buying it and what the organization can do to encourage them to buy more. The organization need this information so the organization can, in effect, clone the organization's best customers.

It is important to really pick apart what motivates them to buy.

The information you glean from a journey into the organization's target audience's brain is often key to the marketing efforts, particularly the positioning of the product. It includes the audience's activities, interests, and opinions. The organization should work through behavioural factors, economic factors, and even interpersonal factors to get to the root of purchasing behaviour.

Answer these questions in the organizations overview:

What do they like about the organization's r product?

What do they like about organization's competitor's product?

What made them decide to buy organization's product?

Did they know which brand they were buying before they purchased it?

What advertising messages had they seen prior to buying?

How much disposable or discretionary income is available for this type of purchase?

What are their hobbies?

What emotional aspects impact their purchase?

What is their social class or status?

Who is the actual decision-maker for this type of purchase?

What values and attitudes play a part in this type of purchase?

Who do they look to when making purchasing decisions?

Now that the organization know their target market and market segments, define the organization's market using concrete numbers and percentages.

In other words, how many users do the organization currently have and how many potential users exist for the product or service?

If the organization is offering a regional service and have found that there are 80,000 potential customers in the geographic area, then this is where the organization put that information.

Explain the growth and other changes the organization see in the market and how the competition is failing, failing or flourishing as a result. Include some market history if it applies to the product and market. Refer to the statistics and data the organization discovered through the market research.

This is where the organization would include the PEST (Political, Economic, Social, and Technology) information the organization gathered about outside influences on the market (i.e. government regulations, union activities, social changes, etc.).

Competitive Overview

In competitive overview the organization should give a complete and thorough overview of the competitive market. In competitive overview the organization should cover not only the directly competing companies the organization face (those who offer a very similar product with similar attributes), but also other product variations the organization may be competing with.

For example, if the organization is selling herbal teas, Is the organization also competing with regular teas? Instant teas? Canned teas? The drink market in general?

We should review these types of competitors as well as the organizations direct competitors.

Describe all of these and answer the following questions:

What are their product's strengths and weaknesses?

What are their strengths and weaknesses as a company (financial strength, reputation, etc.)?

Are there weaknesses the organization can exploit?

What are the differences between the organization's product features and theirs?

What were their sales for last year?

What is their pricing structure?

In what media vehicles do they promote their products?

What is their advertising message?

Where else do they promote their products?

What were their total advertising expenditures for last year?

What is their overall goal (profitability, market share, leadership)?

How are they trying to meet their goals (low prices, better quality, lower overhead)?

What were their responses to changes the organization made in the product pricing or promotions?

Information is often the key to a strong competitive advantage.

The following are the sources of information :

1. Suppliers

They can be good sources of information. We can collect informations by visiting the competitors' locations, Websites, exhibit booths; sample their products.

The organization can also gather a wealth of media and advertising information about the competitors on the Internet.

These firms and many others provide access to databases covering many areas of industry, media, advertising, and competitive information.

Product Overview

The product overview focuses on the following:

The product overview explain the following

The product or service of an organization and its purpose

its features

its current pricing structure

its current distribution channels

its positioning within the market

its current promotions and advertising

its current packaging

The organization should make sure the information is specific and accurate. If the organization's product is new, simply describe the product and its features.

Goals and Objectives

The organization's goals and objectives are simply the hard facts describing where the organization want to be a year from now, or five years from now, or whatever the time frame may be.

The organization should start with their sales goals. In this section, the organization should include goals that are:

concrete and measurable (in terms of rupees and units)

set at a level that is challenging but not impossible to reach

set on a specific timetable for measuring success

linked to projected profits (which should also be estimated in the marketing plan)

To do this, the organization should estimate the market and what the organization can expect to get from the same. There are several methods for doing this.

The first method requires that the organization look at total industry sales over the past five years for the product category.

From that information, one can estimate total industry sales for the next three years for the product category of an organization. From that number, one can figure the market share and extrapolate the annual sales estimates for those years.

The second method is more limited to organization's business itself. Basically, the organization go through the same procedure, but the organization use its own product's sales figures instead of the total product category for the market.

The organization can further break this information down by the specific distribution channel from which the sale came.

The third method is important because it is based on the sales levels the organization need in order to meet the expenses and product costs and make a profit.

Estimate the organizations overhead expenses for the year.

From the organization's expected Gross Margin percentage, subtract the expected profit percentage. This will give the organization's an estimated expense percentage.

Divide the estimated overhead expense by the estimated expense per cent to arrive at the magic number of sales necessary to cover the expenses and make a profit.

If the organization have a new product or business, the organization need to use the industry information to estimate the sales. This analysis should include the average cost of goods, operating margins, overhead expenses, and profit levels for businesses.

Marketing Objectives

This is reflected in the diagram below:

Goals

Opportunities | Resources

Marketing Objectives

Marketing Stratergies (Marketing programme)

Selection & analysis of target market | Development of Marketing Mixes

Diagram of the Objectives of a Business

- Essential marketing objectives include the following:

* Increasing market share
* Expanding product range
* Targeting the geographical representation
* And expansion of marketing opportunities

1. Market share: An increase in a company's market share shows how the company is gaining on competitors. To attain greater market share, the following stratergies, which are generally thought of as sure winners include:
    * More agressive pricing (lowering price or providing discounts)
    * Search for new outlets to distribute your products to
    * A change in some features of your products, to open up to a possibly wider market
2. Product Range: By expansion of a company's product range, a company can attract a wider market than its inital market, and maybe also expand into other markets
3. Geographical Representation: Some geographical markets offer greater market potential than others, and is in the intrests of the firm to invest there to reach these markets wether they be regional, national or international. This allows a company to maximise on its profits
4. Expansion: (I) Through exporting

(II) Maximizing customer service

B. Stratergies to achieve objectives:

Marketing stratergies are the way marketing objectives are achieved. Development of a stratergy involves:

- Selecting and analysing a target market
- Creating and maintaining a marketing mix
- Creation of advertising and promotional ideas

When properly implemented firm achieves objectives.

Selection and analysing of:

1. Target market: This area must be seperated into three areas, as different areas have different needs, these areas are:

(I) Retail market

(II) Wholesale market

(III) Industrial market

Creating and maintaining of:

2. Marketing Mix: This broken down into the four P's, they are:

Marketing Mix - Breakdown:

PRODUCT:	PRICE:	PROMOTION:
Quality	R.R.P. (List Price)	Advertising
Features	Bulk Discounts	Personal/ Direct Selling
Options	Other Discounts?/Offers?	Sales Promotions
Style	Allowances	Publicity
Brand Name	Payment Period	
Packaging	Credit Terms	PLACE:
Sizes		Transport
Service		Channels
Warranties		Coverage
Returns		Locations
Positioning		Inventory

An additional part of the marketing mix now exists, it is called 'Service'. Factors here include:

* Customer Needs
* Guarantees/Warranty
  - period
* Complaints & returns
  - procedures
* Installation, Maintenance, and
  - repairs
* After-sales Service
* Comparison to competitors
* Credit offered Creation of:

3. Advertising and Promotions:

Once the marketing mix has been established, the company's spromotional aspects have now to be completed, these can be made up of plans to do: Advertising.

Personal or direct selling

Sales Promotion

Publicity (Public relations)

Packaging and design

4. Staff Motivation: The effectiveness of the company's market will depend heavily upon the staff, and their degree of motivation.

C. Cost/Benefit Analysis:

As plans and objectives are developed, statements should be produced which should say what the marketing stratergy is to accomplish. There are two ways of evaluating the actual peformance of these plans, these are sales analysis and cost analysis.

1. Sales Analysis: Sales is usually the best way to measure the performance of a marketing plan.
2. This analysis should be broken down into:

- Marketing area (geographical)
- Company devision (eg. NSW devision)
- Individual/Groups of sales representatives (Quota of sales Vs Individual/Group's sale)

2. Cost Analysis: This is a detailed study of the business's operating section of the organisation's profit and loss statement. With cost analysis costs which occurred as a result of the marketing sector of a business are declared as profitable or unprofitable. This can be broken down into: (I) Research costs

(II) Order-getting costs
(Promotional costs)

(III) Order-filling costs
(Distribution and insurance costs)

The marketing objectives should be the means to achieve the organization's sales objectives. By working through the r target market data and the market segment data, the organization should come up with marketing objectives that address every group.

The marketing objectives should follow the same rules as the sales objectives, and be measurable, quantifiable (meaning there is a specific number of some sort assigned to each one), and time specific.

The marketing objective that addresses each group in the organization's target market. For this reason, The organization should have good data about the sizes of the market, potential market, and the present customer base. To this data, the organization add information such as recognized opportunities, the customers' buying rates, and other behavioural issues. This information will help the organization to estimate the numbers the organization need to attach to its marketing objectives.

Strategies

The strategies are the action plans that the organization l use in the marketing mix. The marketing mix is the combination of elements that make up the entire marketing process. By using a variety of modes to reach the r goal, the organization have a better chance of actually doing it.

Traditionally, the marketing mix refers to the four P's: product, price, place, and promotion. In addition to the traditional Ps, and probably the most important when it comes to your marketing communications, is positioning.

Positioning

Think of positioning as the perception that the target audience has of the organization's product. The organization should have total control over this element of the marketing efforts, and it is critical to how the organization develop the rest of the marketing plan.

Planning the organization's product's positioning must involve taking into consideration such issues as the competition and how its products are perceived, the needs and desires of the target audience.

In crowded markets, it is very important to position the organization's product or services more appropriately. It is clear from the present day customers are exposed for various advertising messages and they are bombarded with every day and every minute. In order to stand out, the organization's product has to have a clear position in the audience's mind.

First, the organization should determine a broad positioning. This means determining if the product should fall into a niche, be a low-cost leader, or a product differentiator. These are each very different strategy highways, and will take the organization in different directions when fine-tuning the advertising message.

The positioning focuses on the qualities of the product, its strengths and weaknesses, the opportunities uncovered, the pricing considered, and the target market to determine which broad position the organization will take.

Next, the organization will have to determine specific positioning. This could be based on a certain quality or benefit of the product, such as tangibility, ease of use, durability, reliability, safety, convenience, characteristics etc. In some cases, the organization may even be able to position the product based on two qualities. For example, think of Volvo. Safety and durability are Volvo's primary and secondary positions.

Begin narrowing down the positioning by answering questions such as:

What opinions does the audience already have, and how can the organization tie its product into them?

What are the organization's target audience's needs and desires?

Are there certain company attributes you can build on, such as experience, or being the first in the business?

What are the greatest benefits of the product and how can the organization capitalize on them?

Is there a specific use or application that the organization's product fits particularly well?

Is the organization's target audience identified independently enough to create a position based on their uniqueness?

Can the organization springboard a positioning idea from its competitor's positioning?

Can the organization base the position on quality or pricing strategies?

Can the organization position the product based on opportunities it has discovered in marketing research?

It may help to chart these issues out to compare and narrow the organization's options for positioning. By doing this, the organization incorporate importance levels to some of the issues.

For example, if the organization list the needs and desires of the target market, it might be helpful to rank those according to importance to the target audience.

If the organization list the strengths and weaknesses of the product, it may also be helpful to put those in order from greatest to smallest.

Once the organization determined its product's positioning, the organization should go through these questions to further refine it:

How can the organization simplify the message so it gets through?

Does the name of the product fit with its positioning?

Is the position believable?

Is the position one that the target audience will care about and notice?

Is the position too broad or too narrow?

Is the position clear and understandable?

The product's position, along with pricing and distribution channels, will also determine its value position. The value position is basically the product's perceived ranking of either high-quality/high-cost, average-quality/average-cost, low-quality/low-cost, or even average-quality/low-cost or higher-quality/lower-cost.

What the organization trying to get across to the target audience is the value/cost relationship of the product as it relates to the user.

Thus, the Product positioning involves tailoring an entire marketing programme—including product attributes, image, and price, as well as packaging, distribution, and service—to best meet the needs of consumers within a particular market segment. In this way, product positioning is part of the overall process of market segmentation, but involves a narrowing of focus. "Segmentation analysis tells us how the market is defined and allows us to target one or more opportunities," Glen L. Urban and Steven H. Star wrote in their book "Advanced Marketing Strategy", "Product positioning takes place within a target market segment and tells us how we can compete most effectively in that market segment."

The key to product positioning is understanding the dimensions consumers use to evaluate competing marketing programes and make purchase decisions. It may be helpful for small business managers to create a graph in order to map consumer perceptions along several different dimensions.Once consumer perceptions are understood, the next step is to select the best positioning for the product and take steps to align the marketing programme behind this positioning choice. Some examples of possible positioning choices include quality, reliability, and unique features or benefits. Before delving into product positioning further, it may be helpful to understand the process and goals of market segmentation.

Marketing Mix Strategy

"Marketing mix" is a general phrase used to describe the different kinds of choices organizations have to make in the whole process of bringing a product or service to market. Marketing mix models are defined by the "4P" marketing decision variables:

Product
- How and Where Will the Customer use it?
- What does it look like?
- What size (S), Color(S) and So On,. Should it be?
- What is it to be Called?
- How is it branded?

Price
- Where is the Value of the Product or Service?
- Are there established Price Points for Products or Services in this area?
- How will Your Price Compare with Your competitors?

Place
- Where do buyers look for your product or service?
- How can you access the right distribution Channels?
- Do you need to use a sales force?

Promotion
- Where and when can you get across your marketing messages to your target market?
- When is the best time to promote?

Marketing mix modelling can assist in making specific marketing decisions and tradeoffs, but it can also create a broad platform of knowledge to guide strategic planning.

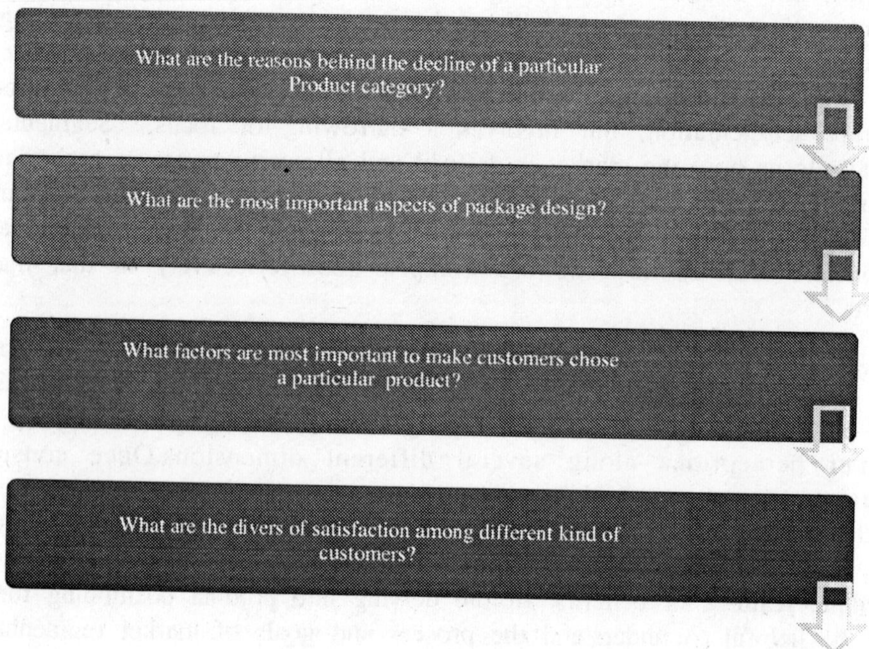

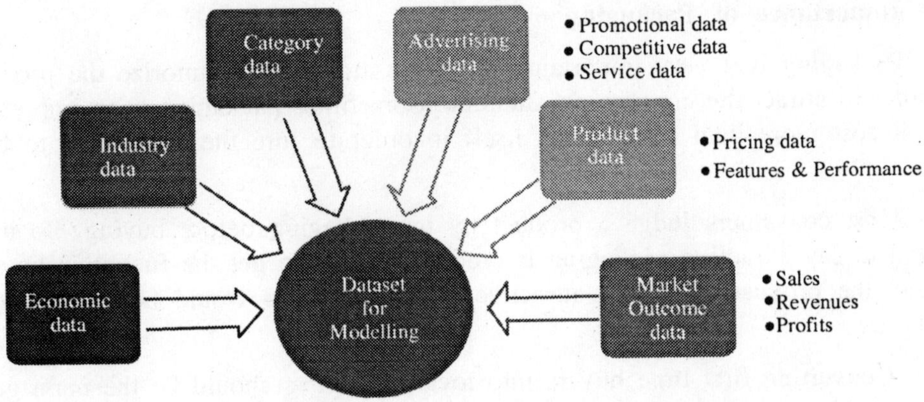

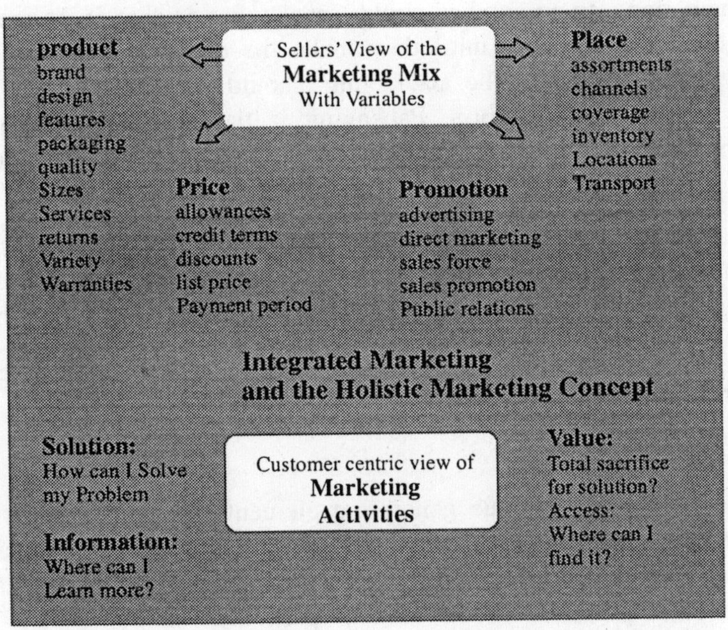

The marketing mix is the combination of elements that make up the entire marketing process. The first P is product, of organizations strategy the organization should know about elements of the product that can be strategic to its success, such as its packaging and warranty. These elements help create the value the customer sees in the product.

The Importance of Packaging

Packaging is a very important marketing strategy to glamorize the product in order to attract the consumer's attention. Sometimes packaging is so important that it cost more than the product itself in order to lure the consumers to buy it.

Most consumers judge a product by its packaging before buying. So it is logical to say attractive packaging is crucial in order to get the first time buyers to buy the products. Without attractive packaging, who would buy it in order to try it?

Converting first time buyers into loyal customers should be the main goal of the business and packaging is the door to it.

The main thing to remember about packaging is that it communicates to the person buying it right up until they make the decision to plunk down their money and take it home. The packaging should be noticeable within three seconds in a store-shelf situation. Packaging is the encasement of products in packages, protective wrappings or other external covering that can provide protection, information, security and marketing benefits.

The same goes for warranties. Particularly if the product is new, the organization should make sure that it give buyers some level of comfort that if the product doesn't do what they thought, they can easily get their money back.

The next P is price.

Price Strategy

Pricing is the only revenue generating elements among the 4 Ps (the other three are product, place and promotion), whereas, Strategy is explained by Henry Mitzberg as a pattern in actions over time and a position that reflects decisions to offer particular products or services in particular market.

Pricing Strategy is defined as the idea and practice of establishing an optimum price for a product or service that will result in the highest profit. Factors that determine the pricing decisions are the competitors, social / cultural / global environment, economic / natural / technological factors, legal / political aspects, the suppliers, the substitutes available, the customers, product positioning/differentiation, demand of the product and the cost involved.

Before deciding the Pricing Strategy the firm needs to answer the following questions to themselves: -

What is their organisational objective?

How much to charge for a product / services?

Why should the price be neutral / higher / lower than the competitors?

Where are the potential buyers?

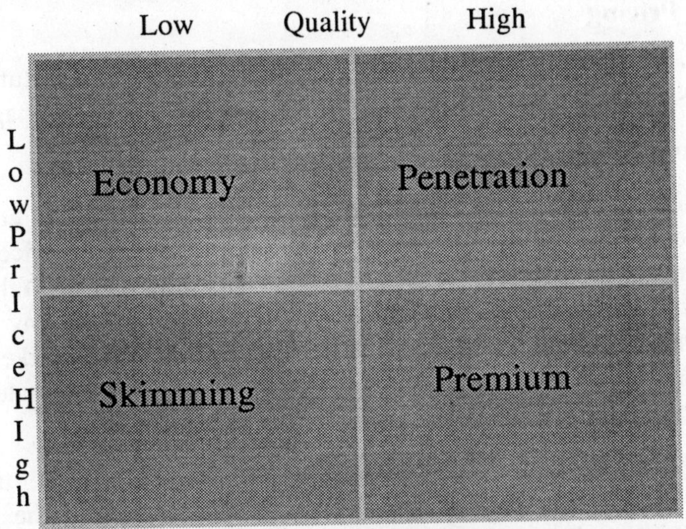

Pricing Strategies Matrix
www.marketingteacher.com

There are many ways to price a product. Let's have a look at some of them and try to understand the best policy/strategy in various situations.

Premium Pricing

Use a high price where there is a uniqueness about the product or service. This approach is used where a substantial competitive advantage exists. Such high prices are charge for luxuries such as the iPhone comes at a premium price of Rs 31,000 and Rs 36,100 for the 8GB and the 16 GB capacity respectively.

Mercedes Benz C 180 and C 200 CDI

These new set of cars from the stable of Daimler Chrysler provide you with all the luxury and can set you back by twenty to twenty three lakhs.

Ford Mondeo from the stable of Ford Motors comes at a price of 14.00 lakhs.

Hyundai Sonata has been re-launched in the country and the car which comes with a 2.4 litre engine and is priced at 13.00 lakhs.

Penetration Pricing

The price charged for products and services is set artificially low in order to gain market share. Once this is achieved, the price is increased. This approach was used by Nirma detergent powder. The Deccan Chronicle launched its Chennai edition at Re. 1 per copy.

Economy Pricing

This is a no frills low price. The cost of marketing and manufacture are kept at a minimum. Supermarkets often have economy brands for soups, spaghetti, etc.

Price Skimming

Charge a high price because the organization have a substantial competitive advantage. However, the advantage is not sustainable. The high price tends to attract new competitors into the market, and the price inevitably falls due to increased supply. Manufacturers of digital watches used a skimming approach in the 1970s. Once other manufacturers were tempted into the market and the watches were produced at a lower unit cost, other marketing strategies and pricing approaches are implemented.

Premium pricing, penetration pricing, economy pricing, and price skimming are the four main pricing policies/strategies. They form the bases for the exercise. However there are other important approaches to pricing.

Psychological Pricing

This approach is used when the marketer wants the consumer to respond on an emotional, rather than rational basis. For example pricing strategies of Bata shows in India.

Product Line Pricing

Where there is a range of product or services the pricing reflect the benefits of parts of the range. For example car washes.

Optional Product Pricing

Companies will attempt to increase the amount customer spend once they start to buy. Optional 'extras' increase the overall price of the product or service. For example airlines will charge for optional extras such as guaranteeing a window seat or reserving a row of seats next to each other.

Captive Product Pricing

Where products have complements, companies will charge a premium price where the consumer is captured. For example a razor manufacturer will charge a low price and recoup its margin (and more) from the sale of the only design of blades which fit the razor.

Product Bundle Pricing

Here sellers combine several products in the same package. This also serves to move old stock. Videos and CDs are often sold using the bundle approach.

Promotional Pricing

Pricing to promote a product is a very common application. There are many examples of promotional pricing including approaches such as Buy One Get One Free.

Geographical Pricing

Geographical pricing is evident where there are variations in price in different parts of the world. For example the shipping costs increase price.

Value Pricing

This approach is used where external factors such as recession or increased competition force companies to provide 'value' products and services to retain sales e.g. value meals at McDonalds.

Place Strategy

The third P stands for place, although it's really referring to distribution.

The strategy behind how the organization sell and distribute the product is a very important element of your marketing mix.

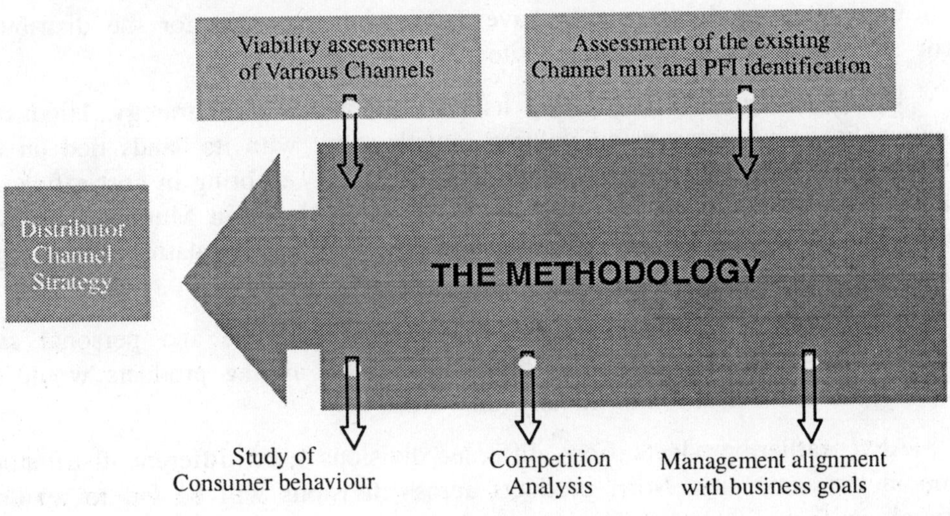

A distribution channel links the manufacturer of a product with the end users i.e. the consumers. Decisions regarding distribution channels are of great significance to the manufacturers. Organizations can have strategic distribution systems that help them to examine the current distribution system and decide on the distribution system that can be useful in the future. In designing a distribution channel for an organization, there are mainly three steps – identifying the functions to be performed by the distribution system, designing the channel, and putting the structure into operation. There are different types of distribution channels depending on the number of levels that exist between the producer and the consumer. In deciding on the kind of distribution strategy to be used, there are various considerations to be kept in mind – considerations on middlemen, customers, product, price, etc. The middlemen should have the necessary financial capacity to carry out the task effectively. Customers should be able to get the products conveniently. Product features to be considered include durability, toughness etc. The price of the product also requires consideration in deciding the distribution strategies.

Steps in distribution strategy

Match the organization's product's "image" with that of the distribution channel and with the customers' perception of the product.

Stay on top of changes in the market that should also make the organization change its distribution strategy.

Make sure the organization's product can get the attention it needs in the chosen channel. Example

CavinKare products usually have 1-2% higher margin for the distributor than similar products from competitors.

Hindustan Unilever is pruning its distribution network strategy. Hindustan Unilever is facing pressure on volume growth. And, with its hands tied on the pricing front, it is restructuring its distribution strategy to bring in cost efficiency with 'Enter: the go-to-market programme'. First tried out in Mumbai, this will now be implemented across all towns and cities with a population above eight lakh, starting with Chennai.

Earlier, HUL had different distributors for its home and personal care division and food division in the same area. Now, all the products would be sold by the same distributor in any one area.

Also, earlier, products from different divisions used different distributors, even in the same city. Now, products across divisions will be fed to retailers through unified distributors.The Go-to-Market model also helps to remove the enormous logistics hitherto faced by the distributors in their back-end operations, thus removing significant costs from the system. More importantly, enabling them to focus on the front-end to deliver better services to end-retail.

Promotion Strategy

The fourth and final P is promotion. This is the communications strategy of the organization's plan.

The promotion section should actually have the following categories:

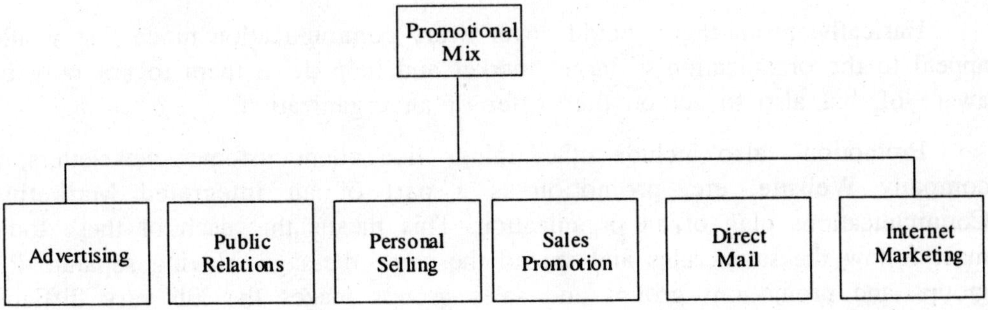

www. learn marketing. net

advertising

public relations and publicity

direct marketing

promotions and events

product/company marketing materials

premium items

sales force or personal selling

A successful product or service means nothing unless the benefit of such a service can be communicated clearly to the target market. An organisations promotional strategy can consist of:

Advertising:Is any non-personal paid form of communication using any form of mass media.

Public relations: Involves developing positive relationships with the organisation media public. The art of good public relations is not only to obtain favourable publicity within the media, but it is also involves being able to handle successfully negative attention.

Sales promotion: Commonly used to obtain an increase in sales short term. Could involve using money off coupons or special offers.

Personal selling: Selling a product service one to one.

Direct Mail: Is the sending of publicity material to a named person within an organisation. Direct mail allows an organisation to use their resources more effectively by allowing them to send publicity material to a named person within their target segment. By personalising advertising, response rates increase thus increasing the chance of improving sales.

Basically, promotion should cover every communication mode that would appeal to the organization's target market and help drive them to not only be aware of, but also to act on the offer of an organization.

Promotion also include other things like client/customer newsletters, a company Website, etc. promotion is a part of an Integrated Marketing Communications plan of an organization. This means that each of these tools must follow the same rules and spread the same message. Having separate PR groups and promotions groups and sales groups makes the job very difficult unless the organization make sure they are all in agreement about what the organization is saying and how the organization is saying it.

Advertising

Advertising is a form of communication used to influence individuals to purchase products or services or support political candidates or ideas. Frequently it communicates a message that includes the name of the product or service and how that product or service could potentially benefit the consumer. Advertising often attempts to persuade potential customers to purchase or to consume a particular brand of product or service. Modern advertising developed with the rise of mass production in the late 19th and early 20th centuries. Advertising is communication used to influence individuals to purchase products or services or support political candidates or ideas. Advertising can be displaced on billboards, newspapers, T.V., websites, movies and more.

The advertising strategy include the following:

Advertising promise – The promise the organization making to its target audience. Support for the promise – Bulleted statements that support the organization's claims

Advertising tone – The emotional images conjured by the organization's message that are appropriate for both the product and its audience

Rationale – Statements referring back to the product/market research that back up its creative strategies

The actual finished creative effort typically comes after (or else during) this exercise and should be detailed in the product's Advertising Plan.

Marketing and Public Relations

Public relations (PR) is the practice of managing the communication between an organization and its publics. Public relations gains an organization or individual exposure to their audiences using topics of public interest and news items that do not require direct payment. Because public relations places exposure in credible third-party outlets, it offers a third-party legitimacy that advertising does not have. Common activities include speaking at conferences, working with the press, and employee communication.

Public relations can be a very powerful tool in the organization's marketing activities. The mantra of your public relations staff should be the Integrated Marketing Communications idea. Their most important function is to ensure that everything the press sees or hears is controlled and is consistent with the image plan. It is therefore recommended that only the organization's public relations people actually communicate with the press. This includes all areas of PR, such as corporate announcements, defensive PR, and marketing PR.

There is a whole set of tools for public relations and publicity, just as there is for advertising. These include:

news releases

feature stories and interviews

exclusives

opinion pieces

photos

speeches or appearances at seminars, conventions, etc.

local, regional or national talk shows and other programmes

online chats and forums

community involvement

lobbying activities

social responsibility activities

There are two elements to a PR plan:

What the organization want to communicate

A public relation message must be newsworthy and interesting

There is a formal definition of the term "public relations," yet its meaning is self-evident; it is the management of relationships between an organization and the constituencies upon which it depends.

Quite literally, public relations is managing relations with various publics, a role that grows in importance as reputation becomes ever more critical to business success. Companies can restore trust in a number of ways, many involving traditional PR strategies, such as:

Using integrity and fairness as criteria for all business decisions

Maintaining an emphasis on quality of services

Openly sharing truthful information with all publics

Actively seeking input from publics and being responsive to concerns

Renewing a commitment to the community

Creating forums to encourage dialogue with constituencies.

An organization's reputation, or the essence of how it is viewed by all of its publics, is the leading factor in its ability to achieve success. With this in mind, the battered image of this organization is no small matter. Restoring trust and helping this organization and others to earn a reputation for credibility will require sound public relations leadership.

The public relations part of marketing plan helps to determine those two pieces of information.

Here are some strategy ideas for types of information to communicate to the press:

Prior to product release, submit sneak previews to the press.

Find a good spokesperson to help promote the product.

Find the right angle for press release.

Include both trade press and consumer press.

Build the excitement (hype-up) in r story by finding a new twist on the information.

Offer co-sponsorships for media to events the organization is planning.

Create the orgnization's own scheduled media blitz.

Schedule press releases so that various media sources publish information that builds on itself and progressively includes new tidbits of information.

Build the newsworthy info on one of the product's benefits used in its positioning.

Develop an interesting and fun idea centered around the product's release or upgrade.

Direct Marketing

Direct marketing, or database marketing, is growing exponentially with the emphasis on very tightly targeted efforts. The growth in e-mail and Internet use, along with the general upward trend in all media subscriptions, is making it an easier and more profitable way to market the product than it was in the past days of mass mailings.

With a database (either a purchased one or own customer database) of names and very specific demographic information, the organization can select specific subsets of groups very easily and send very targeted messages about the product or service. By more finely targeting the marketing efforts, the organization improve the response rates simply because the organization can come closer to reaching the exact profile of its best customers.

Here are some examples uses of direct marketing:

Generating inquiries

Opening doors

Building traffic

Creating awareness

Fund raising

Selling products (mail order)

The direct marketing options include:

direct mail

Self-mailers

Mailing packages that include a letter, brochure, and response card

Post cards (used as inexpensive reminders)

Mailed premium items and other types of gifts

Opt-in e-mail campaigns or permission marketing–The organization should make sure that their clients are requesting their e-mails, otherwise it's spam.

Fax campaigns

Telemarketing

Here are some examples of promotion types used by marketers today:

Price discounts/sales

Coupons

Samples

On-pack or in-pack discounts – or even near-pack discounts (from point-of-purchase displays)

Rebates

Premium items – either in the package or sent by mail

Sweepstakes/games

Packaging

Events

It is important to watch the promotions the competition offers, but the organization should be careful about always reacting with a similar promotion. It is easy to lose market share if the organization overuse promotions.

Customers begin to buy only when the product is on sale. A better strategy is to competitively price of the product in the first place, and then use some of the money would have spent on promotions to improve the products or increase the advertising instead.

Sales promotion Definition: Any activity or material used as a direct inducement to purchase

Sales Promotion Objective is to bolster or complement other promotional mix elements during a specific time period.

Targeted toward:

Sales force

Wholesalers and retailers

Consumers

The following are the Sales Promotion Methods for Consumers Multiple purchase offers,

Frequent-user incentives

P-O-P material

Product placements/tie-ins

Premiums

Classifying Types of Sales Promotion

Promotional

Pricing

Non-price

Promotions

Sampling

Price reductions

Free goods

Tied offers

Money off next purchase

Loss leader pricing

Cheap credit

Contests

Free gifts

Self-supporting offers

Multi-brand promos

Guarantees and added services

Most effective in the early stages of a new product launch

Important for food products

Very expensive

The following are the advantages and disadvantages of Sales Promotion.

Advantages:

Motivation method for special efforts

Short-term sales increase

Defined target audience

Defined role/objectives

Indirect roles (e.g., wider distribution)

Disadvantages:

Only short-term

Hidden costs

Confusion

Price cutting – Brand image

Postponement effect

Significant government regulation

Lack of effectiveness sometimes (learning effect)

Roles of Sales Promotion and Merchandising

Getting customers to try a new service or menu item.

Increasing off-peak sales.

Increasing sales in periods that coincide with major events, vacations, or special occasions.

Encouraging travel intermediaries to make an effort to sell services.

Helping sales representatives get business from prospects.

Facilitating intermediary sales.

Steps in Developing a Sales Promotion and Merchandising Plan

1. Set sales promotion and merchandising objectives.
2. Choose between in-house advertising or agency development.
3. Establish a tentative sales promotion and merchandising budget.
4. Consider cooperative sales promotions.
5. Select sales promotion and merchandising techniques.

Steps in Developing a Sales Promotion and Merchandising Plan

Select media for distributing promotions.

Decide on timing of sales promotions and merchandising.

Pretest sales promotions and merchandising.

Prepare final sales promotion and merchandising plan and budget.

Measure and evaluate sales promotion and merchandising success.

Difference between Special Communication and Special Offer Promotions

Special communication methods: Give the promoter additional options of communicating with potential customers and travel trade intermediaries.

Special-offer promotions: Short-term inducements given to customers, travel trade intermediaries, and sales representatives. Generally, some type of action must take place from the potential customer.

Special Communication Methods

Specialty advertising

Sampling

Trade and travel show exhibits

Point-of-purchase displays and other merchandising materials

Point-of-purchase demonstrations

Educational seminars and training programmes

Visual aids for sales representatives

Special-Offer Promotions

Coupons

Price-offs

Premiums

Contests, sweepstakes, and games

Recognition programmes

Continuity programmes

Gift certificates

Special Communications Methods

Roles and Advantages

Specialty Advertising

Role:

Free items given to potential

Customers or travel trade intermediaries.

Advantage:

Flexibility of use.

Sampling

Role:

Giving away free samples of items to encourage sales, or arranging in some way for people to try all or part of a service.

Advantage:

Gives the recipient a first-hand look at the product and encourages future sales if the recipient is pleased with the services offered.

Trade and Travel Show Exhibits

Role:

Bringing together all parts of the industry (suppliers, carriers, intermediaries, and destination marketing organizations) at one location to show-off their services.

Advantage:

They offer the exhibitor a highly specialized target audience and an efficient alternative to making sales calls to thousand of prospects.

Point-of-Purchase Displays and Other Merchandising Materials

Role:

Used at the point of purchase.

Advantage:

Keeps image of service/product in the minds of its customers longer.

Point-of-Purchase Demonstrations

Role:

Provides the customer with up-to-date and current sales promotions while visiting establishment.

Advantage:

Entices and encourages patrons to purchase a service on the spot.

Educational Seminars and

Training Programmes

Role:

The primary objective is to pass on more detailed information and to help travel agents sell services to clients.

Advantage:

They offer the sponsor a highly targeted and influential audience.

Special Offers

Roles and Advantages

Coupons

Role:

Vouchers or certificates that entitle customers or intermediaries to a reduced price on the coupon service or services.

Advantage:

Coupons deliver greater value in the form of a price reduction to the consumer, thus creating more potential customers in the future.

Price-Offs

Role:

A price reduction that does not involve using a coupon.

Advantage:

These are popular because they can be introduced almost immediately.

Premiums

Role:

Merchandise items that are offered at a reduced price or free with the purchase of services or products.

Advantage:

When consistent with the sponsor's image (position) and target market, the potential for sales increases are great.

Contests, Sweepstakes, Games

Role:

Contests are sales promotions where entrants win prizes based on some required skill that they are asked to demonstrate. Sweepstakes are sales promotions that require entrants to submit their names and addresses.

Games are sales promotion events similar to sweepstakes, but they involve using game "pieces."

Contests, Sweepstakes, Games

Advantage:

Increases advertising readership, are helpful in communicating key benefits, and are good at elevating awareness of the sponsor's services.

Travel Trade Inducements

Role:

Specialty advertising items, familiarization trips, sweepstakes, and educational seminars.

Advantage:

Promotes the product/service to travel trade intermediaries and or potential consumers in order to increase awareness of this product/service so that increased sales are eminent.

Recognition Programmes

Role:

Offers awards to travel trade intermediaries, sales representatives, or customers for achieving or providing certain levels of sales or business.

Advantage:

Increases the use of the sponsor's services and often increases future sales goals.

Continuity Programmes

Role:

Sales purchases that require people to make several purchases, sometimes over a long-term period of time.

Advantage:

Increases the partnerships in marketing hospitality and travel with other industries' services, stimulates more frequent purchases and or builds long-term loyalty for a company or brand.

Gift Certificates

Role:

Vouchers or cheques given away by the sponsor or sold to customers who, in turn, give them to others as gifts.

Advantage:

Encourages recipients to try the services thus inevitably increases awareness of the service and future sales.

The Customer Centred Organisation

Kotler (2000) shows the customer at the centre of this organisational design. Using a value chain framework, we can say that if a whole network of companies used this same general philosophy in organizing themselves, a much greater amount of value could be created for the customer as well as value chain members. However, this model doesn't take into account other stakeholder requirements.

Demand Response

Pine (1993) cited in Walters (2002) shows demand characteristics of the 'new' environment.

Low Market Turbulence	Demand Factors	High Market Turbulence
Stable and predictable demand	Becomes	Unstable and unpredictable
Necessities	Becomes	Luxuries
Easily defined needs and wants	Becomes	Uncertain needs and wants
Slowly changing needs and wants	Becomes	Rapidly changing needs and wants
Low price consciousness	Becomes	High price consciousness
Low quality concerns	Becomes	Concerns for high quality
Low fashion consciousness	Becomes	High fashion consciousness
Low level service requirements	Becomes	High level service requirements

	Structural factors	
Low buyer power	Becomes	High buyer power
Low competitive integrity	Becomes	High competitive integrity
Low/ medium levels of saturation	Becomes	High levels of saturation
Long, predictable product life cycles	Becomes	Short and unpredictable cycles
Low rates of technological change	Becomes	High rates
Narrowly defined marketing channels	Becomes	Broadly defined channels
Local markets for sourcing and sales	Becomes	Global markets
Slow/ medium responses to orders	Becomes	Requests for rapid response
Predictable order volumes	Becomes	Unpredictable volumes
Large frequent customer orders	Becomes	Smaller and less frequent orders
A stable number of order varying in number	Becomes	Points unstable and delivery points

Source: Adapted from Pine (1993) cited in Walters (2002)

The above model of Pine and Walters shows how the low turbulent market turns onto high turbulent market. These changes takes place as the organizations want to become a customer centered.

Customer Strategy

Does the organization have a customer strategy? Most companies have a product strategy and a marketing strategy. Customer-centric organizations also have a customer strategy. Put simply, a customer strategy is a proactive plan for how we want to acquire, retain, and grow our customers! Too many organizations leave it to chance when it comes to retention and growth of customers, focusing most of their resources on customer acquisition. Why would we want to leave the management of our most valuable asset, our customers, to chance?

In order to align our customer experience with our customer strategy, we need to consider how we have created that strategy. A strong customer strategy is built around the interactions we have with our customers, and we are able to maximize the value of every customer touch. In other words, we make each impression with the customer count. Customer service and support may have several opportunities to make customer impressions, and it is often where the rubber meets the road.

How do we handle our customers when there is a problem or a question?

The goal of all these interactions is to increase customer retention and loyalty, which ultimately leads to repeat business and referrals.

Done right, a customer strategy will also build customer trust, strengthen the relationship, and add value to both the customer and the company.

In other words, a customer-focused strategy is a planned approach to how we handle our customers at every touch point. It is more than just giving great customer service. It is more than marketing with certain customer buzzwords. It is more than a great customer experience. It requires a strategic plan to be put in place to address all of those areas, plus the metrics to ensure the success of the strategy.

Customer-focused strategy is defined as:

A plan that emphasizes the needs of a particular customer segment over that of the organization.

Example:

William C. Durant founded General Motors in 1908 but was ousted two years later, so he formed Chevrolet in 1911, intending to make it a powerful lever for regaining control. He did. By 1915, Chevrolet was a force to be reckoned with; by 1918 it was part of General Motors; by the mid-'20s, it was GM's largest volume division — and has been ever since.

More Chevrolet Information

Created by the founder of General Motors, Chevrolet started as a competitor to GM and eventually became a part of the dominant automaker. Early Chevys were largish, medium-price cars with six-cylinder and even V-8 power. The make's historic turn to the low-price field came with the four- cylinder "490" of 1915, named for its advertised list price. It was a big success, outflanking Ford's Model T with more attractive styling and more features. Its closely related successors were Chevy's mainstay products into the late '20s.

However, Chevy didn't pass Ford in production until 1927, the year Dearborn stopped building the aged T to retool for the Model A. Then, in 1929, Chevrolet introduced its new "Stovebolt Six," also known as the "Cast-Iron Wonder." The nicknames stemmed from the engine's cast-iron pistons and numerous 1/4-inch slotted bolts — hardly esoteric, but wonderfully effective and reliable as Old Faithful. By the time this 1931 Chevrolet station wagon was introduced, Chevy was GM's largest volume division.

The Stovebolt was engineered by Ormond E. Hunt from an earlier design by Henry M. Crane that had evolved into the 1926 Pontiac engine. By 1930, it produced an even 50 brake horsepower from 194 cubic inches. With various improvements, this solid, overhead-valve engine would remain Chevrolet's only powerplant for nearly three decades.

For 1934, new combustion chambers prompted the name "Blue Flame," and two versions would be offered through 1935: 60-bhp, 181 cid and 80-bhp, 206.8 cid. The six was then redesigned for 1937 to be shorter and lighter. It also gained nearly "square" cylinder dimensions as well as four (versus three) main bearings. The result was 85 bhp from 216.5 cid.

It was with this engine in 1940 that a young Juan Manuel Fangio won the car-breaking 5900-mile round-trip road race between Buenos Aires, Argentina, and Lima, Peru, at an average speed of 53.6 mph. Fangio continued to race Chevrolets after World War II, but eventually switched to Grand Prix cars and became a legend as the first five-time world champion driver.

Chevrolet Strategy in the Early 2000s

As with archrival Ford, trucks loomed ever larger in Chevrolet's total business picture during the 1990s and into the twenty-first century. Indeed, car sales at both makes were eclipsed by demand for light-duty pickups, sport-utility vehicles (SUVs), and minivans as early as 1990. This reflected a change in buyer preferences that would see light trucks surpass cars in total U.S. sales for calendar 2001.

Chevrolet fought the truck wars well. All-new full-size pickups arrived for 1999 under the Silverado banner, followed by a separate new line of more-competitive heavy-duty pickups, tagged Silverado HD, and redesigned Tahoe and Suburban SUVs. For 2002 came a larger new mid-size SUV, the TrailBlazer, though some of the older Blazer models hung on as price-leaders for that segment.

Also new for '02 was the Avalanche, basically a Suburban with an open cargo box instead of a closed cargo bay, plus "tough guy" styling touches. The box was a short 5.3 feet long, but a "mid-gate" could be folded down with the rear seats to extend load length to 8.1 feet. Avalanche answered a question no one was really asking, but proved fairly popular.

Not so for Chevy's 1984-vintage Astro minivan, which steadily waned in popularity until its 2005 exit. The newer front-drive Venture minivan languished too. On the other hand, the compact Tracker SUV, sourced from GM affiliate Suzuki of Japan, did good business, especially once redesigned for 1999.

Trouble was, the market clamour for trucks led Chevy (Ford as well) to put less apparent effort into cars — understandable, what with the car/truck sales gap widening each year.

As a result, Chevy's replacement car models in this period were usually judged underwhelming against class rivals. And though they generally sold well, they sold more to rental and corporate fleets than retail buyers, to the detriment of both image and trade-in value. Either way, discounts were deep in a market long accustomed to "deal of the week" incentives.

But a sale is a sale no matter who the customer is, and Chevy was happy to keep building around a quarter-million Cavaliers each model year through 2004. Highlights in the Cav's later years included the 1998 return of a Z24 convertible, replacing the LS version, and a mild 2000-model revamp featuring added standard equipment. The ragtop body style was dropped altogether for 2001, reflecting continued lack of buyer interest.

Collectors may one day note the low yearly production for all Cavalier convertibles, which never exceeded 10,000 and was often less than half that (just 4108 of the 1985 Type 10s, 5011 of the '98 Z24s, to cite but two examples).

The Z24 coupe was canned for 2002, but lived on in a similar LS Sport model with GM's new 2.2-litre "Ecotec" twincam four-cylinder, good for 140 bhp and shared with a new LS Sport sedan.

Other models adopted this engine for 2003, shedding the old overhead-valve unit, and all got modest styling revisions. Tellingly, though, the recently standardized antilock brakes moved to the options list (joining newly available front side airbags protecting both head and torso, plus GM Onstar assistance and satellite radio).

Chevy was trying to maintain price parity with small cars from import brands that could set prices more aggressively because they had far less overhead to cover than GM did.

This largely explains why Chevy returned to selling rebadged imports for 2004, adding the little Aveo four-door sedan and hatchback as new bottom-rung offerings pitched below Cavalier. Sourced from low-wage South Korea and a GM subsidiary recently formed from the remains of bankrupt Daewoo Motors, Aveo was a fair sales success. Meanwhile, buy-domestic diehards could opt for a $10,135 Cavalier coupe with no frills and no options.

Customer-Focused Strategy: A proactive plan that emphasizes the needs of a particular customer segment over that of the organization while benefiting both.

It's "proactive" because the organization should be planning how it will meet or exceed customers' needs.

"Customer-focused strategy" as a view on business that puts customers at the centre of business decisions.

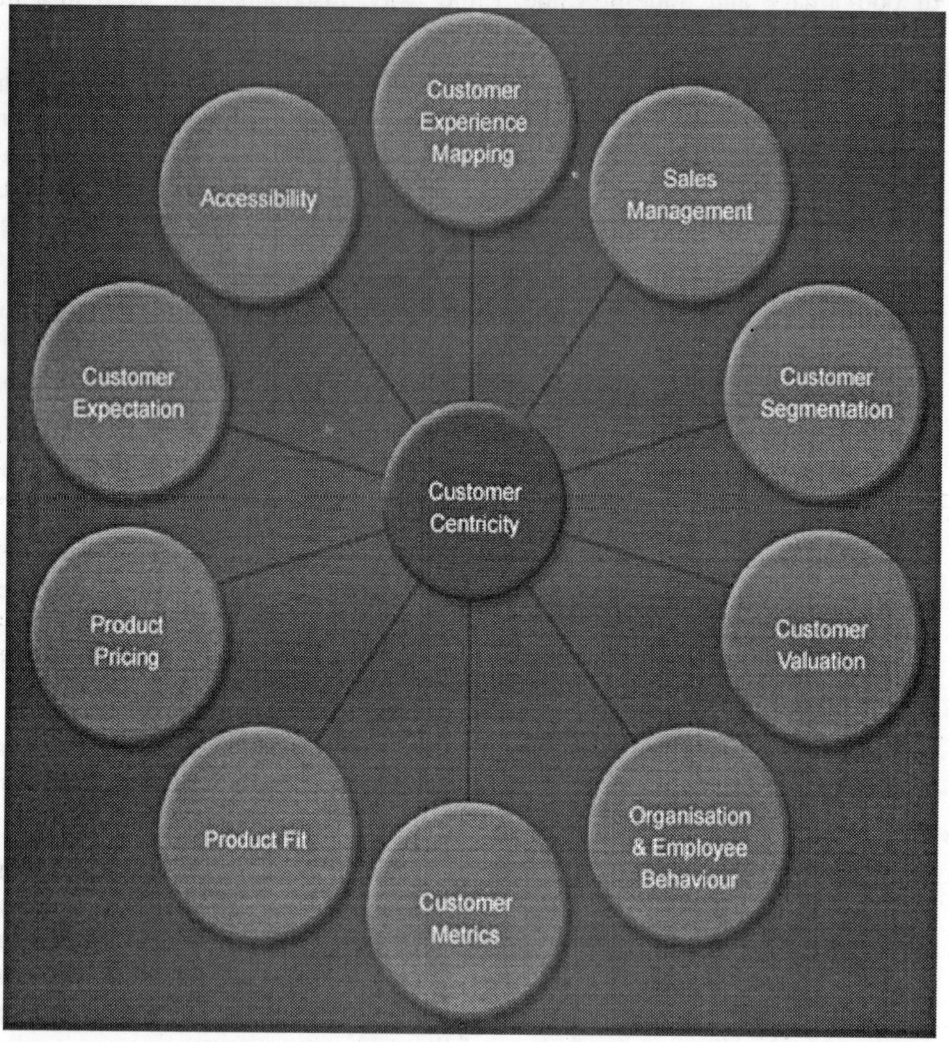

The above diagram shows the customer – centricity of an organization.The customer-centricity organization focuses on the following:

1. product fit
2. product pricing
3. customer metrics
4. organization and employee behaviour
5. customer valuation

6. customer segmentation
7. sales management
8. customer expectation
9. customer experience mapping
10. accessbility

This is crystal clear that the customer-centricity organization introducing the right product and at right price. The customer expectations must be known to the organization, therefore, the organization can add value through its customer experience mapping.

The customer-centricity approach of Amazon Tools, Marketing and Community.

In 1995, Amazon.com sold its first book, which shipped from Jeff Bezos' garage in Seattle. In 2006, Amazon.com sells a lot more than books and has sites serving seven countries, with 21 fulfilment centres around the globe totalling more than 9 million square feet of warehouse space.

The story is an e-commerce dream, and Jeff Bezos was Time magazine's Person of the Year in 1999. The innovation and business savvy that sustains Amazon.com is legendary and, at times, controversial: The company owns dozens of patents on e-commerce processes that some argue should remain in the public domain. In this article, we'll find out what Amazon does, what makes it different from other e-commerce Websites and how its technology infrastructure supports its multi-pronged approach to online sales.

Amazon.com Basics

Amazon.com sells lots and lots of stuff. The direct Amazon-to-buyer sales approach is really no different from what happens at most other large, online retailers except for its range of products. One can find beauty supplies, clothing, jewelry, gourmet food, sporting goods, pet supplies, books, CDs, DVDs, computers, furniture, toys, garden supplies, bedding and almost anything else you might want to buy. What makes Amazon a giant is in the details. Besides its tremendous product range, Amazon makes every possible attempt to customize the buyer experience.

When one arrive at the homepage, one willl find not only special offers and featured products.

The Gold Box

There's probably a little "Gold Box" icon at the top of the Amazon.com homepage every time one visit. This box holds special treats for the visitor who visits the homepage of Amazon.

Time-sensitive discounts: Once the visitor click on the Gold Box and view an offer, one have to complete the transaction (if one want it) in a specified time period. After that time period, the offer disappears.

The goal is pretty straightforward: "To be Earth's most customer-centric company where people can find and discover anything they want to buy online." The implementation is complex, massive and dynamic. Amazon's marketing structure is a lesson in cost-efficiency and brilliant self-promotion. Amazon's associates link to Amazon products in order to add value to their own Websites, sending people to Amazon to make their purchases. It costs Amazon practically nothing. Some associates create mini-Amazons — satellite sites that do new things with Amazon data and send people to the mother ship when they're ready to buy.

In the 2003 holiday season, Amazon processed a top-end 1 million shipments and 20 million inventory updates in one day. Amazon's sales volume means that hundreds of thousands of people send their credit card numbers to Amazon's servers everyday, and security is a major concern. In addition to automatically encrypting credit card numbers during the checkout process, Amazon lets users choose to encrypt every piece of information they enter, like their name, address and gender.

Amazon employs the Netscape Secure Commerce Server using the SSL (secure socket layer) protocol. It stores all credit card numbers in a separate database that's not Internet-accessible, cutting off that possible entry point for hackers. Customers who are particularly cautious can choose to enter only a partial credit card number over the Internet and then provide the rest by phone once the online order is submitted.

5.2 CUSTOMER FOCUS

The ISO/TS 16949:2002 Standard represents specific automotive OEMs concentrates on the customer focus of an organization.

Top management shall ensure that:

Customer requirements are determined and met Aim is to enhance customer satisfaction (also see clause 7.2.1 and 8.2.1)

Key Explanation Points and Tips:

- Organizations depend on their customers. Accordingly, one must understand current and future needs of customers; develop customer focused processes; establish customer goals and objectives; measure customer satisfaction against these goals and objectives; have customer focused internal and external communications; and ensure that the orgnization's personnel are competent and trained in understanding and achieving customer requirements.
- As this standard represents specific automotive OEMs, the organization's QMS must provide objective evidence that the QMS processes can identify and manage these requirements and that customer-specific requirements are effectively implemented. Review specific requirements at OEM customer.
- The organization must communicate its OEM's current and future product programmes within the organization as well as flow them down the supply chain in terms of sub-products, price, timing, delivery communication and support.
- The organization must have an effective communication process between the customer and the organization, for discussion, review, timing, action and responsibility on the above issues.
- The organization must have an effective process for communication and review of the above requirements to relevant personnel or departments within the organization.
- It is top management role to provide the leadership and commitment of time and resources to ensure this happens. Auditors will be looking for evidence of this.
- Clause 7.2.1 gets further into the details of understanding and processing customer requirements.

Clause 8.2.1 sets requirements for monitoring and measuring customer satisfaction.

- Clause 5.2 provides the top management's overall responsibility for customer relationship management (CRM), while clause 7.2.1 provides the front end and clause 8.2.1 provides the back end, of the underlying and detailed activities of CRM.
- The organization will notice that customer focus can be included in the following processes – business planning; communications; sales and marketing; and customer satisfaction feedback.

- Clause 5.2 does not require a 'documented' procedure. However, The organization must identify and document (e.g. process map; process flow diagram; etc.) the processes listed in the paragraph above as part of your QMS.

The organization must also identify what specific documents are needed for effective planning, operation and control of these processes (clause 4.2.1d).

Examples of such documents may include – a documented procedure; business plan; statement of customer related policies and objectives; etc.

In a world where products become commodities in record time, service has become the crucial differentiator for long-term sustainable success – developing a Customer-Centric Enterprise with a focus on the needs of its customers is the key to ensure sustainable success for today's enterprises.

A number of businesses focus on satisfying the customer and a business can have millions of satisfied customers. Unfortunately, having satisfied customers is not enough to have sustainable growth. A satisfied customer does not imply that they will talk about your organization or service to others and that they might refer others to you. An organization can lose out on potential increments in revenue, customers and profits, if it fails to attract the customer.

An impressed customer is not only a satisfied customer but also a LOYAL customer. In order to develop customer loyalty and the attraction effect, organizations need to consistently provide service quality that is above and beyond the customer's expectations. In other words, every interaction that the customer has with your organization needs to have the attractive factor.

In doing so, the organization gains customer loyalty and increased customer retention. Loyal customers, and customers that feel that the organization met and exceeded their expectations will talk positively about their experience and will refer others to the organization.

For the organization, this is critical, because the longer a customer stays with the company, the higher the revenue and profitability from the customer. the lifetime value of a customer increases exponentially with the number of years they have been the organization's customers.

It is clear that organizations need to focus on developing higher customer loyalty in order to increase revenues, profits, and to achieve sustainable success and most organizations will accept this fact.

When an enterprise defines its "customer"as a combination of its customers, employees and partners, and when the whole organization is designed to provide the best customer experience at every interaction – that's when the enterprise truly becomes a Customer-Centric Enterprise. And a Customer-Centric Enterprise is exactly what will be required for an organization to achieve sustainable growth.

Merging elements has developed a model, 'Relationship Model', to better understand the importance of all three players in a Customer-Centric Enterprise.

The Relationship Model presents a number of concepts that are important to understand when developing a Customer-Centric Enterprise plan.These concepts are described below:

Core Values: The values upon which the leadership has build the foundation of the company. Core values are the ideals, principles, and philosophy at the centre of the enterprise. These are the values that drive the decisions made by each and every employee within the organization from major decisions to performing their day-to-day functions.These values need to reflect the company's focus on the customer, since these are the guidelines that will drive the Customer-Centric Enterprise.

The Core Values of an organization are the foundations upon which the company's Customer-Centric strategy is created. Hence it is at the centre of the Relationship Model. Customers, Employees and Partners – The three corners of the triangle, represent the three elements in the enterprise that combined make the organization customer-centric.

One of the first steps that all organizations need to take in the process of architecting a Customer-Centric Enterprise is to define the company's customers, employees and partners. This step is essential in order to know the company's target market, customer profiles, customer needs and expectations, employees needs, partner profiles and their roles and needs before developing its customer-centric strategy.

Interactions: Represented in the model as the arrows connecting the customers, employees and partners. The interactions between the players and the rest of the organization play a pivotal role in determining their experience with the organization. As the channel is the primary touch-point determining the user experience, the organization needs to develop a channel strategy as a part of the overall business strategy. The channel strategy needs to define the channels to be used by the different players, the services to be provided via each channel, cost of supporting each channel and other channel matters.

When developing a channel strategy, organizations also need to focus on consistency in service quality between the different channels.

Relationship Infrastructure: It is the underpinning infrastructure required in order to support the different players in the Relationship Model. The Relationship Infrastructure is what defines the technology and processes that an organization.

Matrix Diagram

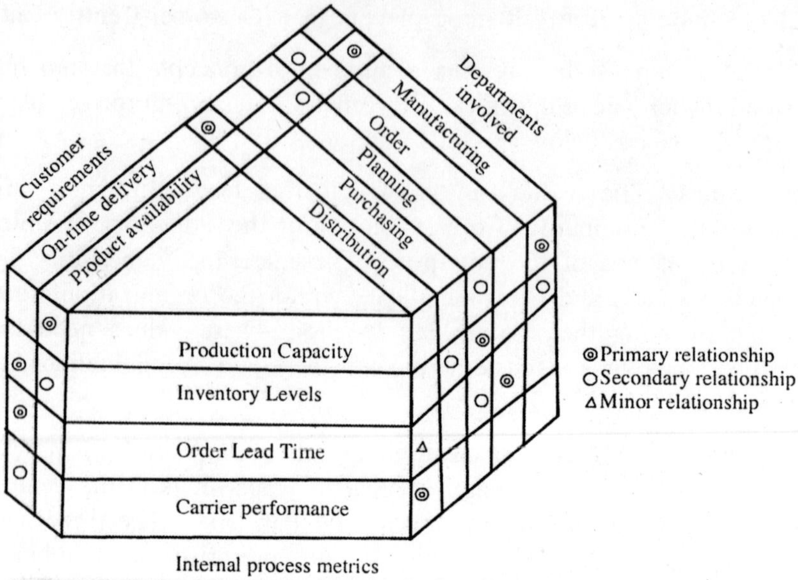

© - Strong relationship O - Moderate relationship Δ - Weak Dr polental relationship No relationship	↑ Postive relationship O Neutral relationship Negative relationship
S - Supplier C - Customer D - Doer O - Owner	↑ item on left at top ← item at top influences item on left The arrows usually are placed next to another symbol indicating the strength of the relationship

The above shown matrix diagram shows the customer requirements and the level preparedness of an organization.

Rolls-Royce (who makes aircraft engines, not just luxury cars) that is well worth reading to learn about how different business model elements can be combined to create a successful company. Some key points to look for:

The company made a big bet on a particular underlying technology for jet engines.Their initial attempt failed, requiring a bailout from the British government, but these efforts led to a winning design for a family of engines. Key lessons: Learning from failure is a good thing, but it does required capital to see you through. Whether or not a government bailout is appropriate, there are certain decisions for any company which are "bet the company". Choose wisely.

Rolls-Royce evolved into a highly customer-centric model that combines manufacturing and services. In many industries, services are separated from the product, often provided by different companies. In aircraft engines, however, the ability to make the product provides key knowledge to service the product. This knowledge is not enough, however, for the model to work. For Rolls-Royce, getting access to customer operational data on engine performance is required to solidify their competitive edge in services and to feed this information back into engine design.

Why does the customer want to provide critical operational data back to a supplier? Many customers would be fearful of this approach.Yet Rolls-Royce has created a win-win contractual structure that aligns incentives. Instead of selling the engine, they sell "power by the hour". Since the customer only makes money when their engines are running, they only pay Rolls-Royce for that time when the engines are running. For this model to work, Rolls-Royce needs access to the data that lets them continuously monitor performance. Great example of a win-win customer-centric business model.

What's a customer-centric business and what's its value?

A customer- centric business puts its valuable customers at the core of its strategy and day-to-day operations. Every action is first evaluated by its impact on its customers.

Valuable customers is an important term. It describes the most profitable customers, rather than the largest number of customers. Many companies make the mistake of trying to grow their customer base regardless of value. This generates costs with little returns and has a negative impact on satisfaction.The end result is a decline in profitability and damage to the brand. Customer focus is the key to success.

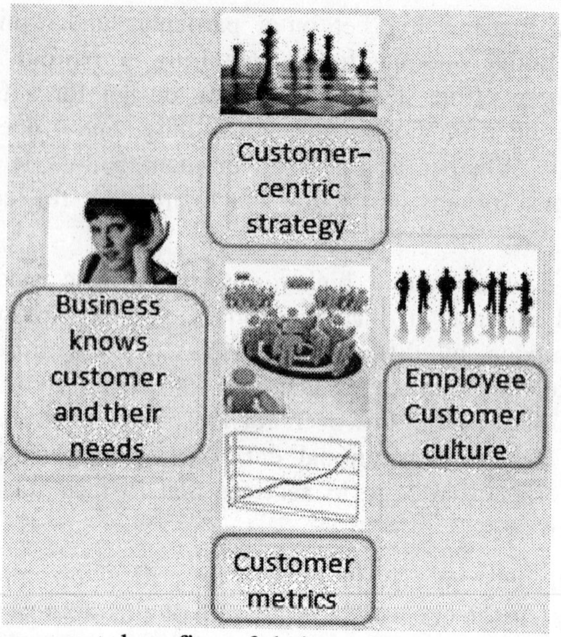

Here are some great benefits of being customer-centric:

A profitable customer base

Clear understanding of how to grow your business and profits, based on a deep knowledge of your customers; An ability to respond quickly to your customer needs and changes in your business environment; A faster, more efficient organization, as everyone beats to the same drum; Better protection in downturns, due to more loyal customers.

In the next few pages, we'll show you how you can evaluate your business for customer-centricity and take steps to become customer- centric.

What does a customer- centric business look like?

Customer-centric businesses exhibit four key attributes:

They know their customers: they understand their value, needs and they listen to them.

Customer-centric business strategy: the business is built around their core customers.

Customer culture: employees live and breath their customers.

Customer metrics: the business tracks its customers as part of key business performance tracking.

Good examples of customer-centric businesses are companies such as, Apple, Amazon and HMV. All are very focused on their customers and have done an excellent job at achieving success based on this approach.

Is your business customer-centric?

The customer-centric checklist

Take a look at the criteria below for a customer-centric business and score yes or no for each question.

Do you have a clear idea of who your customers are and what are their needs?

Do you know which of your customers are most valuable to you?

Does your business strategy/mission mention anything about your customers?

Do you hire/develop your staff with your customers in mind?

Do you have a process by which customers and employees can give feedback and review/act on this within your business?

Do you have a customer complaints process which enables quick resolution of customer problems?

Are all your employees empowered to deal with customer complaints?

Do you know how satisfied or loyal your customers actually are?

Do you provide specific services or incentives for your most valued/loyal customers?

Do you deliver what you promise in your advertising/marketing to your customers?

If it's a new or small business it's relatively easy to build in customer-centricity. If, however, your business is somewhat larger, it maybe more challenging, as you'll need to bring your entire organization on the journey. Whatever your business, here are some simple steps you can take to achieve customer-centricity.

Lead from the top: To make a customer-centric programme work within your business, you'll need to lead this from the top.

If you have a management team, it's worth taking time to get everyone on board. If a boss of a business can show they are customer-centric, it's an easier sell to everyone else. Dig into your customers

Set up a process to measure customer satisfaction and the drivers that affect it. Begin reviewing customer feedback with your people.

Identify who are your customer groups, based on their value and needs.

Look at what the competition is doing to deliver great customer experience (why re-invent the wheel?)

How to make your business customer-centric: part 2

Building a customer-centric strategy

Familiarise your management team with your customer needs.

Amend your business strategy/mission to focus on your customers.

Continue to update your business with customer findings

Test your strategy against your customers

Define a process to track the success of your strategy. For example, measure the number of customers, their satisfaction and loyalty.

Build a marketing strategy for your valuable customers and make sure you deliver on your promises.

Build a customer-centric business culture: Set up a process with your staff to review customer feedback and customer satisfaction data regularly.

Run workshops with your staff, focussing on how best to service your customers.

Set customer-centric objectives for all staff

Set up a process to deal with customer complaints

Create incentives for staff who excel in customer service

Make sure you hire and develop your staff with a view to customer-centricity.

4.7 ADVANTAGES AND DISADVANTAGES

Being customer-centric is the best way to supercharge your organization. Let's explore the benefits of transitioning your organization to becoming more customer-centric.

First and foremost are profits

"Companies that improve their ability to consistently meet their customers' needs will produce positive bottom-line business results." (Mikel Harry, Richard Schroeder, <u>Six Sigma</u>). The financial perspective is a direct benefit that starts most organizations on the journey to increased customer relevance.

There are many other reasons, of course, but let's focus on two that are even more important.

First, customer-centricity produces freedom for an organization.

"The customer is in world class organizations, not outside...If left outside, the customer gets treated with indifference at best, and offers the same in return." (Richard Shonberger, AchieveGlobal). Freedom empowers everyone in the organization to customize their treatment of customers rather than to deliver lackluster performances that customers feel are indifferent. Freedom rises out of the confidence that all employees understand why and for whom they are working. Freedom also manifests itself when a company is proactively working on customer solutions, rather than reactively handling complaints and resolving customer issues. All of this translates to fewer worries, coupled with brand new opportunities to achieve greater heights in terms of innovative and creative solutions.

Secondly, companies will enjoy stronger employee loyalty if they embrace strong customer relationship values. While your employees certainly want to receive a paycheque from you, they really care more about their customers than they do about you. Sorry to break the news to you. Much of employees' satisfaction comes from delivering strong, commonsense solutions to their customers. Customer-centric organizations rise above internal procedures, which the customer does not care about, and focus on a logical service or product which makes the customer's life easier. Employees' answers to our surveys always confirm that the way their employer treats customers is one of the most important drivers of their satisfaction as workers. If employees are empowered to take care of their customers, they will like working for you much better. Not a bad combination, is it? Happier, more committed employees and customers at the same time.

Companies that outperform the competition have "customers" as a core competency. Teach everyone in your organization the benefits of being customer-centric. Don't assume that they know. Communicating the positive results of thinking like a customer in every aspect of your business will serve as a foundation or touchstone that will accelerate the transition within your organization. Being custome-centric aligns everyone around one purpose–to make the customer successful – and the customer loves you for it. But, your organization also reaps the benefits in ways most leaders haven't considered. Those other benefits are the real reasons that you start the transformation.

According to Jonathan Narducci, the following are the essentials for successful implememtation of customer-centricity.

(1) The company's vision and mission mention the customer and their success (not just making them more "competitive") as a goal and the company promotes as its highest principle "Do everything we can to make the customer successful!"

A corollary: A company knows why their customers can fail and does what it can to prevent it.

(2) The company takes on the following attitude: A "risk" taken by the company is also a risk taken by their customers, so company and customers work together to manage or mitigate it.

For example, implementing new technology is always risky, so companies work with their customers to make sure it can be "installed," their people can be trained to use it, and support personnel are located in the right place for the right time (i.e., the company anticipates or knows when support will be needed).

(3) A major company goal is to "make life easier" for the customer. Customer-centric companies make it easy to, for example, return goods, get ans ness and the businesses of their customers.

(4) The company's loyal customer, "best" customer, and successful customer have well defined criteria that segment them into these categories, which is useful for focusing value propositions.

For example, the most loyal customer may not be the most successful, but when they buy, they buy from the company; the "best" customer may be the one that promotes the company's business the most, but may not buy the most; and the most successful customer may sell more goods and services than their competition but may not be the most loyal. Knowing this information, a company can develop a customer-centric strategy for each customer type.

(5) The company focuses enterprise activities – those designed to cut across the entire company down to those designed, specifically, for each individual – on what it means to retain customers and create repeat buyers.

This means that company strategies are developed to include the results that customers can expect from the successful implementation of the associated initiatives. It means that when designing jobs, the company makes sure they start with defining the customer's needs and expected results as the foundation for the job's activities and standards.

(6) The company is aligned around the total value proposition for each customer segment, not just the products and their related services that are at the core of each proposition.

For example, providing industry consultative services to certain customer groups via (possibly) the sales force is a part of the total value proposition and, although not a core service (one that's related to core products) the sales organization has to align itself – taking into account their skills, processes, tools, physical locations, customer needs, etc. – with the appropriate customers to effectively deliver the service.

(7) The company receives value back from their customers in the form of, for example, market promotions, feasible self-sufficient support, applicable co-branding programmes, and useful, hard to get industry information (e.g. a "heads up" to technology breakthroughs or impending market shifts).

(8) Essential corporate information (e.g. product availability, account status, problem reports) is available to all customers in "real time" as if they were internal to the company.

(9) The company gathers information about their customers' customers and suppliers, how "information" flows around their customers' enterprises, how their customers operate, about their customers' strategies, and so on. More importantly, the company asks for some of this "non-transactional" information.

In other words, the company knows everything possible about their customers so they can constantly innovate their business, with and for their customers, to provide unique solutions for their unique problems or needs.

(10) Companies know that customer-centricity is implemented via a set of skills and processes supported by a set of tools and not just by installing the tools. They take the time to define the skills and processes they need to become customer-centric – e.g. analytical skills and a process for "learning about the entire customer business" (see bullet above) – before they purchase and install tools to make them effective.

Use these ten criteria – along with business objectives, core value propositions, business goals, and targeted marketplaces – to identify and select the following, vital to robust customer-centric strategies:

In today's ultra competitive market place where customers are highly empowered, competitors are trying every trick in the book to lure away customers from other companies and collaborators have become highly technology savvy. The best way for any company to move forward is by adopting a customer-centric philosophy.

As the term indicates, customer-centric philosophy or customer-centricity is an ideology, a value system where in companies' activities are centered around the requirements of customers. As simple as it may sound, it is probably one of the toughest things for any company to incorporate into their corporate strategy and structure. Businesses till now have been following the dominant product centric philosophy (of product centricity).

Product centricity refers to an internal alignment with focus predominantly on operations, productions and internal controls. As such, the deciding factor on many decisions was the production efficiency. Further, a product focus results in a more transactional and short-term interaction with customers.

On the other hand, customer-centricity refers to an external alignment with focus predominantly on the customer and the way in which customer wants and needs are satisfied whereby value can be created both to the customer being served and the organization that is serving the customer. Customer-centricity is also in line with service-centered dominant logic for marketing in that customer-centricity goes well beyond selling products to customers and entering a whole new world of providing comprehensive solutions. As such, customer-centricity emphasizes building long term relationships with customers.

Do these two ideologies result in tangible systems for companies and ventures beyond definitional jugglery? The answer is an emphatic yes. Customer-centricity offers companies certain key advantages hitherto not offered by product centricity. Further, it enables companies in building sustainable competitive advantage.

Product development and design will be more in tune with the needs of the customers rather than being just to reflect the technological prowess or superiority of the company.

Pricing would be more in line with the value perception of the customer and his/her willingness to pay rather being an exercise to cover the cost of manufacturing.

Innovative ways of reaching customer in order to provide them convenience will replace logistic oriented distribution where places where the product ends up at is decided by a number of other operational and financial factors with no emphasis given to customer convenience.

Communications, advertising and promotions will also be line with the receptivity of the customer rather than bombarding the customer as dictated by the demands of selling a prerequisite number of products.

Co-creating value along with customer becomes possible as a customer-centric culture of an organization would establish systems that would enable a constant dialogue with customers.

Effectiveness of marketing can be shifted from the traditional market share and sales figures to more comprehensive measures such as the customer lifetime value, satisfaction scores, and strength of customer loyalty.

Given the emphasis on relationship building in a customer-centric culture, it allows companies to don a more long-term perspective rather than a short-term perspective with focus purely on quarterly results.

The customer-centric philosophy will increasingly be adapted by businesses in their quest to master the new requirements and role of marketing – customer loyalty.

Four Principles to Customer-Centricity

Oracle OpenWorld, and Melissa Boxer, vice president of product marketing for those products, outlined the four basic principles to customer-centricity:

(1) Understand your customers: know who they are and how their behaviour is changing.What are your customers' preferences — where and how do they buy, what do they like or don't like?

(2) Reward, recognize, and differentiate: Once you have a rich repository of customer data, leverage the insight gleaned to recognize differences in customers and their behaviours and think beyond basic loyalty points. Really think about what's meaningful to your customers to deliver a personalized, differentiated experience via every channel and interaction.

(3) Engage across channels with relevant interactions: Customers aren't listening to traditional marketing. They are looking for rich dialogues with you — and you need to be able to do that through any channel.

(4) Build powerful communities of loyal customers: by doing so, you will build brand affinity and value for customers.

4.8 SUMMARY

In defining a market, it is important not to focus only on products/services that currently meet the customer need. For example, the two wheeler manufacturer who believed that their market was the "two wheeler market" would have made some poor marketing decisions unless he had seen the arrival of products such as higher end models – which also satisfy the same need – "to provide convenient travel". Thinking about customer needs first – and then identifying the products that meet those needs – is the best way to define a market.

However, it is also important not to define a market too broadly. For example, it is not particularly helpful for a marketing manager to define his or her market as the "food market" or the "transport market". The purpose of market definition is to provide a meaningful framework for analysis and decision-making. Innovative ways of reaching customer in order to provide them convenience will replace logistic oriented distribution where places where the product ends up at is decided by a number of other operational and financial factors with no emphasis given to customer convenience.

Communications, advertising and promotions will also be line with the receptivity of the customer rather than bombarding the customer as dictated by the demands of selling a prerequisite number of products.Co-creating value along with customer becomes possible as a customer-centric culture of an organization would establish systems that would enable a constant dialogue with customers.

Effectiveness of marketing can be shifted from the traditional market share and sales figures to more comprehensive measures such as the customer lifetime value, satisfaction scores, and strength of customer loyalty.

Given the emphasis on relationship building in a customer-centric culture, it allows companies to don a more long-term perspective rather than a short-term perspective with focus purely on quarterly results.

The customer-centric philosophy will increasingly be adapted by businesses in their quest to master the new requirements and role of marketing-customer loyalty.

4.9 SELF ASSESSMENT QUESTIONS

1. Explain the essentials for successful implementation of customer-centricity.
2. Discuss the Customer-centric businesses's key attributes.
3. What are the advantages and disadvantages of customer-centric organization?
4. Explain the Steps in Developing a Sales Promotion and Merchandising Plan.
5. What is customer-centric strategy? Discuss the merits and demerits .
6. Discuss the customer-centricity focuses of an organization.
7. Explain the factors to be considered in organization's focus and marketing success.

□□□

5 Chapter CUSTOMER-CENTRICITY

Objectives

After going through this chapter, you will be able to understand:

- To identify about the customer-centricity
- To familiarize about the customer relationship strategies
- To identify the issues in customer relationship
- To know about the customer relationship management
- To learn about the importance of customer relationship management

Structure:

5.1 Definition of Customer-Centricity

5.2 Customer Relationship Strategies.

5.3 Why Customer Relationship is Important?

5.4 What is Customer relationship Management?

5.5 Importance of Customer Relationship Management

5.6 Summary

5.7 Self Assessment Questions

5.1 DEFINITION OF CUSTOMER-CENTRICITY

According to business dictionary, customer-centric is defined as "An approach to doing business in which a company focuses on creating a positive consumer experience at the point of sale and post-sale. A customer-centric approach can add value to a company by differentiating themselves from competitors who do not offer the same experience."

Customer-centricity refers to the orientation of a company to the needs and behaviours of its customers, rather than internal drivers.

Customer-centric is defined as a comprehensive customer orientation – ie, gearing actions to customers and their various needs when designing products and developing services.

5.2 CUSTOMER RELATIONSHIP STRATEGIES

Definition of CRM

"Customer Relationship Management is an integrated effort to maintain and build up a network with individual consumers and to continuously strengthen the network for mutual benefits of both the sides, through interactive, individualized and value added contacts over a long period of time."

Shani and Chalsani

"Customer Relationship Management is to focus on an individual or one to one relationship with the customers that integrate database knowledge with long term customer's retention and the growth strategy."

Peppers and Rogers

"The coherent management of contacts and interactions with customers". They identify that "The essence of a CRM system is that customer data is collected from all touch points and deposited into one central data pool for more effective marketing, better order processing, production and accounting."

The chartered Institute of Marketing

Objective of CRM

- CRM aims at integrating all business strategies that places the customer at the centre of a business consciousness.
- Aligning of organization towards customers.
- Integrating your customer touch points.

- Knowing and understanding your customers and potential customers.
- Establishing and managing relationships with customers.

PRINCIPLES OF CRM

Differentiate Customers

All customers are not equal; recognize and reward best customers disproportionately. Understanding each customer becomes particularly important, and the same customers' reaction to a cellular company operator may be quite different as compared to a car dealer. Besides for the same product or the service not all customers can be treated alike and CRM needs to differentiate between a high value customer and a low value customer.

What CRM needs to understand while differentiating customers is:

Sensitivities, preferences and personalities

Lifestyle and age

Culture background and education

Physical and psychological characteristics

Differentiating offerings

Low value customer requiring high value customer offerings

Low value customer with potential to become high value in near future

High value customer requiring high value service

High value customer requiring low value service

Keeping existing customers

Grading customers from very satisfied to very disappoint should help the organization in improving its customer satisfaction levels and scores. As the satisfaction level for each customer improves as well as customer retention with the organization.

Maximizing lifetime value

Exploit up – selling and cross selling potential. By identifying life stage and life event trigger points by customer, marketers can maximize share of purchase potential. Thus the single adults shall require a new car stereo and as he grows into a married couple his needs grow into appliances.

Increase Loyalty

Loyal customers are more profitable. Any company will like its mindshare status to improve from being a suspect to being an advocate. Company has to invest in terms of its product and service offerings to its customers. It has to innovate and meet the very needs of its clients/ customers so that they remain as advocates on the loyalty curve. Referral sales invariably low cost high margin sales.

What is CRM (customer relationship management)?

CRM (customer relationship management) is an information industry term for methodologies, software, and usually Internet capabilities that help an enterprise manage customer relationships in an organized way. For example, an enterprise might build a database about its customers that described relationships in sufficient detail so that management, salespeople, people providing service, and perhaps the customer directly could access information, match customer needs with product plans and offerings, remind customers of service requirements, know what other products a customer had purchased, and so forth.

According to one industry view, CRM consists of:

Helping an enterprise to enable its marketing departments to identify and target their best customers, manage marketing campaigns and generate quality leads for the sales team.

Assisting the organization to improve telesales, account, and sales management by optimizing information shared by multiple employees, and streamlining existing processes (for example, taking orders using mobile devices).

Allowing the formation of individualized relationships with customers, with the aim of improving customer satisfaction and maximizing profits; identifying the most profitable customers and providing them the highest level of service.

Providing employees with the information and processes necessary to know their customers, understand and identify customer needs and effectively build relationships between the company, its customer base, and distribution partners.

Many organizations turn to CRM software to help them manage their customer relationships. CRM technology is offered on-premise, on-demand or through Software as a Service (SaaS) CRM, depending on the vendor. Recently, mobile CRM and the open source CRM software model have also become more popular.

Customer Relationship Management is the process of understanding and acting on information about customers better and more efficiently than the competition. He who has the best relationship with the customer wins. The relationship yields knowledge that allows the company to provide more relevant product/service offerings. The ability to do that consitently through time helps to differentiate the company from the competition and ultimately becomes a key competitive advantage.

The organization should consider it Customer Relationship Marketing and, it is the cultivation of a true relationship with the customers insuring minimal sales base erosion and strong trial visit activity.

In customer relationship marketing, the products of an organization being enveloped by insightful customer orientated relationships, anticipating and satisfying the customer needs beyond their expectations.

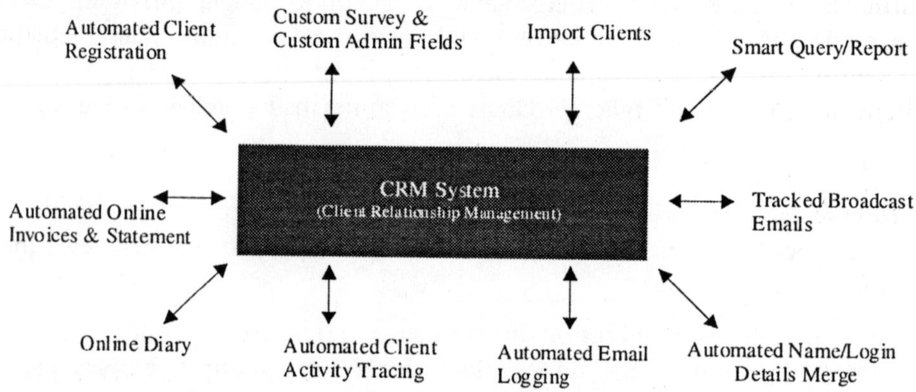

Adapted from Hotcode Designs Limited

The CRM diagram shows that relationship between the organization and its clients. Managing client data is vital to enabling you to provide a high level of responsiveness and service to your clients and to maximize your sales opportunities and create a more efficient business.

The sort of data helps to store and easily access and manage includes:

contact information

sales related data

contact activity

e.g. phone calls, appointments, e-mails and their contact with your business through your website, etc. classification data

e.g. their business type, their unique needs, etc.

5.3 WHY CUSTOMER RELATIONSHIP IS IMPORTANT?

Companies that need customers in order to build a profit need to have a system in place that effectively and successfully manages the customer/client relationship. Customer relationship management teaches the tools that are needed to reach a customer in a way that instills trust and confidence. Some of these tools include methods in the way the customer is approached. Building up a level of common ground with the customer is an effective way to start building that confidence. Studies show that people are drawn to what they are attracted to. When a customer is approached by a salesperson that is confident, well dressed, and can communicate well, they are more likely to listen from the beginning to the end.

Contact management is all about teaching companies to successfully manage all the contacts that they initiate over a period of time. It's one thing to develop those contacts, but it's important that you know what to do with them when you have them. Contact management teaches tools that allow employees to take those contacts and turn them into profits and sales. Customer relationship management and contact management are effective tools for generating profits that more and more companies are using to improve their leverage in the market. With the level of competition today in any industry, companies need to have the edge up on all the others. This means utilizing customers and contacts as strongly and effectively as possible without losing one along the way. With these types of tools at their disposal many more companies are watching their customer sales improving.

A CRM system will also help an organization a lot in expanding its business. As CRM systems are capable of handling enormous amounts of data, CRM systems will help a lot in coping with the increased numbers of customers and data. With a CRM Customer Relationship Management system installed and properly utilized, the organization can be sure that all data is maximized and used to ensure that the business will be successful and the customers a lot more satisfied than before.

CRM Customer Relationship Management is one of the newest innovations in customer service today. CRM stands for customer relationship management and helps the management and customer service staffs cope with customer concerns and issues. CRM involves gathering a lot of data about the customer. The data is then used to facilitate customer service transactions by making the information needed to resolve the issue or concern readily available to those dealing with the customers. This results in more satisfied customers, a more profitable business and more resources available to the support staff.

Furthermore, Customer Relationship Management systems are a great help to the management in deciding on the future course of the company.

As mentioned, there is much data needed for the CRM system to work. These fields include the customer name, address, date of transactions, pending and finished transactions, issues and complaints, status of order, shipping and fulfilment dates, account information, demographic data and many more. This information is important in providing the customer the answer that he or she needs to resolve the issue without having to wait for a long time and without going to several departments. With just a few mouse clicks, a customer support representative for example can track the location of the customer's package or order. This is infinitely better than the cumbersome process of tracking shipments previously. Furthermore, the customer service representative will also be able to see the previous concerns of the customer. This is a great help especially if the customer is calling about the same issue since he or she will not have to repeat the story all over again. This results in less time in resolving the issue, thus, higher productivity of the support staff.

Customer Relationship Management systems are also important to the top management because it provides crucial data like customer satisfaction and efficiency of service by the frontline crews. A piece of customer relationship management software will also be able to generate the needed reports for product development or new concepts. Customer Relationship Management systems helps an organization to identify the individual requirement of a customer. Furthermore, this system will also be a great help for the top management in deciding the company's future course of action, whether it involves phasing out one of the products on the shelves or making adjustments to one of the products sold.

The reports generated by CRM systems are also invaluable to an organization's advertising and marketing planners, as they will be able to pinpoint which ideas works and which do not. Because of CRM systems, it will be able to release advertisements or plan marketing campaigns more in tune with the target market. This will also lead to more responses to the advertisement and a more effective marketing campaign.

Successful integration of a CRM

Customer Relationship Management system in the company, however, might not be as easy as it seems. The following might give you an insight why CRM systems fail in some companies... Most companies fail to prepare for CRM systems. By this, most companies fail to integrate all the departments that need to share the information for it to be effective. Furthermore, CRM units scattered all over the company's departments is often more effective than just making one big CRM department. This will ensure that each department will get the information and data that they need.

A CRM system will also help a lot in expanding the business. As CRM systems are capable of handling enormous amounts of data, CRM systems will help a lot in coping with the increased numbers of customers and data. With a Customer Relationship Management system installed and properly utilized, one can be sure that all data is maximized and used to ensure that the business will be successful and the customers a lot more satisfied than before.

Three converging trends have enabled the emergence of CRM applications as a major force in the marketplace. The first trend is the availability of robust, scalable decision support technology. Data warehouse software is helping companies collect vast quantities of data from multiple, heterogeneous sources, such as accounting, manufacturing, human resources, sales force automation, and customer service applications. This provides the technological foundation for building a consolidated, enterprisewide view of the customer, rather than a limited perspective offered by departmental applications. Data warehousing can also be used to deliver consistent information to any customer touch point, such as a Website, e-mail, call centre, or customer self-service application. Customers hate getting inconsistent information from different business units in the same organization. Data warehouse technology is also leveraged by analytical software, such as OLAP and data mining tools, which are extremely useful in analyzing customer relationships.

The second trend is the emergence of front-office applications. This software category has made it easier for companies to identify and track customers. Front-office applications tend to focus on the sales and the marketing departments, and are essentially transactional in nature. This limits their use in analysis – something that is essential for complete customer understanding. Some vendors have recognized this limitation and are adding OLAP capabilities to their applications.

The third trend is the recognition that a new, individual customer-focused marketing model is needed to maintain a competitive advantage in the late 1990s. The emergence of the one-to-one marketing phenomenon has helped put a rationale in place for companies to have their marketing activities focus on the customer, rather than on their products, distributors, sales force or suppliers. One-to-one marketing helps drive an analysis of customer share, rather than market share.Customer share is the concept of increasing your share of the customers' business, enhancing their value to the organization and leveraging the investment the company made in courting them in the first place.

CRM is more than sales force automation (SFA), marketing automation or call centre software, although it incorporates elements of all these applications. An enterprisewide CRM solution may include data mining functions to enable analysis of the attributes and behaviour of large groups of customers or prospects. It also may include external data from sources that collect and maintain large databases of consumer profiles obtained from a variety of public and private sources.

Like most new technologies, this is a space that is changing rapidly. New vendors are popping up like mushrooms. Siebel Systems Inc. is an enterprise sales force automation market leader, and is now delivering analysis capabilities as well. SAP AG recognizes the need to add customer management features to R/3, but isn't shipping anything yet. E.piphany, Annuncio Software and Rubric focus on delivering marketing applications for CRM on the Internet.

So what should the company do about a CRM solution? The first thing to do is understand what products we need to implement such a solution. For example, if we work for a bank or other service establishment, we need to be concerned with defining the attributes of your best customers, with the goal of reducing churn and improving customer loyalty. Evaluate various products on the market, and look for scalability, industry expertise, and an open, customizable solution. Be sure to pick a platform that will scale up to support both the anticipated growth in data, as well the complex queries the users will want to execute.

Customer Relationship Management systems are also important to the top management because it provides crucial data like customer satisfaction and efficiency of service by the frontline crews. A piece of customer relationship management software will also be able to generate the needed reports for product development or new concepts. Furthermore, this system will also be a great help for the top management in deciding the company's future course of action, whether it involves phasing out one of the products on the shelves or making adjustments to one of the products sold.

In whatever we do as a business, the end goal is to get a happier customer resulting in more business. The primary element here is to know exactly what the customer wants / would want in the future – every year from now on say for the next 10 + years and be the first player in the market to lure the customer with that need / product / service. It is in this context that it becomes important to look at convergence keeping the customer perspective in mind. The key business drivers are around customer centricity, synergies and brand value.

The first step of convergence is the fusion of the marketing of the products of either the triple players (Voice, Video, and Data) or quadruple-players.

(Voice, Video, Data and Mobility). Beyond quadruple play, convergence starts assuming a significant change in approach and implementation – both in terms of vertical convergence and horizontal convergence.

So what is convergence from a customer perspective? To an end customer, the limits of convergence are endless. The customer needs:

- All the possible services as a single entity
- A single bill (converged bill for family accounts)
- Option to choose one or more or part or whole of those services.
- Best user experience within the services
- Use based pricing model

These customer needs can be best explored in the context of three key areas:

Have a single equipment in their static location which caters to all his different needs of communication, related to media and entertainment (called Static Device). Do we have such a single device today?

Have a single equipment while they are on the move, dynamic location, which caters to all his different needs of communication, media and entertainment (called Dynamic Device): Do we have such a single device today?

Single Customer Care Programme for the needs: Are we running this at an optimal level to the satisfaction of the customer? The exploration of each of these items needs to be looked in depth:

Static Device: e.g. Cable, Internet Services, DVD Player,CD Player, Palmtop, Laptop, Wireless (Phones, Features), Land Line, Ability to access one/ multiple features for different family members and others, Media channels and information, Entertainment (Games etc.)

Dynamic Device: e.g. All the features of static device + Portability Single Customer Care Programme: e.g. Flexibility and Innovativeness of Plans and Pricing, Simple and Easy Billing, Scalability and Family Pricing.

Yet another modern-day buzzword, CRM stands for Customer Relationship Management.

Of course, any good businessman has always understood the importance of developing and nurturing strong equations with the customers. This is as true of large conglomerates such as the Detroit auto majors and the Tatas as it is of a small neighbourhood grocer who spends the time of day chatting up the families in the locality.

However, as the scale of operations gets larger and the number of customers grows, such actions are not always possible. It becomes difficult to remember the likes and dislikes of each customer, his or her birthday, and the like.

Nonetheless, the need for personalised attention and service exists; in fact, it becomes even greater as the world is getting ever more competitive.

As businesses get larger, software packages come to the rescue. The CRM industry has grown to keep pace with the requirements of different industries.

A typical CRM software package offers the following facilities:

Stores individual details of a huge number of customers

Tracks transactions with these customers

Records, across multiple points of interaction with the customer (call-centre, sales points, service centres), details of each fresh transaction

Analyses this database to group customers based on their demographic profile, preferences, behaviour patterns and profitability

Identify problem areas such as a reduction in the business from a particular customer.

Alerts / reminds operatives of issues such as customers' birthdays

Alerts / reminds operatives of more important issues such as payment reminders to enable cross-selling of services to the customer and has rigorous security mechanisms in place to ensure that such vital information cannot be misused.

An important concept in CRM is Mass Customisation. Let us say person 'A' and 'B' log in each morning to google.com to catch up on the news. 'A' likes to read the business news first, followed by the day's music concert listings in his city, and then the national political news. 'B' is far more interested in city news, followed by the astrology.

If google.com decides to mass customise the news page, then it could identify the person based on the log-in id and then show the news in order of preference. As can be seen from this example, Mass Customisation means being able to provide individual customers their own preferred service, and doing this for a large number of customers.

CRM packages come in many sizes — from full-service offerings to small applications that solve one particular need or the other. The industry continues to grow, but sometimes suffers because managers tend to think the software can solve all the requirements. The software can only be a tool that can execute what a customer-oriented team of managers can think of offering as a service.

5.5 IMPORTANCE OF CUSTOMER RELATIONSHIP MANAGEMENT

The level of competition is increasing in every industry in the last few decades. More companies enter into every industry and that makes the rivalry extremely high. There is no monopoly industry in the world today. Every company has to fight for their survival in the extreme competitive situations. All companies are trying to innovate to satisfy their customer and remain competitive in the market. The corporate war amongst the players of different industries are pulling the customers towards their respective organizations.Companies come up with different strategies to find their way to outcome the rivals. But it is not that easy as the competitors also attack them in the similar way. The competitor are trying to lure the customers by offering various bundle of offers. It becomes very crucial for the managers to take the right decision for the organizations.

In this competition market organizations must show their commitment on Customer relationship. In every business the main focus is the customers. Whatever strategy the company make, the ultimate aim is to satisfy the customers. Customers have various kind of demand. Companies must try to understand that and try to fulfil it better than the rivals. Companies fail to identify customer need cannot able to sustain in the long run. Many case studies of successful companies show the evidence of this argument. The main reason of their downfall is the lack of understanding of customers need. To remain competitive in the market you have to understand the customers. You have to ensure a superior Customer Relationship Management.

Customer relationship is one of the major focusing points of the companies these days. The successful accomplishment of vision required the company to fulfil their objectives. It can be financial or strategic objective. Both of the objectives are equally important for the companies. But it is important for the organizations to realize that the successes in gaining objectives are largely depending on the Management of the customers. If you cannot ensure a high quality Customer Relationship Management you cannot expectations the achievement of objectives according to your plan. That is why it is becoming so important for the companies to focus highly on Customer Relationship Management.

5.4 WHAT IS CUSTOMER RELATIONSHIP MANAGEMENT?

Many experts define customer relationship management in different ways. But the core concept is having a good relationship with the customers. That is becoming very important for the companies these days. When customers buy a product or service they need a continuous support form the company. Some time it may be related to know additional information about the product or it may be related to repair of the product. Many other situations can also occur. In those situations customer require support from the company to overcome from it. To fulfil the demand of these customers companies often establish a separate department and that is known as Customer Relationship Management. Most of the companies around the world establish their customer service centres to satisfy their customer. Customer Relationship Management also shows organizations commitment toward the customers. In every city you find a customer care service of your company. This was not a common scenario few years back. But the nature of the competition in the industry and changing customers demand force the companies to make this move. But ultimately it has a positive impact on the customers. Current competition demands that companies should have a strong bond with their customers. Today customer has many options to choose their product. There is no monopoly business around the world. Also globalization makes the competition much more intense. Organizations previously had to face competition with their domestic rivals. So the intense of the competition was limited. But today they have to face competition with their foreign competitors as well. It becomes very difficult to survive in the market for the organizations. To ensure their survival in the industry organizations must have a close tie with their customers. Customer Relationship Management can provide support in this area. As a manager you need to understand this need of the customer.

As the competition increase in the market companies are find it difficult to survive in the market. The corporate world has never seen such fierce competition in the market before. And this intensity of rivalry is likely to increase in the future. So as a manager you need to take appropriate strategy to become effective in the market. You need to ensure a good relationship with your customers. At the end of the company become successful who have a loyal customer group. To ensure such relationship the role of customer relationship management is very crucial.

Most of the companies realize the importance of customer relationship management and they become very focus in this section. The think of Management approach has change a great deal in the past decades. Customer relationship management cannot be an accepted approach in the past. But today it becomes a common scenario in many organizations. This changing trend can be effective in the business environment. The responsibility of the organizations is not over when they sell a product to the customers. It was believed in the past that you just need to sell the product to the customer. You don't have any more responsibility after that. But those marketing concepts did not last for a long time because they did not create value for the customers. Today the companies realize the importance of having an excellent relationship with the customer to secure their position in the market.

Customer Relationship Management set a new ways for the company to be connected with the customers. Previously most of the people thought the responsibility of the company is over when they sell the product to the final consumers. But that is not true. Company need to provide some assistance to the customers for a long period of time. That will increase the satisfaction of the customers. With the change in the business environment it becomes essential for the managers to change their thinking as well. Otherwise you cannot hold a strong position in the market. It is important that you create more value for the customers compare to your rivals. In this way you can have a unique image in the customers' mind. And that give you a competitive edge in the market. With the proper establishment of a Customer Relationship Management you can have a competitive advantage in the market. Have a competitive advantage in the market in the dream and vision or every organization.

Why Customer Relationship Management?

One of the success factors of the corporate depends on the investment in the right area of the business. The resources are limited for the companies. So they have to ensure a proper utilization of their available resources. So it is very crucial for the top Management to take the right investment decision. Many people hesitate to invest a large amount of money in the area of Customer Relationship Management. You might think why organizations spend such a huge amount on to improve their relationship with the customers.

We always think of the return from the investment so we remain profitable in the final calculation. Some people think the return they can get from this investment in the area of Customer Relationship Management. But it has already proven that organizations get higher return from the investments. It has a long term positive impact of the company. Organizations spend a lot of money on the area like research and development, marketing, production etc. But investment on these areas does not always give the expected return to the company. But Customer Relationship Management is an investment to improve their relationship with the customers. And customers are the profit generators for the company. So this investment can only generate value for the organization as well as for the customers. It creates a winning situation for both the company and the customers. That is a rarity in other strategies. Customer Relationship Management can be an investment that can bring huge benefits for the company.

The technological improvement changes the nature of the market for both the buyer and seller in the market. With the help of improved technology companies can make better products. They can add many attractive features as well. But technological improvement helps the buyers as well. Customers have huge information about the product than the past. They can identify the best offer in the market very easily. Organizations cannot make any over promise in their offers. Customers are very much aware of their rights today. There was a time when customer did not know much about their option of products. They had little or no idea about the benefits of the product. It was difficult for them to make the differentiation among the companies. But those days are gone. Today customers know how to differentiate product between organizations. They take the reference from other people as well search for information in different places like electronic media, internet, newspaper etc. It the product or service quality is not up to the mark they make complain of that. So this change in the customer's behaviour forces the companies to change their approach as well. Companies need to show their commitment to the customers. They need to come up with the best offer in the market. Today customers are the king. Companies are trying to do everything just to satisfy them. Customer relationship management is playing an important role in this whole process.

A company can have different types of assets. That increases its brand value in the market. Companies spend a lot of money to gain high brand value compare to the competitor. But sometime they forgot the most important assets for the company is their customers. It might not have a monitory value. For the overall assets in contributes a lot. Loyal customers bring positive results for the company in many ways. The customer's lifetime value can only get through the loyal customers. That can increase the overall profitability of the company for a longer period of time. Repurchase is the one benefit that loyal customers bring to the company. But we cannot ignore the importance of the reference they have made to the other people. Their free word of mouth advertising can be a unique asset for the company. These loyal customers influence their friends and other family members to purchase the product of the company. Today attracting new customer is not an easy task for the companies. Beside it is very expensive as well. To attract new customers, companies need to spend more money rather than retaining the existing customer base. These loyal customers work like a strategic partner for the company. This is the best thing a company expects from its customers. So we can understand how good relationship with the customer can bring positive results for the company. That's why the establishment of Customer Relationship Management is so important. This change will bring positive result for both the customers and for the organizations.

History of Customer Relationship Management

In the past when little or no preference given to customers. Companies did not try to know the demand of the customer. The basic philosophy during that time was to increase production. The organizations were under the impression that whatever that they produce they were capable of selling them in the marketplace.In marketing it referred as a production concept. The main focuses of the companies were to increase the production level. They believed customers buy product if that was readily available to them at a cheap price. Customers did not have other demand. But that was not true. Customers have different set of demands of products. As a service provider or as a manufacturer we should recognize it. As the companies did not try to know the preferences of the customers there was not Customer Relationship Management during that time. The customers of the organizations were neglected altogether. The production concept was followed by the product concept.

The production concepts receive many criticisms all over the world. Many experts suggest companies should change this concept. Then we see the introduction of product concept. Unlike the production concept it emphasizes the customers. They try to know the customers' need and meet the demand with quality product. So the scenario starts to change little bit during the phase of product concept. But the problem was companies tried to give better product to the customers but they made a mistake. They did not try to know what customers want from the product or service. They define the quality in their own language. There might be a difference between customers and organizations thinking in terms of quality. The expectations of the customers with regard to quality were not known to the organizations. But the organizations were unable to identify that or not willing to identify that. They put the features in the product that they believe important for the customers. In this stage the companies fail to create a better customer relationship. Customer's satisfactions were not at a pick.

It makes the organizations to seriously think about the alternative approach in the market. The level of competition is also increasing during that period. Finally in the mid 1950s the marketing concept was introduced. In marketing concept the organizations started giving much importance to the satisfaction of the customers.That makes a revolutionary change in the marketing system and especially the relationship between the organizations and the customers. Organizations recognize the importance of customer in the business. They also understand the importance of having a good relationship with the customers. First time companies think about different strategies to manage the customers. That was not in the consideration previously. Many organizations establish their Customer Relationship Management department. These brought a huge change in the business environment. The level of competition has increased. Most of the companies put a large effort in their Customer Relationship Management. They realize to have a better relationship with the customers to remain competitive in the market as well as earn high profitability.

Importance in Current Business World

Customer Relationship Management was ignored by the early Management theories. But today it is rated one of the most important factors for the top Management. How a company performs in the market is often determined by their relationship with the customers. We cannot ignore its value in maximizing stockholders wealth. Most of the companies try to attract new customers to increase their profitability. But it is not that easy. Customers are much more knowledgeable these days. We need to spend a lot of money to attract a new customer. These costs make it difficult for the companies to remain cost effective in the market. Most of the large organizations spend large amount of money in activities like promotion or advertising. But most often they cannot get the desired result. That's why it is often suggested by the marketing experts that we should give more importance on customer retention rather than attract.

The above concerns make it more important for the companies to have a proper customer retention policy. But the successful customer retention cannot possible without the proper contribution of Customer Relationship Management. Organizations need to have a good relationship with the customers than its competitors. This is easier to say than done. But the organizations should take necessary steps to make this objective successful. This cannot be done for one or two months. It is a continuous process and organizations have to practice it for a long period of time. As the market is getting more competitive, successful retention strategy can give an organization more profit than attracting new customers. The higher retention rate of the customers also shows the commitment of the customers toward the company. The highest brand loyalty of the customers can generate a greater profitability for the company compare to the other firms in the industry. These companies enjoy a unique image in the market. Their brand equity will raise that result a greater return for the stockholders. To ensure all of these factors at first the organizations need to establish an efficient Customer Relationship Management.

In this competition market if the firms want to remain profitable they have fully utilize the lifetime value of every customers. To ensure customers lifetime value the role of Customer Relationship Management is massive. Only with a better relationship with the customer can bring the total value of customers. Customer lifetime value means the total amount of profit generated by a single customer over his or her lifetime. It consists of the product consume by him and also the referral he make to other people to buy the product. When the other people buy the product he is also generating profit for the company. So a customer can make profit for the company in many ways. But the customers need proper motivation to do that. When he receives a superior value from the company he induces other people to involve with the company.

These loyal customers make free advertising for the organization most of the time. They work as a reference group for other people. The word of mount advertising of the people is a strong mean to induce the other customers to buy their product. But to get this free service the organization have to properly manage them. Only a better Customer Relationship Management can ensure this. Organizations need to invest more on this area because of the final outcome. It has a large impact on the future. An organization who wants to have long term benefit should invest on Customer Relationship Management. Many examples can see around us that having a competitive advantage through efficient Customer Relationship Management.

Benefits of Customer Relationship Management

Proper management system ensure success for any department or an overall growth of an organization.That provides a require guideline for the people who operate it. The Management sets the objectives to achieve. So everyone knows what their responsibility in the organizations is. Customer Relationship also requires a proper Management system to ensure the desired outcome. Many firms want to make better relationship with the customers. Companies should have an effective Customer Relationship Management to achieve its vision and objectives. Once we established a Customer Relationship Management we receive many benefits. Some of them are discussed below.

Excellence in customer services

Providing a better customer service is becoming vital for the companies. As the market is getting more competitive, firms are looking to satisfy the customers more. The increasing competition is also increase the demand of the customers. The customers are much more knowledgeable these days and have a higher expectation from the companies. As they have many options they can easily switch to other competitor if the company unable meets their expectations.

That's why companies are in tremendous pressure to meet the satisfaction level of the customers. That's why customer service is becoming so important for the companies. Customer Relationship Management can play a vital role in this whole process. They can trained up the employees on how to deal with the customers, how to provide best services. Customer Relationship Management can deal with all the problems of customers and provide necessary services to them. As we see the number of customer service centres increase all over the world. Many industries set their customer service in different region. Some of these organizations even provide customer service through internet. Without better service it is almost impossible for the companies to survive in this competition market.

Customer Relationship Management can help the company to serve better its customers. Customer Relationship Management can record the data of different customers group, their age, preference and other attributes. These factors help the organizations to understand the unique need of the customers and give them customized service. It becomes so important for the companies to look customers individually through customized service. In this process customers feel they are important to the company. And that enhances their brand loyalty to the company. There is a higher chance that this satisfied customer group make free word of mouth advertising for the company. That increases the revenue of the company. Customer Relationship Management helps the organizations to adjust the level of service to reflect the customer's importance or status. Also this data collection process of Customer Relationship Management helps the employees to better inform about each customer's specific needs and transaction profile.

Customer Relationship Management helps the organizations to provide best services to customers. It can help the organizations to achieve some of its strategic objectives as well. In today's market every company has a desire to increase its customer loyalty. Organizations focusing on the customers, as the basis of survival are with the customers in modern world. Loyal customers are the asset of the company. The lifetime value of a customer can only get through the loyal customer. Also the costs of attracting new customers are increase quite a lot in the recent times. That's why no organizations want to loose its current customers. That's why customer retention is a very important factor for the companies. Customer Relationship Management also helps the company to get the important feedback from the customers. This feedback helps the company to make appropriate strategies and steps for the future. So the importance of Customer Relationship Management in providing better service can be understandable from the above discussion.

Helps in understanding the characteristics of the segments

Marketing experts suggest that at first try to know your customers. After that we can meet the expectations of the customers. So it is very important for the company to have a genuine knowledge about their customers. In this competitive situation we cannot make a single mistake in understanding our customer. That gives an opportunity to our rival to attack us. Proper understanding of customers requires a specific procedure that can only perform by Customer Relationship Management.

Every group of customer has their own identity. No two groups respond similarly. That's why it is important for the company to identify the differences among the groups so they can provide unique service to all of them. Not all offers are equally important to different segments. The requirement of people of different groups varies. So we need to have the proper idea about the preference of different groups. Customer Relationship Management records all the important data of the customers. It is the best way for the company to know the differences among the group.

When Customer Relationship Management collect data of some of the people of the segment it is likely that the characteristics of the other member of the group are more or less same. Company can make a prediction about the remaining members of the groups. Company can use this department efficiently for their strategy decision. To fulfil the vision of the company they need support from every department. Customer Relationship Management can be an important mean to achieve the overall goals of the organizations. It can increase the wealth of the stockholders. For the long term Profitability Company should focus on Customer Relationship Management.

Can Make Cross Sale

Efficient divisions of a company cannot confined themselves on a specific set of activities. Traditionally most of the division like marketing, finance, accounting, human resources, and production focuses on their individual work. They try to ensure superior performance in their own department. But that should not be the goal for the departments. To achieve the vision of the company every departments need to work together. Cross functional activities are very much required for the success of the company. Today efficient Customer Relationship Management widens their activities. Customer Relationship Management can serve the other purposes of the company. It can play a vital role in increase the sales of the product of company. They have a frequent interaction with the customers. There is possibility for Customer Relationship Management to induce the customers to buy more product of the company. They can provide the latest and additional information to the buyers that make them interested to buy the company products. This influence is tending to be greater when the customers receive a good service from the company. They might like to associate with the company and show more interest on the company's other products. The expert employees of Customer Relationship Management make proper use of this situation.

Today we find many examples where Customer Relationship Management helps the company to increase their sales. Many people might not think to increase their sales with the help of Customer Relationship Management. Previously the sales were the complete responsibility of the marketing department. They face a huge pressure in meeting the annual sales target of the company. Help from the other department make the job of marketing little bit more easy. Customer Relationship Management provides the support to marketing department.

Customer Relationship Management developed some unique ways to sell the product to customers.They are not identical with the techniques of marketing. But they are very much effective. The most common method using by the Customer Relationship Management is known as cross selling. It means try to induce customers to buy complimentary products based on their previous purchases. The superior communication skills of employees of Customer Relationship Management have often able to convince customers to buy the product. The second method that is used by Customer Relationship Management is known as up selling. This method is different compare to the first method. In this case Customer Relationship Management is offering customers premium products in the same category. In increasing the sales of the company both the selling methods has proven effective. It reduces the burden of marketing department to take all the responsibility of sales. So the role of Customer Relationship Management can be two-fold. In one side they are ensuring the satisfaction of the customers so they remain loyal to the company. On the other side it helps in increase the sales of the product.

Quick Customer Response

The nature of the business transactions changes a lot in the past few years. In this busy schedule customers want the service very quickly from the companies. It is not enough for the companies to only become efficient in providing good quality product or service. In this age they have to perform the job at a rapid pace. Quick customer response is a high demand in the current market. Customers do not allow the organization to take a long time to complete the task. To be one of leading company in the industry the organization has to adjust with the changing trend in the market. Otherwise the organization may find it difficult to attract the customers. Companies are also looking new ways to perform the task quickly. Much technological advancement has been observed in different sectors just to increase the pace of the work. Some of the multinational companies have shown their willingness to invest a lot for the improvement in their response time. But it is important for the companies to realize that quick customer response can only be achieved through proper deployment of Customer Relationship Management. "If senior executives don't believe in CRM, it will never fly," said Peter Weedfald, vice president of strategic marketing and new media for Samsung Electronics America Inc., who models the CRM behaviour he expects from his staff by spending at least 50 per cent of his time with customers.

Those companies have a good Customer Relationship Management are very often give a quick response to its customers. Employees tend to perform better when they have a clear guidance of their responsibility. Then they might know what to do in a specific situation. Also a proper guideline defines the necessary steps of a particular job that help to perform the job faster. Customer Relationship Management can ensure all of the factors that is required for quick customer responses. The employees also receive the require training from Customer Relationship Management to improve their ability. That helps in performing the job better. They learn how make complete the job faster than the other people. They can increase the customer satisfaction through quicker and more efficient responses to customer leads and customer information. Every customer do not have same sort of needs. Most of the customers have different sets of needs and wants. That sometime create problem for the managers. But with proper training and experience employees learn how to deal with different situations. And Customer Relationship Management provides that experience to the employees. With a short period of time they also learn how to handle the downstream customers. Many experts of marketing and Management discover many theories that help the organizations to perform their job better. For the improvement of Customer Relationship Management there are some theories exist. These theories help employees to understand the importance to be more efficient. The large companies spend a huge amount of money in establishing Customer Relationship Management. The expectation of the company is to provide better service to customers and gain the satisfaction of them. At the end of the day that is make difference between the companies. There is a high possibility that customers can easily switch the companies that have slow response time. People give preference of response time more than anything else today. This is especially true for the developed countries. The establishment of customer Relationship Management is more than essential for achieving quick response time. Management should not overlook this opportunity.

Represent the Organization

Customer Relationship Management can represent the whole organizations to the customers. They are the closest to the customers. The quality they can provide to these customers that represent the commitment of the company to the final customers. The quality of their service reflects the organization culture, their value and other factors. That's why it is important for the organizations to establish an effective Customer Relationship Management system. The image of the company and the product is largely depending on the success of Customer Relationship Management.

Many organizations set a poor Customer Relationship Management that gives a negative signal to its customers. Customer cannot see the top Management or their strategy. They can just see the people who serve them. Poorly arranged Customer Relationship Management cannot create value for the company. Customer Relationship Management can be a unique way to create a better communication channel. It can make the life easier for the company as well as the customers.

Managing relationships with one's guests and making them happy has come under the limelight in the wake of competition, where guest satisfaction is the only key to one's existence and success. The focus on guests and giving them exactly what they want has been present in almost all organisations, hence the discussion on CRM or Customer Relationship Management.

CRM, a methodology of creating golden guests, is not a new concept. It can help us not only retain existing guests but also widen our customer base and help us track our opportunities better and focus on those guests who help us to rake in that much more – not just in terms of volume but also in terms of profitability.

CRM is a multifaceted strategy that helps the hotel industry and other companies understand, anticipate and manage customer needs. The focus is on CRM and all about building brand loyalty – something hotels are in desperate need of – especially during these competitive and tough times.

CRM is an information technology industry term for methodologies, strategies, software and other Web-based capabilities that help an industry like ours organise and manage customer relationship. The need for accurate and timely information to the sales team is really important, the advantages being that the knowledge gathered by a particular person who has been interacting with the guest, now lies with the organisation and not with the person alone.

Promise and Trust

At its core, CRM is based on the pillars of promise and trust. It is with the help of these promises that a hotel can build and maintain the relationship with its customers. The other face of the picture is that if one does not keep its promise then the relationship with the customer deteriorates. Thus, it is important to fulfil promises to achieve satisfaction and loyalty.

Trust is another important component in the relationship-building process. Only if a hotel keeps its promises can it expect to gain the trust of its customers. An establishment should learn to establish, maintain and enhance the relationship with its customers by becoming loyal, trustworthy and faithful since a relationship based on mere trust is not always long term.

The only difference is that until recently the service industry was more concerned about the 'whats' than the 'whos' so as to say the hotels were focused on selling as many products and services as possible without giving importance to who was buying them.

We must shift from being service-centric to customer-centric, stress upon what they need or want than stressing on what we can give them. Traditional marketing theory and practice have focused on attracting new customers and making the sale. Today, however the emphasis is shifting. Beyond designing strategy to attract new customers and make transactions with them, companies now are going all out to retain present customers and build lasting customer relationship with them.

Hotels today are facing some new marketing realities regarding the cost of attracting new customers. In fact, it costs five times as much to attract a new customer as it does to keep a current customer satisfied.

Types of CRM

There are four types of CRM :-

1. To win-back or save customers
2. To attract new and potential customers
3. To create loyalty among existing customers
4. To up-sell or cross-sell services

Implementation of CRM

Identify the key customer merits relationship management

Assign skilled relationship managers to each key guests

Develop a clear job description of relationship managers

Have each relationship manager develop annual and long range customer relationship plans. These plans should state objectives, strategies, specific actions, and required resources.

Appoint an overall manager to supervise the relationship managers. Other benefits include:

1. Faster response to guests' inquiries
2. Increased efficiency through automation
3. Deeper understanding of customers
4. Increased marketing and selling opportunities
5. Identifying the most profitable customers
6. Receiving customer feedback that leads to new and improved facilities or services
7. Obtaining information that can be shared with business partner

CUSTOMER LIFE CYCLE

Customer Life Cycle is a term used to describe the progression of steps a customer goes through when considering, purchasing, using and maintaining loyalty to a product or service. Marketing analysts Jim Sterne and Matt Cutler have developed a matrix that breaks the customer life cycle into five distinct steps: reach, acquisition, conversion, retention and loyalty.

This means getting a potential customer's attention, teaching them what you have to offer, turning them into a paying customer, and then keeping them as a loyal customer whose satisfaction with the product or service urges other customers to join the cycle.

The customer life cycle is often depicted by an ellipse, representing the fact that customer retention truly is a cycle and the goal of effective CRM is to get the customer to move through the cycle again and again.

There are many types of current and savings account, and you wish to buy property and so take out a mortgage. You could take out a car loan, to buy a vehicle to get you to work. It would also be advisable to take out pension. As you progress through your career you begin your own family, and save for your own children education. A number of savings plans and schemes and ultimately ICICI offer you pension plannings.

THE CRM BUSINESS CYCLE

As shown in the diagram, for any organization, business starts with the acquisition of customers. However, any successful CRM initiative is highly dependent on a sound understanding of customers.

UNDERSTAND AND DIFFERENTIATE

Organizations cannot have a relationship with customers unless they understand them, what they value, what types of service are important to them, how and when they like so interact, and what they want to buy. True understanding is based on a combination of detailed analysis and interaction. Several activities are important:

Profiling to understand the demographics, purchase patterns and channel preference.

Segmentation helps to identify logical unique groups of customers that tend to look alike and behave in a similar fashion. While the promise of "one-to-one" marketing sound good, we have not seen many organizations that have mastered the art of treating each customer uniquely. Identification of actionable segments is a practical place to start.

Primary research to capture needs and attitudes.

Customer valuation to understand profitability, as well as lifetime value or long

CUSTOMER SATISFACTION

Customer satisfaction means giving the customers what they really want, when they want it and the way they want it. It involves understanding customer expectations and meeting them fully.

It can be defined as an outcome of purchase and use resulting from the buyer's comparison of rewards and the costs of the purchase in relation to the anticipated consequences. (Churchill and Superman 1982, 493)

Customer is an individual or an organization. Their requirements are very similar. Conformance of services to their requirements and its performance in actual stage

Competitive prices

Quality and reliability

Prompt delivery

Service

IMPORTANCE OF CUSTOMER SATISFACTION

Differentiation strategy: -

Satisfaction is quickly becoming the key to competitive posture within an industry. Initially, products or services secure life in the market by fulfilling a basic need. But only offering minimal functionality grants a product nothing than a commodity status. To ensure long-term market success, businesses have created brands. Brands allowed businesses to develop and sustain an image, differentiating one another's products in the eyes of customer. Today most companies are leveraging branding to its maximum benefit.

To further differentiate brands, customer satisfaction is the most likely next strategy. Companies are realizing that the brand that best satisfies its customers not only keeps them longer, but also benefits from positive word of mouth.

Improved profitability: -

There is both an intuitive belief and empirical evidence that improved customer satisfaction will increase organizational profitability.

Improved customer retention: -

Satisfaction extends customer lifetimes and lifetime values. Also focusing on satisfaction helps to estimate negative word if mouth of dissatisfied customers. Losing a not satisfied customer is more severe than it sounds because one dissatisfied customer may speak to as many as nine others, increasing its dissatisfaction by nine folds.

Improved market share: -

There are always four sources of business for a firm. Four sources of customers in any purchase decision have been identified as: retained customers, customers switching from competition, customers new to the category and customers leaving the category. Different probabilities of success are associated with each of these four classes of customers because retained customers exhibit probability for additional business, they deserve more attention and focus than they currently receives.

Customer Satisfaction has long reaching impact on the current and perhaps future viability of an organization. The cycle suggests that satisfied customers tolerate higher margins that can be used to better pay employees. This boosts employee moral, reducing employee turnover, which in turn helps to produce more satisfied customers and so on.

HOW TO ACHIEVE CUSTOMER SATISFACTION?

CUSTOMER RETENTION

The trend in marketing towards building relationships with customers continues to grow and marketers have become increasingly interested in retaining customers over the long run. Marketing analysts have identified satisfaction as a key determinant in a consumer's decision making, relating to keeping or dropping a given product or service relationship.

According to Oliver, satisfaction is the consumer's fulfilment response. It is a judgment that a product or service feature, or the product or service itself, provided a pleasurable level of consumption related fulfilment, including level of under or over fulfilment.

Banks do spend a lot of money through different media to attract new customers to the business. Attracting new customers requires substantial skills and effort. However, these skilful efforts will be of little use if the bank suffers from high customer churn. Unless organizations pursue customer retention strategies, the problem cannot be solved. It is important to know how much loss the bank makes when it losses customers.

The key to customer retention is to offer continuous satisfaction to customers.

According to Philip Kotler, a highly satisfied customer

- Stay loyal and longer.
- Buys more as the companies introduces new products and upgrades existing products.
- Talks favourably about the company and its products.
- Pay less attention to competing brands and advertising and is less sensitive to price.
- Offers product or service ideas to the company.
- Costs less to serve than making new customers because transactions take place in a routine manner.

It is necessary, therefore, to measure customer satisfaction regularly by surveying the customers to know whether they are highly satisfied, indifferent, dissatisfied or highly dissatisfied. Customer complaints are one of the important sources to track the level of customer satisfaction. Speedy recovery of complaints results in a stronger customer base. In the words of Albrecht and Zemke, between 54% and 70% of the customers who register a complaint will do business again with the organization if their complaint is resolved.

The key to customer retention is relationship marketing. The service company should develop overtime the means of monitoring and evaluating the quality of relationship. There are two basic approaches that can be pursed to monitor the relationship: relationship survey and customer database.

The "three "levels of retention strategies:

- Level one : Financial Bonds
- Level two : Financial and Social Bonds.
- Level three : Financial, Social and Structural bonds.

1. Financial Bonds :-

At this level, customers are offered financial incentives either for greater volume purchases or for continuation of relationship for a long time.

2. Financial and Social Bonds:-

At this level, the firm intends to develop long-term relationships with customers through social as well as financial bonds. The customers are identified by name and services are customized to fit individual needs. Marketers are looking for new ways to keep in touch with their customers by providing a personal touch and building informal relationships.

3. Financial, Social and Structural Bonds:-

The strategy is to develop structural bonds along with financial and social bonds. Structural bonds are created by providing highly customized service to the clients. Specific customer needs are brought into organizational system to design new ways and to improve the offerings to the clients.

In service business, sometimes there is a possibility of things going wrong. Under such circumstances, a recovery strategy needs to be designed for retaining customers. Effective recovery is essential to save and even build relationships. Therefore, service firms should track and anticipate recovery opportunities.

Overview

- ICICI Bank is India's second largest bank.
- The bank has total assets of Rs. 3,997.95 billion and profit after tax of Rs. 41.58 billion for the year ended March 31, 2008.
- The bank has around 1,308 branches and 3,950 ATMs in India and presence in 18 countries.
- ICICI Bank offers wide range of banking products and financial services to corporate and retail customers.

- ICICI Bank has subsidiaries in the UK, Russia and Canada, branches in USA, Singapore, Bahrain, Hong Kong, Sri Lanka, Qatar and Dubai International Finance Centre and representative offices in United Arab Emirates, China, South Africa, Bangladesh, Thailand, Malaysia and Indonesia. Our UK subsidiary has established branches in Belgium and Germany.
- ICICI Bank's equity shares are listed in India on Bombay Stock Exchange and the National Stock Exchange of India Limited and its American Depository Receipts (ADRs) are listed on the New York Stock Exchange (NYSE).

Global Recognition

- "Bank of the Year" and "Best Multi-Channel Strategy"– The Banker, UK
- "Best managed bank in Asia" – Euro money
- "Best Bank in India" and "Best Trade Finance Bank in India" – Global Finance
- "Best Consumer Internet Bank in India" – Global Finance
- "Bank of the Year from the Emerging Markets"– The Banker, UK
- "Excellence in retail banking" – Asian Bankers' Journal

ORGANISATION STRUCTURE OF ICICI BANK

HISTORY OF CRM IN ICICI BANK

The CRM initiatives in India's ICICI Bank hold together its compelling story of growth. Its growth in customer base, channels, and product and service offerings. Since its inception in 1995, the bank has grown to have 15.8 million customers, holding about 17 million accounts. The bank's network has expanded to 610 branches and standalone counters and over 2,000 ATMs.

CRM has been envisioned by the bank to support its goals in sales, customer service, and analytics. Already, about 30.40% of the bank's home loans are cross-sold to existing customers. Similar ratios have also been reported in the sale of insurance policies. Ratios of about 50.60% have been seen out of the credit cards and personal loans business. The bank's stated intention is to take these ratios to as high as 60.75%. ICICI Bank states that these high levels of relationship maximization are made possible by how its CRM system is able to "know and understand the customer better." which customer is most suitable for what kind of product and at what point in time."

In the area of service, the bank receives as many as 150,000 customer requests per day, a challenge not only to channel capacity but also to how the bank is able to ensure that each request is recorded, tracked, and resolved. Last, customer analytics have been used to support various strategic decisions of the bank. Recent strategic decisions of note are several anti attrition programmes, the intended attrition of unprofitable customers, the imposition of fees, and various customer segment tactical initiatives.

ICICI Bank's CRM capability is built on a "Teradata" data warehouse that integrates data from multiple sources, including the Oracle database and various flat files. The system provides users with information about each customer's checking accounts, fixed deposits, credit cards, and other financial information. The bank has taken on the end-to-end proposition of SAS for enterprise intelligence, which offers a credible integrated approach to analytics, including data detection, data cleansing, data preparation, event detection, reporting and business intelligence, and campaign analysis. The bank estimates that it is able to track more than 1,200 parameters concerning demographics, transactions made, channel usage, and product relationships. Through Behaviour Explorer and views, business users develop customer profiles and run ad hoc queries. Analysts then use the information to guide product development and marketing campaigns that are intended to address each individual's total requirements, instead of just pushing a product. The success of cross-selling to existing customers has also been enabled by the bank's growing capabilities in lead management. The home loans business unit, for example, has built a lead management system rolled out to about 700 users. The system is able to allocate leads, schedule meetings, provide a record of all interactions with the customer, and give reminders for customer follow-ups. A lead generation tool has also been developed in-house to capture and route Product applications made over mobile phones.

CRM OF ICICI BANK

1. What is your understanding of CRM?

CRM, according to ICICI consists of following approaches:

[A] Getting personalized information on customers.

[B] What is the value of the relationship?

[C] Customized offerings to the customers

[D] Converting a prospective customer into a true customer.

[A] GETTING PERSONALIZED INFORMATION ON CUSTOMERS

The bank collects all the information about the customers for processing. ICICI Bank has mainly 4 service offerings viz: loan account, saving account, current account and fixed deposits. Moreover, the bank has many customers in each category. So, they collect the data on one server and thus the company gets the personalized information on each customer by asking them to fill the information in customer application form.

[B] WHAT IS THE VALUE OF THE RELATIONSHIP?

After the collection of the personalized information on every customer, the department checks out the value of the relationship with each and every customer. Later, they decide how to approach the customer for knowing what his needs and wants are? After this is done, the company offers him the customized product.

[C] CUSTOMIZED OFFERINGS TO THE CUSTOMER –

The step which comes after deciding the value of the customer is that the company offers the person the customized product. Moreover, they also practice a concept called cross-selling over here. Cross-selling refers to offering another product from the service offering of the bank to the customer which he has not gone for. Example If customer has saving account with the bank then we offer him loan, insurance and other investments.

[D] CONVERTING A PROSPECTIVE CUSTOMER INTO A TRUE CUSTOMER.

The last approach of CRM, according to ICICI Bank, is that they try to convert the prospective customer into a true customer. Right from the moment the inquiry comes, they follow-up the customer and then make him to come to the bank occasionally and then regularly.

The processes for delivering CRM

The tools and the processes are as follows –

- Customer application form
- Centralized software where the whole data is collected.
- Wide range of offering
- Cross-selling and
- Feedback forms

Customer application forms

Bank collects all the data from customer application form and gets the personalized information to know which product to offer to which customer. This process helps in collecting the data and knowing what the customer wants.

Centralized software where the whole data is collected

The data collected through customer application forms is available at one server and can be accessed anytime, anywhere. So, this helps in the further process of customized offerings and cross-selling.

Wide range of offering

After collecting the data from the customer, team decides what product to offer to which customer. In case the bank recognizes you as a valuable customer then it offers a more customized service.

Cross-selling

It refers to offering another product from the service offering of the bank to the customer which he has not gone for. For example if customer has savings account with the bank then they offer him an insurance, fixed deposits etc.

This depends on the value of the customer to the bank. Cross-selling is not offered to every customer. It depends on how loyal the customer is to the bank. The more business he gives us, the more are his chances of being special services offered.

Feedback forms

The bank distributes feedback forms at all its branches. The customer feedbacks on the service, technology used, employee behaviour and promptness in solving customer's problems, are taken and they are analyzed.

CRM of ICICI different from other banks

Most banks have their own databases but because of the huge technological investments done by ICICI the databases in all the branches are integrated, which means they can be accessed from anywhere and at anytime. ICICI Bank has tied up with Terradata Company for making their software and is the only bank doing this.

The difference can be known through matching tool parameter. This refers to, on the server of ICICI sum standards are set in terms of value of the customer and whenever the customer reaches the set standard, the server automatically informs the department to offer him another product.

How is CRM helping you in retaining and increasing the market share?

CRM helps to know the needs and wants of the customer. So, on the basis of this company can decide which product to offer to which customer.

More over, under CRM, we have identified that cross-selling is the best weapon. It enhances the relationship value with the customer. This satisfies the customer and that is the reason why the customer keeps on coming again and again to the company. This helps in retaining the market share.

Now, the satisfied customers help in the word- of- mouth promotion of the bank, which eventually increases our market share.

Does technology helps in practicing CRM?

Yes, the whole base for practicing CRM is technology. It helps in collecting the data, processing the data and then according to the available information offering different products to the customer through e-mails, call centre, pop ups during the transaction in the ATM.

DIFFERENT CHANNELS FOR ACCESS SERVICES

Bank Branch ATM Phone Banking

Internet Banking Insta Banking Mobile Banking

Call Centre

BANK BRANCH

You can find a host of ICICI retail products at our widespread Bank Branch network – Bank Accounts, Credit and Debit cards, Bonds, Demat Accounts, Loans against Shares, etc.

ATM NETWORKS

More than 3500 networked ATMs across the country

Make balance enquiries

Make cash withdrawals

Free access to all ATMs

Trilingual ATMs

Payee name available on the Mini statement

Mini statement shows last 10 transactions

Ledger Balance available in Mini statement

PHONE BANKING

24-hour manned Customer Care Centre

Interactive Voice Response (IVR) facility available

Bill pay requests

Stop payment request

Balance enquiries

Give standing instructions for payments

Open a Fixed Deposit

Dial-a-draft

INTERNET BANKING

Payment of Utility Bills – electricity, phone etc.

Online Railway ticket booking

3-in-1 Demat Account

Inter Bank funds transfer (available in select cities)

Third party transfers

Credit Card bill payments

Enable mobile banking alerts

Importance of Internet Banking for customers

Bill payments

You can pay your bills like electricity, telephone, gas etc., mobile phone bills and insurance premium bills etc. online, or through phone banking. Just log on to icicibank.com or call the phone banking number to do the same.

Check the status of the payments made

Query on all the bill payments made by you

The bill pay service is absolutely free of cost.

Mobile Banking

ICICI Bank mobile banking enables you to bank while being on the move.

ICICI Bank mobile banking can be divided into two broad categories of facilities:

Alert facility: ICICI Bank mobile banking alerts facility keeps you informed about the significant transactions in your accounts. It keeps you updated wherever you go.

Request facility: ICICI Bank mobile banking requests facility enables you to query for your account balance.

INSTA BANKING

ICICI Bank's "Insta Banking" enables you to conduct banking transactions anytime from anywhere. You can avail of this anywhere-anytime banking service through our 24-hour channels like ATM, Internet Banking, Instant Voice Response (IVR) Banking and Mobile Banking, and from 8 a.m. to 8 p.m.

These unique and user-friendly channels have brought banking services to your fingertips. From balance enquiry to checking cheque status to ordering a new cheque book, you can communicate with ICICI Bank from the comfort of your home or in the middle of a busy day at the office.

CALL CENTRE

MUMBAI CALL CENTRE

- Handle 25 different products with 10 million customers with 620 positions.
- Call centre is a cheaper channel than the branch, and often it is more convenient for the customer.
- The ability to serve across all product categories from a single location has enabled the bank to provide a level of service qualitatively superior to its competitors, and this is offered as a complementary extension of the branch capabilities.
- The relationship between the branches and the call centre is very good, and the branches are discovering how to focus their efforts on more rewarding service relationships.
- The biggest challenge is the people management side of the equation: your call centre service is going to be as good as your people. They have to be motivated; they have to empathize with the customer.

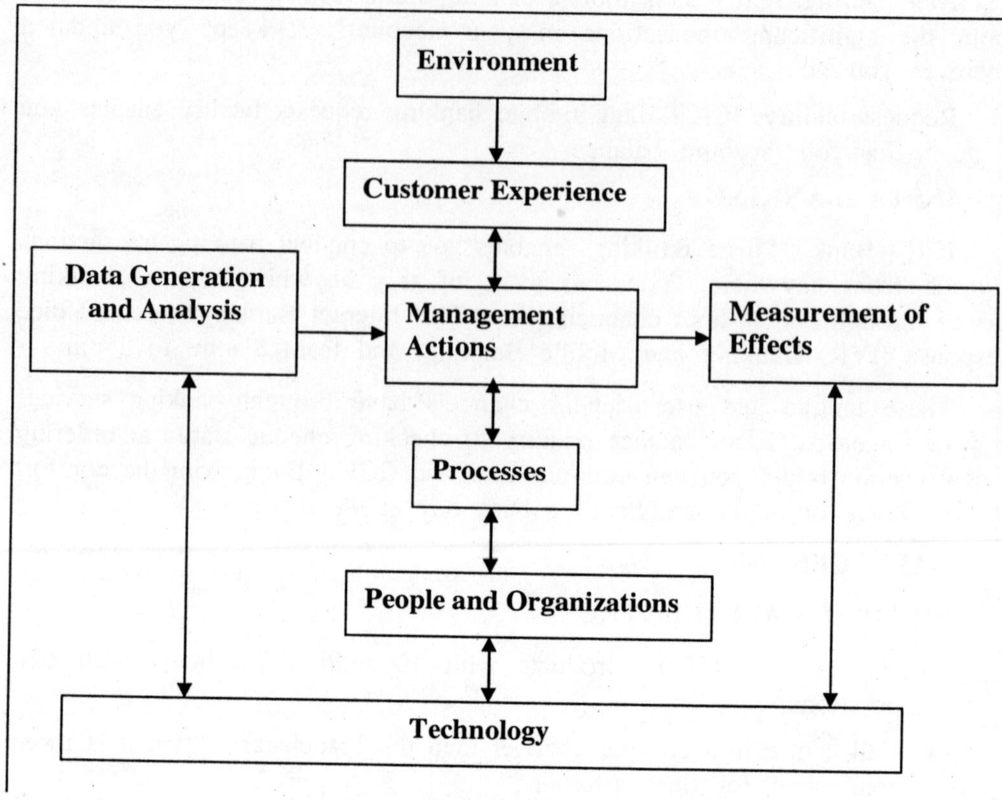

Fig: CRM Framework

The above diagram shows the CRM framework.The CRM framework focus on the technology, data generation and analysis, customer experience and measurement of effects etc.There is a interlinkage between the technology and its environment.There is a two-way relationships between the customer experience and management actions, processes and management actions and people and organizations and technology.

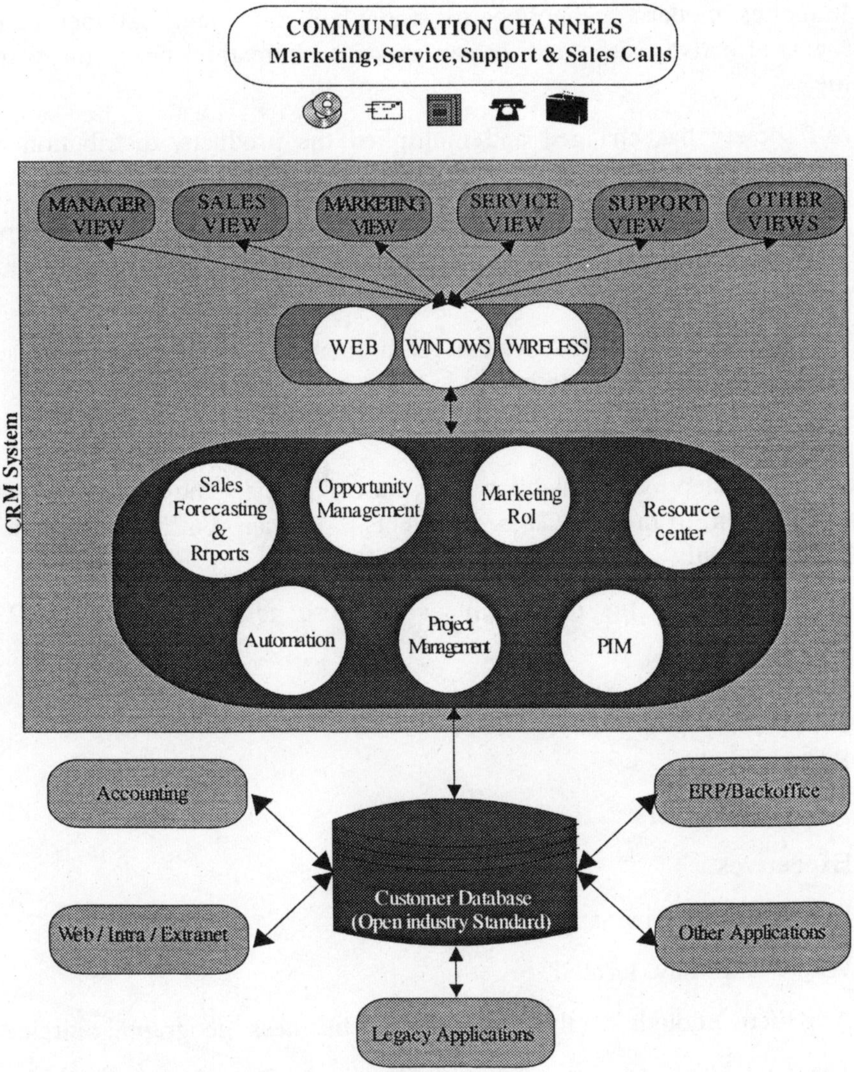

source: sienna Solutions

The above diagram shows the CRM systems, customer database and CRM software.The customer database forms the basis of CRM initiatives in an organization.CRM software focuses on the functional areas of an organization.The various communication channels are showing the customer contact points of an organization.

CRM – Client Relationship Management is a term that is gathering serious attention from attorneys, accountants, merchants, bankers and financial advisors.

CRM applies modern technology to strengthen the client/customer relationship on a cost-effective basis and it can have a dramatic impact on your future income!

As society has changed and multiplied the products, distribution channels have undergone radical transformation.

Those old, personal relationships are a matter of history. Major corporations are spending millions on CRM tools, but the insurance agent can do it relatively inexpensively.

For example , A CRM system for a financial advisor/life insurance agent has several basic components:

Defining the present clientele.

The first step is to establish two cut-off levels. The higher separates the Class A clients from the Class B clients. We can build our practice most effectively by only acquiring new Class A clients.

What would be the demographics of those new Class A clients?

Are they Retired?

Self-Employed?

Professional?

Business Owners?

Executives?

In a particular industry or occupation?

Where are they located?

Are there enough of them within our business geographic circle?

The next level separates our Class B clients from the Class C customers.

The Class C customer is someone who initially or on an ongoing basis pays the organization so little that the organization pulling down the opportunity for income growth.

Our goal with Class C customers is to gradually raise the bar and shut off these unproductive customers.

Sometimes a middle group Class B client grows into a Class A status through job performance, investment success inheritance or good fortune. It is important to retain these clients effectively and harvest from them as many quality referrals as possible.

5.6 SUMMARY

Customer centric is defined as "An approach to doing business in which a company focuses on creating a positive consumer experience at the point of sale and post-sale. A customer-centric approach can add value to a company by differentiating themselves from competitors who do not offer the same experience."

Customer centricity refers to the orientation of a company to the needs and behaviors of its customers, rather than internal drivers.

Customer-centric is defined as a comprehensive customer orientation – i.e., gearing actions to customers and their various needs when designing products and developing services.

The key to customer retention is relationship marketing. The service company should develop overtime the means of monitoring and evaluating the quality of relationship. There are two basic approaches that can be pursed to monitor the relationship: relationship survey and customer database.

5.7 SELF ASSESSMENT QUESTIONS

Part – A

1. What is customer relationship management?
2. Define CRM system.
3. What is customer Interaction Management (CIM) solution?
4. What is the need for customer relationship focus?
5. What are the organizational capabilities?

Part – B

1. Discuss the methods to be carried out by the organization while executing good strategy.
2. Explain the Components of Building a Capable Organization towards customer-centricity.
3. Explain the steps involved in the customer focused action plan.

□□□

Chapter 6

DESIGNING A CUSTOMER - CENTRIC ORGANISATION

Objectives

After going through this chapter, you will be able to understand:

- To identify about the new organizational capabilities
- To familiarize about the Translating strategy into design criteria
- To identify the issues in designing a Customer-Centric Organization
- To know about the Aligning management processes, reward systems, and people practices to support the new design
- To learn about the implementing the Customer-Centric Design

Structure:

6.1 Identifying New Organizational Capabilities

6.2 Translating Strategy into Design Criteria

6.3 Issues in Designing a Customer-Centric Organization.

6.4 Problems Identification and How to Overcome?

6.5 Evaluating Designs, Anticipating Implementation Challenges

6.6 Aligning Management Processes, Reward systems, and People Practices to Support the New Design

6.7 Implementing the Customer-Centric Design

6.8 Summary

6.9 Self Assessment Questions

Introduction

WHAT IS CUSTOMER-CENTRICITY?

The customer-centricity is an approach to doing business in which a company focuses on creating a positive consumer experience at the point of sale and post-sale.

According to *BusinessDictionary.com,* "A customer-centric approach can add value to a company by differentiating themselves from competitors who do not offer the same experience."

In customer-centricity we are putting customer focus at the heart of everything we do, in order to achieve customer satisfaction and loyalty.

Further, aligning resources of the organization to effectively respond to the ever changing needs of the customer, while building mutually profitable relationships.

The above definitions show that customer-centricity is the main focus area of the organization.

Customer Focused:

The customer focused means the continuous improvement resulting in more loyal customers. The organization keep on focusing on the creation of loyal customers through its products or services.

Customer-Centric:

Customers are an extension of the organization and act as raving fans, having a stake in the organization's success. Both the rational and emotional needs of the customers are considered and met.

Organizations often promote at the level of customer-centric but deliver at customer focus, resulting in disappointment and unmet expectations.

6.1 IDENTIFYING NEW ORGANIZATIONAL CAPABILITIES

According to BusinessDictionary.com the organizational capabilities are the ability and capacity of an organization expressed in terms of its

(1) Human resources: their number, quality, skills, and experience,

(2) Physical and material resources: machines, land, buildings,

(3) Financial resources: money and credit,

(4) Information resources: pool of knowledge, databases, and

(5) Intellectual resources: copyrights, designs, patents, etc.

The organization's capability is depending on the type of human resources, their efficiency and effectiveness play a vital role. For example the Scandinavian countries are having largest workforce having post graduate qualification, resulted in innovative products produced by the organizations and dominating the global market. The expertise of work force thus plays an important role in the customer focus of an organization. The organization's other physical infrastructure, financial resources and intellectual capabilities are ensuring the more focused approach towards the customers.

6.2 TRANSLATING STRATEGY INTO DESIGN CRITERIA

The organization's capability need to translate into organizational design so that the organization can reach its desired objectives. The organization now focuses on the implementing and executing the strategy for the betterment of the organization's capability. The following diagram shows the components of Implementing and Executing Strategy

Strategy Implementer's Action Agenda

Figure 6.1:The Eight Components of Implementing and Executing Strategy Adapted from the website of victoronline.net

The components of implementing and executing the strategy starts with allocation of required resources such as human capital, financial resources and other infrastructures etc., then the next step dealt with establishing strategy supportive policies followed by instituting best practices for continuous improvement, installing support system, achieving key strategic targets, shaping corporate culture, exercising strategic leadership and building a capable organization.

The following diagram shows the components of building a capable organization.The organization should focus on the following:

(1) The recruitment of strong management team and talented employees

(2) Developing core competencies of an organization

(3) Structuring the organization as a powerful entity.

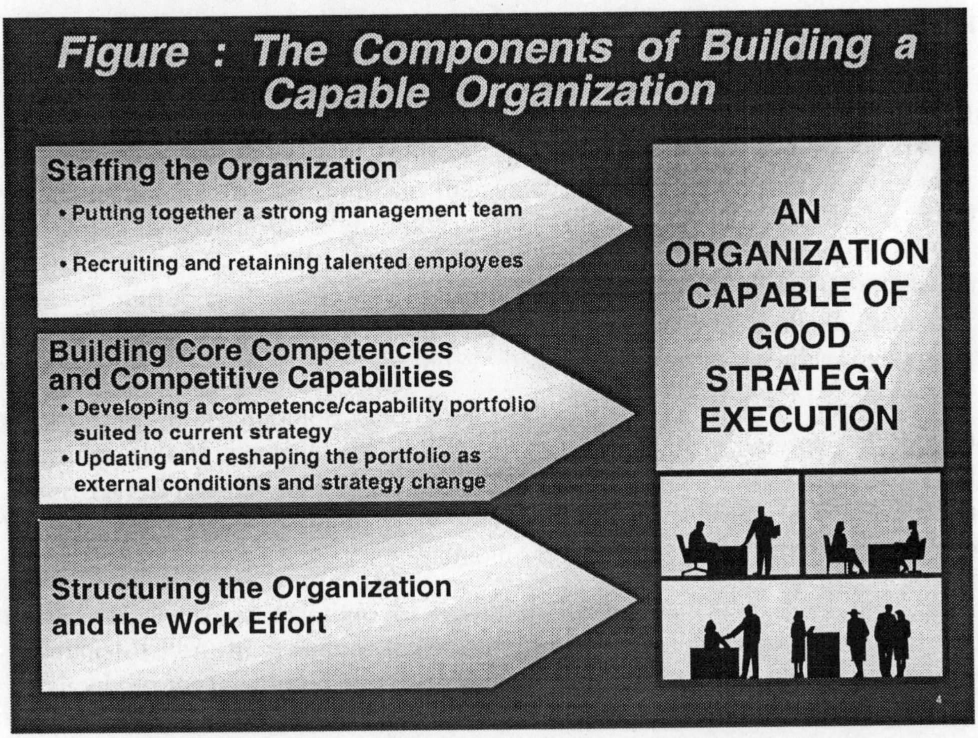

Figure 6.2: The Components of Building a Capable Organization

The organization now becomes a capable organization and capable of meeting its set priorities.

6.3 ISSUES IN DESIGNING A CUSTOMER-CENTRIC ORGANIZATION

The following are the issues in designing a customer-centric organization

1. Global orientation of the organizations
2. Focus on the shifting set of customers and customer needs
3. Innovation of the product or services
4. Core competencies of the organization
5. Changing customer's tastes and preferences
6. Growing competition
7. Available human resources.

Global orientation of the organizations

Established in 2003, Custommerce is India's only forum dedicated to Customer-Centricity. Far from being a management fad, refashioning business processes to align with customer's needs is critical to competitiveness today. As markets become more intensely contested, earning and retaining customer loyalty is perhaps the key arbiter of a company's sustained success. The objective of conducting Custommerce is to highlight the benefits organizations can gain by improving and enhancing customer response. The forum attempts to identify challenges faced in customer interaction and provides possible strategies to achieve a customer-driven economy.

As a part of a Custommerce, Servion Global Solutions is a fast-growing company that specializes in Customer Interaction Management (CIM) solutions. With more than 400 customers and over 1000 installations spread across 41 countries, Servion's products and solutions handle more than 500 million voice/fax/ACD/Web/e-mail interactions per month.

Servion takes a consulting-led approach to optimize customer interaction for its clients. Servion offers solutions across eight segments of the CIM industry (technology consulting, Contact Centre intelligence and reports, agent productivity, outbound interaction management, self-service, workforce management, quality monitoring, and process management) to a wide range of verticals such as banking and finance, telecommunications, business process outsourcing, transportation, retail, and hospitality.

These CIM solutions are delivered through Servion's Consulting and Engineering arms using five different services – application maintenance, custom development, product development, systems integration, and research and development.

Customer Interaction Management Blueprint (CIM-B) is a knowledge framework and implementation methodology. CIM-B is –

A specialized diagnosis methodology to assess the maturity of customer interaction management of an organization;

An optimization model that attempts to arrive at the improvement opportunities for customer interaction based on its strategic alignment to the enterprises' positioning;

A 'top down' design methodology which cascades decision making from the business layer to the financial layer to the operation layer and then finally to the technology layer;

A knowledge framework which has practices seen in a wide variety of centres across the world arranged and indexed by their natural influence to impact 'cost per call', 'customer experience' and 'revenue per call' as the key levers to optimize;

A benchmarking tool to assess Contact Centres on their maturity to introduce and operate good practices in their centres (***Source:*** www.servion.com).

The present day organizations are taking all the necessary steps to offer world class customer experience to the customers. Organizations exceed customer expectations by focusing improvement efforts in three areas:

Customer friendly processes, employee commitment to customer service, and customer dialog, according to Eberhard Scheuing in his book "Creating Customers for Life". Therefore the organization must be excellent in all three areas to achieve excellent customer service.

According to Britannica online encyclopedia, the world class customer service is defined as "When a company provides a client with world-class service, it often becomes a legendary experience that the client retells to others in a form of free publicity, which can't be bought."

World-class customer service is more than a process; it is a purpose meeting customers' expectations, providing customers with assistance, information, explanations and options to meet their needs and concerns, and the commitment to providing value added services to veterans, dependents and survivors, including attitude knowledge, technical support and quality of service in a accurate, clear, concise and timely manner.

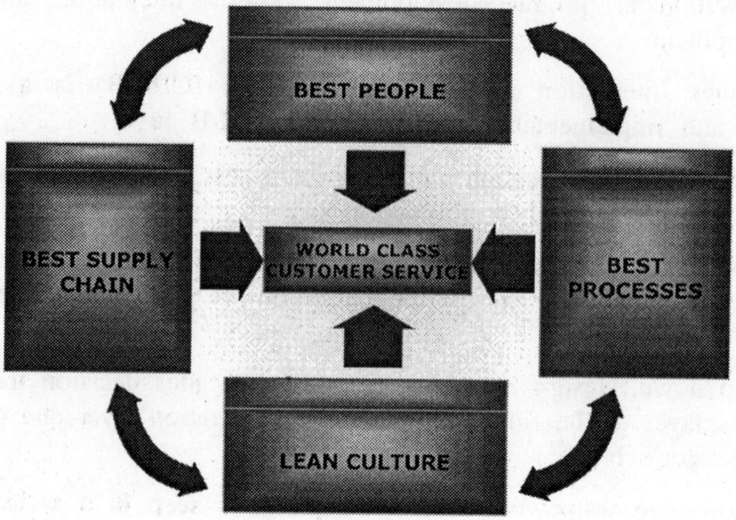

The above diagram shows the components of world class customer service. They are as follows:

1. Best people
2. Best processes
3. Lean culture
4. Best supply chain

The world class customer service should meet these requirements as apart of the customer-centricity approach.

Focus on the shifting set of customers and customer needs.

The present day customers are more demanding in nature. The aspirations and lifestyles are totally different; therefore organizations are finding it very difficult to match the customer expectations and customer needs.

According to Bryan Foss, the typical objectives on the shifting set of customers and customer needs are discussed as given below:

- Develop and achieve sustained movement towards a customer-driven culture, embedding essential values including integrity, commitment, professionalism and more.
- Improve the productivity of the sales force, while ensuring that they find and recruit customers that will stay, be profitable, grow over time and will recommend others. A UK executive recently said 'we don't need people recruiting bad or low value customers….'.

- Increase the number and percentage of staff that consider themselves important to the delivery of an exceptional customer experience, helping to retain and grow profitable customers. While rewards don't always need to be financial, a company's staff do need to understand how they are contributing towards the organization and its customers.
- Ensure that middle management's leadership contribution is encouraged and rewarded.
- Help top executives 'walk the talk' through sustaining a focus on new strategies and ways of working, avoiding the easy traps of reverting to previous and long held cultural traditions.

6.4 PROBLEMS IDENTIFICATION AND HOW TO OVERCOME?

The following are the problems faced by the customer-centric organization.

(1) The existing line of business is suitable to the present and future customers of an organization

(2) The available technology platform is conducive or not

(3) The existing competition among the players of a given industry

(4) The capability of an organization in shifting from the product-centric model to customer-centric model

(5) The customer experience with the organization's customer service staff, after sales service staff, customer experience with the products or services of an organization

(6) Unable to understand customer requirement

(7) Retention of customer and increasing the customer value

(8) Competitive advantage over the competitors

(9) Ability to track down the individual customer's need, want and demand

(10) Feedback mechanism to know the expectations and present satisfaction of customers

(11) Ability to understand the problems of the customers and steps to be taken to mitigate the same

(12) Process orientation of the organization

(13) CRM initiatives of the organization and its ability

(14) Tracking down the customer experience at the top level of the management

(15) Absorption of newer technology and its impact on the products and services of the organization

(16) Views of the customers over the deployment of the newer technology.

The organization may overcome these problems by focusing on the following:

The company's vision and mission should mention the customer and their success as a goal and the company promotes as its highest principle "Do everything we can to make the customer successful!"

A major organization goal is to "make life easier" for the customer. Customer-centric companies make it easy to, for example, return goods, get answers to all types of questions, call the CEO, understand warranties and guarantees, get training on their terms, optimize phone time, and voice their quality needs. Organizations knows that having "making life easier" skills and processes are a cost effective benefit for both their business and the businesses of their customers.

The organization's loyal customer, "best" customer, and successful customer have well defined criteria that segment them into these categories, which is useful for focusing value propositions.

For example, the most loyal customer may not be the most successful, but when they buy, they buy from the company; the "best" customer may be the one that promotes the company's business the most, but may not buy the most; and the most successful customer may sell more goods and services than their competition but may not be the most loyal. Knowing this information, a company can develop a customer-centric strategy for each customer type.

The organization receives value back from their customers in the form of, for example, market promotions, feasible self-sufficient support, applicable co-branding programmes, and useful, hard to get industry information (e.g. a "heads up" to technology breakthroughs or impending market shifts).

Essential corporate information (e.g. product availability, account status, problem reports) is available to all customers in "real time" as if they were internal to the company.

The organization gathers information about their customers' customers and suppliers, how "information" flows around their customers' enterprises, how their customers operate, about their customers' strategies, and so on. More importantly, the organization asks for some of this "non-transactional" information.

According to Jonathan Narducci, "If a company's business objective is to be a product innovator, then customer-centricity means something different than if its objective is to offer commodity products with world-class service. The first strategy might mean the company co-designs innovations with customers, while the second might mean physically organizing the company close to customer sites".

Finally, implementing strategies will have to help institutionalize centricity into the business' culture, that is, make it "natural" to have everyone think of the results of their activities in terms of customers. It can't feel like it's a "tacked on" behaviour or appear as a temporary programme to customers.

Think about the results of implementing quality management systems over the past two and a half decades: quality, while it's still measuring products and services to predefined standards, has also become a way of operational life. Companies now think of the quality of information, skills, how well resources are managed, and so on. They have, for the most part, integrated their "quality goals' procedures and standards" into their everyday activities, involving every individual as a result.

The same has to be true with customer-centricity! Because being a customer-centric company can't feel contrived; it has to feel normal. It requires a concerted effort by the entire company: All of its activities and all of its results must be focused on the customers' explicit and implicit goals. Why? Because, customer-centric businesses are the answer to today's economic reality.

6.5 EVALUATING DESIGNS, ANTICIPATING IMPLEMENTATION CHALLENGES

Effective implementation achieves the desired results within the stipulated time and budget. This can often be the key to success or failure of an initiative a customer-centric organization may take. Many programmes in the corporate sector are complex in nature. They are often started with great anticipation, only to fail during implementation.

Key determinants which contribute to capacity for implementation include management support and strengthening of customer service department.

Programme management and evaluating design of the capability of an organization:

If there is a weak coordination of implementation by various stakeholders, the set up need to modified. In case of lacunae in financial and administrative systems, the same should be rectified.

Roles and responsibilities of top level of management in monitoring, evaluation, and oversight to be fully realized.

The following Customer focus related issues are to be addressed:

Sub-optimal capacity for implementation

Weaknesses in customer information and monitoring systems

Barriers to access and utilization of services.

Example

Customer-Centric Selling (R) (CCS) is a proven methodology for predictably improving revenue growth and sales performance. Founded in 2002, CCS helps clients worldwide to implement repeatable, auditable and scalable sales processes that, when combined with Sales Ready Messaging (R), guides marketing and sales to have meaningful conversations with customers and prospects. This results in winning high-value deals, retaining and growing client relationships and improving the predictability and accuracy of sales forecasts.

Major global organizations such as Microsoft, Hewlett Packard, Business Objects, Rockwell Automation, EMC and Raytheon have deployed CCS worldwide.

In 2005, Ixonos first enlisted the help of Petteri Laine, Customer-Centric Selling (R) Business Partner based in Finland, to evaluate their challenges and define the sales process that would best address those challenges and help them achieve their sales and business goals. Ixonos' main challenge was finding a way to improve sales performance that would drive greater revenue results for the company. The most significant result has been in the accuracy of forecasting compared to where it was several years back.

Before the Customer-Centric Selling (R) methodology was implemented, forecasting accuracy would either be up or down 20 per cent from the actual, whereas now it is within just a few percentage points of accuracy.

In applying the Customer-Centric Selling (R) approach, Ixonos' sales organization is now able to improve resource planning with an optimized impact on day-to-day sales management, while the sales force has a common set of tools within the defined process to help them better manage opportunities. In taking this customer-centric approach, Ixonos sales staff has greatly improved forecasting accuracy and significantly streamlined pipeline management, all of which has positively impacted Ixonos' revenue performance.

The challenges in front of the customer-centric organizations:

1. New market entrants grab market share not only with innovative product and services, but also with ever-improving ways of providing them to customers.
2. Mergers and acquisitions create monumental problems around caring for customers—in both front and back offices.
3. Absence of complete information pertaining to the customers.
4. Lack of customer-centric business processes and services to provide a seamless customer care experience.

These challenges forces the organization to consolidate the customer profile through implementing the following:

customer relationshipmanagement (CRM),

customer information file (CIF) systems,

operational data stores (ODS), or

data warehousing (DW).

AN ORGANIZATION CAPABLE OF GOOD STRATEGY EXECUTION

The organization is capable of adopting the good strategy execution through the following methods:

1. Building Core Competencies and Competitive Capabilities
2. Developing a competence/capability portfolio suited to current strategy
3. Updating and reshaping the portfolio as external conditions and strategy change
4. Structuring the Organization and the Work Effort
5. Key Human Resource Practices to attract and retain Talented Employees
6. Spending considerable effort in screening job applicants, selecting only those with Suitable skill sets
7. Energy and initiative
8. Judgment and aptitudes for learning
9. Ability to adapt to firm's work
10. Environment/culture
11. Put employees through training
12. Continuous training programmes throughout their careers

13. Offering the employees challenging, interesting, and skills-stretching assignments
14. Rotate employees through jobs with great content, spanning functional and geographic boundaries
15. Encourage employees to be creative and innovative, Challenge existing ways of doing things and offer better ways
16. Submit ideas for new products or businesses
17. Foster a stimulating and engaging work environment
18. Exert efforts to retain high-potential, high performing employees with excellent salary and benefits
19. Staff organizational units with the specialized talents, skills, and technical expertise needed to develop and build core competencies to meet the demands of the customers
20. Build competitively valuable organizational capabilities in providing the superior customer experience.

6.6 ALIGNING MANAGEMENT PROCESSES, REWARD SYSTEMS, AND PEOPLE PRACTICES TO SUPPORT THE NEW DESIGN

The Most Valuable Organizational Capabilities are discussed below:

Contribution of the organization towards better strategy execution

Provide a differentiating factor in delivering the product or services to the utmost satisfaction of the customer

Customers can see and value the organization through the differentiation of a product or services

Difficult for rivals to match the organization's offerings

Aligning control systems with corporate strategy.

A well designed organizational structure, effective reporting systems backed by the requisite IT infrastructure and well thought out compensation and incentive plans are integral components of a good control system. A well-designed management control system ensures that there is internal consistency between the company's long term objectives and day-to-day operations.

The starting point in designing the management control system is a good understanding of the company's strategies. The following questions should be asked:

1. Is the strategy internally consistent?
2. Is the strategy consistent with the environment?
3. Is the strategy appropriate in view of the available resources?
4. Does the strategy involve an acceptable degree of risk?
5. Does the strategy have an appropriate time horizon?
6. Is the strategy workable?

A strategy should be consistent both with the environment and with the organizational goals and objectives. Strategy formulation should keep in view the resources available and the risk-taking capabilities of the management. Appropriate criteria should be developed to assess whether the strategy will work given the organizational capabilities. Since implementation of strategy involves commitment of resources, the management should determine the time frame over which a given strategic choice will have its impact. This is necessary to understand whether the company has adequate staying power till the strategy is satisfactorily implemented.

Planning and control play an important role while implementing any strategy. The management first decides what the organization plans to achieve in a given time period. This is the planning aspect. It is followed by the measurement of what is happening. Managers have to decide whether the difference between the desired state and actual state is significant or not. Accordingly, they need to take corrective action, where necessary. This is the control aspect.

Control systems in an organization typically involve the following functions:

(i) Planning

(ii) Coordination

(iii) Information sharing and reporting

(iv) Deciding the action to be taken based on targets and performance

(v) Influencing people, changing their behaviours and aligning their goals with those of the organization.

About the management Process Selecting and implementing significant change is one of the most challenging undertakings that faces an organization. If the change involves the entire organization and also requires new paradigms that will replace established ways of doing business the challenge is daunting.

According to David G. Thomson, the following are the essentials of aligning management processes, reward systems, and people practices to support the new design

1. Create and Sustain a Breakthrough Value Proposition

   Deliver higher-order benefits or "exceptional value" as perceived by customers.

2. Exploit a High Growth Market Segment

   Target a high growth market segment within a large market.

3. Marquee Customers Fuel Exponential Revenue Growth

   The organization's best customers serve as an extension of the organization's sales force and advisors to guide the growth. They provide exponential revenue growth on a per customer basis.

4. Leverage Big Brother Alliances for Breaking into New Markets

   Establish long term win-win partnerships to fill portfolio gaps, fortify supply chains or for breaking into new markets.

5. Become the Masters of Exponential Returns

   Companies that are cash flow positive and have little long term debt are the masters.

6. The Management Team: Inside-Outside Leadership

   A complementary Inside-Outside Leadership pair leads the organization. One is outside-facing focusing on customers, alliances and the community while the other is inside-facing focusing on operations. Inside-Outside Leadership is applied throughout the organization.

7. The Board of Directors: Comprised of Essentials Experts

   Balance investors and management with Essentials Experts: customers, alliance partners and a CEO who has grown a company larger than the organization itself.

Example:

The last economic slowdown, at the turn of this century, was a multiple whammy for Maruti Udyog. It was not merely the industrial slowdown, but also the new reality of rampant competition, resulting in a slump in our market share to 45 per cent and a Rs 269-crore loss in 2000-01.

There was a need to save the company, Maruti Udyog. The Maruti Udyog was build on the successes of the past, pay the price for their shortcomings, venture into new areas of business like finance, insurance, accessories and find new ways of doing things.

Above all, Maruti Udyog had to persuade thousands of employees who had grown up in the belief that they were the best, as well as hundreds of managers and workers who had earlier been commended for being pioneers, leaders and path-breakers that they had to reinvent themselves to survive.

Maruti Udyog took the call that the Indian car market was destined for rapid growth, and whenever that happened, Maruti should be ready to harvest it. New businesses, two voluntary retirement schemes, drastic measures to increase worker productivity, and cutting costs sharply were just a few of the various new initiatives. But it was not easy getting the organisation to share the vision. For some time, management's actions seemed confused. Case in point is the VRS scheme which conveyed that Maruti Udyog needed fewer people and lean operations. Yet at the same time, Maruti Udyog was recruiting in service, sales and R&D.

The existing incentive schemes were designed to reward workers who made more cars. With competition, the waiting periods disappeared and customers now had a choice. It was no longer how many cars one produced— rather, a variety of parameters influenced this decision. Incentives were now linked to sales, quality, productivity, etc.

A large number of the senior people in the company, well-meaning as they were, wondered why a manufacturing company was venturing into services like finance, insurance, accessories, preowned cars, etc. Maruti Udyog set up two groups consisting of middle and senior managers from various divisions. The Vistaar team, an internal team to spearhead the new forays, and AT Kearney, engaged by Maruti Udyog, were told that before they brought up the business plans to directors, they would have to get them cleared by these two groups. It worked. When the plan was eventually presented to directors, it was defended not so much by the Vistaar team as by the managers in those groups.

For Maruti Udyog dealers, the change from being a dominant player to one that was struggling in a flat market was shocking. From being distributors they now had to sell. There was a sharp fall in profits. Some were incurring losses. Maruti Udyog's authorities met them, individually and in groups, and heard them vent their anger. Maruti Udyog said the cycle would turn and business would look up. Maruti Udyog did workshops on how to improve profitability, showed them the huge opportunity in new services, offered to train their sales force, and supported them with sales promotions.

The rules of the game had changed drastically for component suppliers. Earlier, when Maruti Udyog launched a model, the prices of its components were fixed according to their import price.

As Maruti Udyog tried to keep the final price of the car on a tight leash, it moved to "target pricing". For instance, Maruti Udyog would decide that a 1,000cc car could not be sold for more than Rs 3.4 lakh. Then they worked backwards — to sell it at that price, what should be the price of each component. Maruti Udyog had two or three vendors for each component and asked them to match the target price. The nearest quote was selected.

Maruti Udyog used the last downturn as an opportunity. Their objective, now redefined, was clear to them. However, the task ahead of aligning any issues that the stakeholders may face due to this redefinition was addressed by effective communication and a buy-in from every affected stakeholder — perhaps the reason why Maruti has not reported another loss, and its market share has stayed above 50 per cent.

This is an example aligning of an organization as per the requirement of the market.

6.7 IMPLEMENTING THE CUSTOMER-CENTRIC DESIGN

Customer-centric design is design centered on what the customer wants (as opposed to what the company wants). To do this, the organization always keep in mind why the customer came to the organization's site and make it as easy as possible for them to accomplish their goals. The customer focus is the essence of the organization. The organization changes the dynamics of the relationship between the organization and the customer. The customer is more empowered, more in control. To keep in touch with the customers the organization should have a customer-centric website.

According to Gerry McGovern,"Most organizations aren't focusing enough on the customer. Their marketing material might talk about how important the customer is, but the culture of most companies is organization-centric — they focus on themselves. The problem with this approach is that organization-centric websites fail. The customer-centric websites are the ones that succeed". Customer-centric design actually makes it easier to accomplish the organization's goals. Customers who can find what they're looking for are much more likely to make a purchase or return later for more information and services. Most importantly, they're likely to recommend the organization to their friends and colleagues, which is one of the most powerful ways to increase sales.

There are three major phases for the Web: Infrastructure, Architecture, and Content.

In the early days (1994-1999), the major focus was on Infrastructure. Just getting everything technically working was not that easy. There was a big fascination with technology and a belief that all one needed to do was get the right technology and everything else would fit into place.

Around 1999, a greater emphasis on Architecture began to emerge. People had experimented a lot with layout and navigation, and there was a sense that it was time to begin formulating some rules. Large organizations, which often had totally different designs for their many websites, began to develop best practices and standardize.

In 2003, content began to be recognized as important. The infrastructure and architecture challenges had matured somewhat. There was more time to think about content. Print content was copied and just put up on the Web. From 2003 onwards, the better organizations recognized that there was indeed such a thing as web content, and that if it was professionally managed it became the engine of value for the website.

Being customer focused is not some 'nice thing to do.' Customer focus is about hard-edged business. Customers are hugely impatient on the Web. They don't need to hang around a website that is not directly focused on them. Customer focus is the beginning, middle and end of a successful web strategy.

The following diagram shows the customer experience with the organization and its importance, corporatewise programme focused on customers and the organization's overall approach towards the customer experience management. The survey conducted by the Forrester Research with 74 US based organization's clearly shows that 57% of these organizations have undisciplined approach towards their customer experience management.

According to Matthew E. May, Observe—watch the customer. Designers at Whirlpool know that customers can't always articulate the problem that needs solving, so they study their products as they're used in the home. In a usability session involving a new refrigerator design, three separate cameras captured the difficulties in finding and replacing the water filter. Stop-action and slow-motion review of customer movement lead designers to the solution. Not only do Whirlpool designers watch and video-record the action in the kitchen, but they accompany technicians on service calls to gain insight into quality and dependability.

1-1 Customer experience is critical or very important to most firms

"What role will customer experience play in your firm's competitiveness over the next three years?"

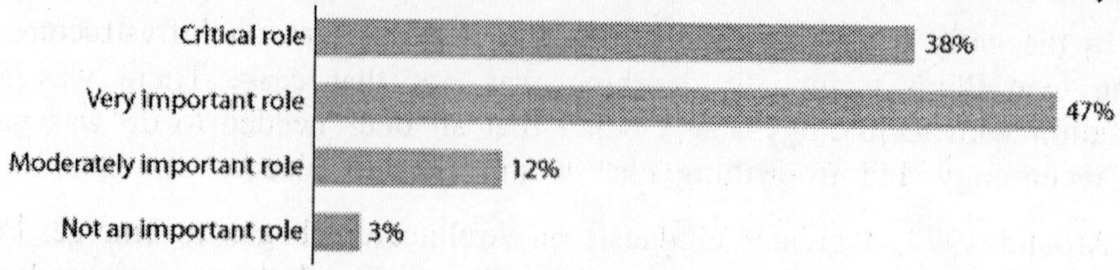

1-2 Most firms are at least considering corporatewide efforts

"To what extent has your company put in place any of the following?"

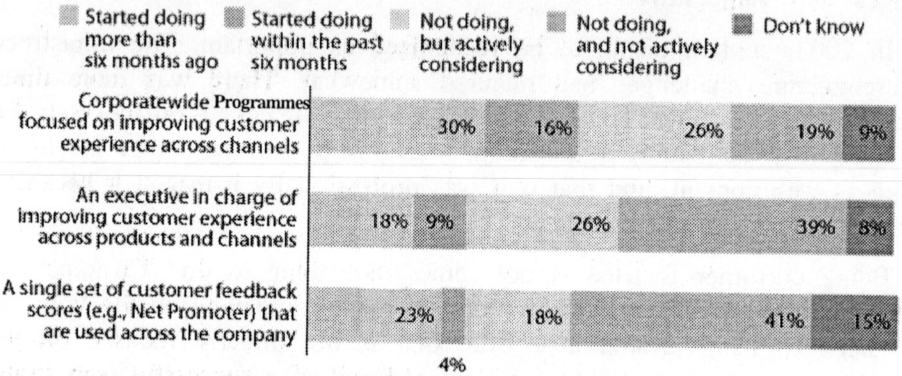

(percentages may not total 100 because of rounding)

1-3 Companies lack customer experience discipline

"How would you describe your company's overall approach to customer experience management?"

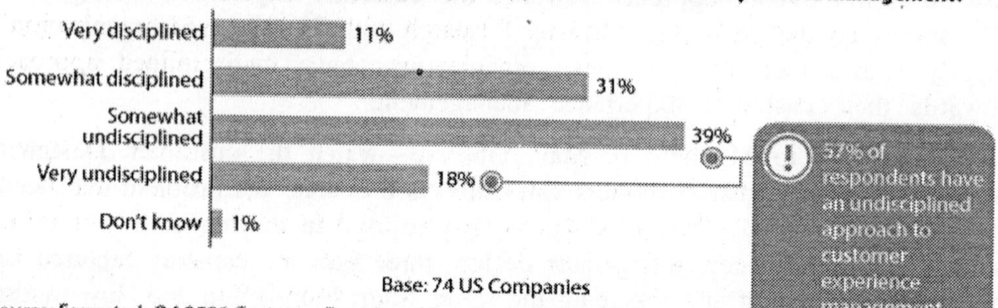

Base: 74 US Companies

Source: Forrester's Q4 2006 Customer Experience Peer Research Panel Survey

43539

Source: Forrester Research, Inc.

Infiltrate—become the customer. When Harley-Davidson sales dropped in the mid-1980s, CEO Vaughn Beals directed his senior management team to attend biker rallies and go on all the big Harley rides. Vice president of design Willie Davidson, grandson of the founder, saw that every Harley had been customized. He took the modification ideas and adapted them to future designs—sculpting gas tanks, chopping the chassis, adding chrome, and painting flames.

Collaborate—involve the customer. Intuit's "Follow Me Home" programme allows software designers to sit with the first-time user in his or her home or office. Designers learn what other programmes reside on the person's hard drive, how navigation between those various applications works or doesn't work, and what paper and electronic sources of data the user pulls from to input into Intuit's software. But they don't stop there. They "co-create" and ask the user to essentially play designer. Incorporating many of the resulting customer ideas and configuration suggestions leads to the development of various targeted versions of financial software.

Therefore the right approach in creating the customer-centric organization is to collaborate with the customer and involving the customer for higher benefits.

Example:

Hershey Direct, the Hershey Foods division that is responsible for e-commerce sales to consumers and corporate customers, designed, developed, and launched its new online store within five months of project kickoff. The redesigned site reflects the high-quality Hershey brand and provides consistency in printed and online catalog brand presentation. Built with Microsoft Commerce Server 2002 on the Microsoft. NET Framework, the site provides Hershey with in-house control of content and product merchandising. The site's consumer-centric design enables easy browsing and searching, as well as a streamlined checkout process. Hershey's return on investment in the new site is reflected in increased sales, larger orders, and a shift in orders from traditional channels to the Website.

According to Tim Brown, "design thinking": a holistic approach to innovation, including in-depth customer insight and rapid prototyping, aimed at getting beyond the assumptions that block effective solutions. This means addressing the look and feel of the product being designed, as designers conventionally do. But it also means reconsidering the way it meets consumers' unspoken needs, as well as reworking the infrastructure that enables the product and the supply chain that delivers it.''

Among the examples of this approach described in Brown's new book, Change by Design: How Design Thinking Can Transform Organizations and Inspire Innovation (Harper Business, 2009), are the Nintendo Wii, which ignored the industry fixation on improved graphics and focused instead on gestural controls; HBO, which sought to stop relying on cable TV distribution and began to offer its programmes for new platforms such as mobile phones; United Airlines, which set up "premium service" featuring larger seats, finer food, and expanded in-flight entertainment options between selected cities in the U.S.; and the Aravind Eye Institute in India, which cures cataracts for as little as Rs 3250 by emulating a no-frills assembly line.

The customer-centric design depicts the changing parameters of customer's perception and views. The customer-centric design approach is carried out in India by the pharmaceutical manufacturers in their supply chain network as discussed below:

1. In 1970s the pharmaceutical industry was dependent on clearing and forwarding agents to distribute the products
2. In 1980s company owned sales depots all over India were distributing the products
3. In 1990, the pharmaceutical industry started their hub to cover either southern India or northern India.

Thus the customer-centric design is the creation of new methodologies and technologies to support customers and companies in the design and development of massively customizable new products.

According to quality India article on creating customer-centric organizations, the following customer focus is needed for a good customer-centric design of an organization.

Customer focus cannot be developed in an organization merely by having systems and procedures specifying the responsibilities of various departments and functional groups. The organization need to create organizational culture of sensitivity and empathy with respect to the customer. A culture of customer focus can be developed only through the total commitment of top management, which should be reflected both in a formal Quality Policy and in concrete action by management.

This involves the following action plan:

1. Before top management assumes responsibility for creating an environment conducive to customer focus, it needs to be convinced that such an action makes economic sense. This would require the

establishment of a clear linkage between customer satisfaction and the profitability of the organization.

2. Communicate the customer-focus philosophy and the policy of top management to the entire organization. This communication should highlight the importance of customers to the company's profitability and growth. It should be explained that the main purpose of everyone in the organization is to attract customers, satisfy their needs and secure their loyalty. The total satisfaction of customers should be the objective of the company. Studies have shown that whereas a satisfied customer may share his experience with two or three persons, a dissatisfied person may influence 7 to 10 other potential customers.
3. Every department or group in the company should identify its internal customers. It should take pains to understand and define the requirements of their internal customers so that everyone in the group is aware of the customers' expectation. There should be frequent interaction with internal customers to understand their issues, as discussed in earlier sections. They should proactively obtain feedback from their internal customers so that corrective action can be taken when their internal customers find some deficiency in the product or service. This step can be taken further by establishing interdepartmental teams to assure better coordination and problem resolution.
4. It should be realized that customer expectations always keep on rising. In an environment of intense domestic and international competition, companies have to continuously improve the quality of their products and services to enhance customer satisfaction. For this, the best approach is to appoint an inter-disciplinary team to take input from the market and from existing customers, for the development of improved products and services.
5. Customer-facing personnel in any company have a particularly important role in providing customer satisfaction. Studies have shown that 40-50% of dissatisfaction with products is not due to the product itself, but with the way it is delivered and serviced. Thus it is important to train the front-line staff to develop a customer-friendly attitude. In case of errors or deficiencies in service, the staff should not get into arguments about the cause of problem– instead they should empathize with the customer and should be empowered to pacify angry customers (within reason) by offering free service or some other compensation so that the customer is not lost.

6. Provide easy accessibility for the customer by extended hours of service and easy telephonic access. Often the first customer contact with any company is through the telephone. Automated customer response systems may be economical for the company, but they need to be managed in such a way that the customer can speak to the desired person without having to wait for eternity listening to music and the bland message "you are very important to us. Our customer service representatives will attend to you shortly". Long wait times can put off any customer. If you must use these mechanisms, it would be much better to provide an indication of wait time up front — so the customer is not wondering if they will be on hold for 15 seconds or 15 minutes. To facilitate customer access, some companies have dedicated customer service representatives for major clients. These clients can approach their relationship executive at any time through his or her mobile phone. This goes a long way in assuring the client that the company really cares about them.
7. Promote customer focus in the organization by publicizing notable successes in achieving customer satisfaction. Reward individuals and teams for outstanding performance in handling difficult customer situations or for getting special appreciation from customers.
8. Monitoring the progress of the company toward a customer-driven organization. Devise schemes for conducting customer satisfaction surveys and encouraging customers to provide feedback on products or services. In service organizations some companies employ decoy customers to get independent inputs about the treatment given to a normal customer. Take appropriate measure to improve the weaknesses found by the monitoring process.

Example:

The Ford India Limited customer-centric design is as given below:

FORD INDIA PVT. LTD.

Background

Ford Motor Company (FMC) is the world's second largest automotive company after General Motors. Ford had revenues worth US$ 164.5 billion in 2003 and is spread across 200 countries with over 327,000 employees.

Ford sells vehicles under various brand names such as Aston Martin, Ford, Jaguar, Land Rover, Lincoln, Mercury and Volvo.

In 1995, FMC established a joint venture company with Mahindra & Mahindra (M&M) to assemble and distribute the Ford Escort, the company's first model to be showcased in India. The company was re-christened Ford India in 1999, following a change in equity holding, with Ford buying out a majority stake. Ford India is a part of Ford Motor Company's regional operating unit, Ford Asia Pacific (FAP).

Ford India set up its 250 acre manufacturing plant near Chennai with an investment of over US$ 354 million. It today has the capacity to manufacture 100,000 vehicles per annum. In 2003, Ford India had about 900 employees and a turnover of over US$ 200 million.

Ford is present in the C-Segment with the Ikon, and in the D-Segment with the Mondeo. Ford India has also launched Endeavour, in the sports utility vehicle segment.

Ford ranked highest in the J.D. Power Asia Pacific 2003 Sales Satisfaction India (SSI) survey. In the J.D. Power Asia Pacific 2002 India Initial Quality Study (IQS) Study, Ford Ikon ranked the highest in the entry mid-size segment as it did in 2001, achieving a 126 PP100.

SUCCESS STORIES

Challenges and success factors

- Uncertainty and fluctuations in the Indian car market
- Reluctance of Indian consumers to upgrade cars.

Initially, this had resulted in lower than expected sales volume in the C-Segment.

Ford India, however had a strategy to overcome these challenges.

Wide product portfolio

To improve the appeal for its products and maintain product differentiation, Ford introduced new products in various segments as well as variants for existing products.

- Ford India sells Ikon in five variants viz. Ford Ikon, Ford Ikon NXT, Ford Ikon 1.3 CLXi NXT, Ford Ikon Sxi, Ford Ikon Flair
- Ford launched 'Flair', at a price aimed at attracting the B Plus segment of car customers
- Ford Mondeo comes in two different variants: Ford Mondeo, Ford Mondeo Ghia

- Ford launched Endeavour to cater to the Sports Utility Vehicle (SUV) market High degree of localization. A high degree of localisation has enabled Ford to keep its manufacturing costs low. Ford India's localisation programme has crossed the 90 per cent mark. Ford India has entered into a strategic tie-up with Hindustan Motors India Limited (HMIL), which manufactures engines and transmission units for the Ford Ikon at its Pithampur manufacturing facility.

  Maintaining quality and customer satisfaction Ford India is a customer-centric company and has launched various promotion programmes to increase its brand recall and customer satisfaction among Indian consumers.

- Ford India launched "Quality Care" in 2001 to provide superior after-sales-service from its dealer locations throughout the country.
- Launched in 2000, "Ford Assured" is a venture in which Ford India dealers buy, recondition and sell various models of "used" cars.
- The quality of manufactured cars is ensured through a quality check programme based on the principles of NOVA - C (New Overall Vehicle Audit-Customer) wherein daily random checks are conducted from a customer's point of view. Routine calls are also made to Ford dealerships to check the quality of cars delivered to them.

Constant monitoring of its supplier base Ford uses a monitoring system to ensure that suppliers adhere to high quality standards and deliver shipments on time. This gives it an assurance of the inventory management.

Ford India follows its US parent Ford Motor Company's policy of sourcing components from Q1 certified vendors. Achieving the Q1 certification is a collaborative effort of Ford and its vendors.

Ford India's purchasing policy requires that all primary suppliers achieve TPM, TQM, ISO 9000, ISO 14000, QS and TS 1649 certifications.

Excellence in manufacturing

Ford India's facility is designed with a focus on scalability and speedy expansion in the future. With a unique plant design of an inverted 'E', the facility is capable of supporting volumes both for the domestic and the export markets.

Ford has implemented its global processes and standards at its manufacturing facility in Chennai. For example, the processes used in the paint shop and other facilities in India are just the same as in any other plant in the world.

Reaching untapped markets

Ford India has made improvements in its distribution network to reach the markets with low penetration.

As a result, company sales grew by 41 per cent to 25,936 units in 2004.

- Improvement of distribution networks: Ford India shares equal branding with dealers. Ford India increased its number of dealers from 33 in 2001 to 90 in 2003 across 71 cities. Ford India was expected to have a presence in 105 dealer locations by the end of 2004.
- Entering smaller towns: Ford has made a foray into relatively small towns like Allahabad, Gwalior and Trichy to reach a larger number of customers.

Leveraging the India Advantage

India's IT advantage

Ford set up Ford Information Technology Services India (FITSI) in Chennai, which caters to the software requirements of Ford Motor Company in the region and around the world. FITSI develops solutions for Ford worldwide. For example, it developed a web-based customer relationship service for Ford India, Australia and South Africa. In addition, Ford has shifted the CAD/CAM development, e-mail processing and application development from its worldwide operations to India's FITSI.

Ford India awarded the Q1 supplier status to 10 suppliers, to help them export their products to Ford worldwide.

Ford India exported 28,000 units of Ford Ikon in completely knocked down (CKD) form to South Africa, Mexico and Brazil in 2003. Ford has also exported Ford Ikon components worth over US$ 10 million per annum to China since 2002.

Future plans

Following the launch of Fusion, its new car in 2004, Ford India now plans to increase exports from its Indian manufacturing plant. The company also plans to double its production capacity in India to reach a target of 100,000 cars a year and simultaneously expand the distribution network across the country.

The customer-centric design involves the following strategies:

Identify strategy-critical value chain activities of a customer-centric organization

Decide value chain activities to perform internally and those to outsource

Make internally-performed strategy – critical value chain activities the main building blocks in the structure

Decide how much authority to centralize at the top and how much to delegate to managers and employees

Provide cross-unit coordination and collaboration to build/strengthen internal competencies and capabilities

Provide the necessary collaboration and coordination with outsiders

Step 1: Identify Strategy-Critical Activities

Which activities are strategy-critical depends on

Particulars of a firm's strategy

Value-chain make-up

Competitive requirements

External market conditions

Identify strategy-critical activities

1. What business processes have to be performed extra well or in timely fashion to achieve competitive advantage?
2. In what value-chain activities would poor work performance impair strategic success?

Appeal of Outsourcing

Outsourcing non-critical activities allows a firm to concentrate its energies and resources on those value-chain activities where it

Can create unique value

Can be best in the industry

Needs strategic control to

Build core competencies

Achieve competitive advantage

Manage key customer-supplier-distributor relationships

Potential Advantages of Partnering

By building, improving, and then leveraging partnerships, a firm enhances its overall capabilities and builds resource strengths that

Deliver value to customers

Rivals can't quite match

Consequently pave the way for competitive success

Partnering makes strategic sense when the result is to enhance organizational capabilities.

Advantages of Decentralized

Decision-Making and Empowerment

Fewer management layers

Less bureaucracy

Shorter response times

More creativity and new ideas

Better motivation of employees

Greater employee involvement

Increased organizational capability

Options to Supplement the Basic Organization Structure

Coordinating teams

Cross-functional task forces

Dual reporting relationships

Informal networking

Incentive compensation tied to group performance

Teamwork and inter-departmental cooperation

Organizational Structures of the Future: Overall Themes

Revolutionary changes in how companies organize work have been triggered by

New strategic priorities

Rapidly shifting competitive conditions

Tools of organizational design include

Empowered managers and workers

Reengineered work processes

Self-directed work teams

Rapid incorporation of Internet technologies and cutting-edge e-commerce infrastructure

Networking with outsiders

Organizational Structures of the Future: Overall Themes

Traditional, authoritarian structures have often proved to be a liability where

Market conditions are fluid

Customer preferences shift from standardized to customized products

Product life cycles grow shorter

Flexible manufacturing replaces mass production

Customers want to be treated as individuals

Pace of technological change accelerates

Organizational Structures of the Future: Requirements for Success

Decentralized structures with fewer managers

Small-scale business units

Reengineering to decrease fragmentation

Development of stronger and newer capabilities

Collaborative partnerships with outsiders

Empowerment and self-directed work teams

Lean staffing of corporate support functions

Electronic information systems

Accountability for results

Use of e-commerce practices in daily operations. The customer-centric organization should meet the following objectives:

- Strategy – what do we want to be for our customers?
- How to operationalize the corporate strategy so employees can deliver?
- What ròle does the call centre play in that strategy?
- Ensuring that capabilities are assessed and built around the desired customer experience. Understanding the gaps.
- We know of the strong link between customer experience to customer recommendation and loyalty-
- Is there greater risk today as experiences and feedback is very public and widespread for millions to read?

The Journey to Customer-Centricity

- Understand and grouping of customers-who are they?
- Understand what they want – rationally and emotionally
- Design processes around those needs and implement a mechanism to easily change processes as required.

  The critical issue is HOW to best design these processes
- Focus employees around the strategy and defined processes
- Build the capabilities
- Implement clear metrics and incorporate customer input into the feedback mechanism

The following diagram shows the importance of the customers and how the profiling of the customers are keeps on changing over the last few years. The modern organizations started focusing on the customers as they are the co-creators of value. Therefore the customer-centric design will be effective when the customers as viewed as the collaborators of an organization and meet their expectations.

The outcome-based method–Customers.

	Customer as a passive audience		Customer as active players	
	Persuading pre-determind group of buyers	Transactions with with individual buyers	Lifetime bonds with individual customers	Customers as co-creators of value
Time frame	1970s, early 1980s	Late 1980s and early 1990s	1990s	Beyond 2000
Name of business exchange and role of customer	Customers as seen as passive with a predetermined role of consumption			Customers are part of the enhanced network, they co-create and extract business value. They are collaborators, co-developers, and competition
Managerial mind-set	The customer is an average static group of buyers pre-determined by the company	The customer is an individual statistic in a transaction	The customer is a person, cultivate trust relationships	The customer is not only an individual but also part of an emergent social and cultural fabric.
Company's interaction with customers and development of product and services.	Traditional market research and inquiries; products and services are created without much feedback	Shift from selling to helping customers via help desks, call centres, and customer service programmes; identify problems from customers, then redesign, products and services based on that feedback	Providing for customers through observation of users identify solutions from lead users, and re-configure products and services based on deep understanding of customer services.	Customers are co-developers persualised experiences. Companies and lead customers have joint roles in education, shaping expectations and co-creating market acceptance for products and

Purpose and flow of communi-cation.	Gain access to and budget predetermind groups of buyers one-way com-munication.	Database marketing two-way communi-cation.	Relationship marketing two-way communi-cation and access,	active dialog with customers to shape expect-ation and create buzz. Multilevel access and communi - cation.

C.K. Prahalad, and V. Ramaswamy, 2000. Co-opting Customer Competence, Harvard Business Review, p. 79-87

Case Study: Standard Chartered's CRM

Banking on customer relations

Standard Chartered Bank was looking for a tool that would help it analyze the huge volumes of data captured by its OLTP systems. The objective was to analyze new business opportunities, provide better customer service, and boost profitability. by Soutiman Das Gupta

Standard Chartered Bank (SCB) previously used OnLine Transaction Processing (OLTP) system, which facilitated and managed transaction-oriented applications. "The system was reliable but provided little scope for in-depth customer analysis, which is the key to survive in the fiercely competitive financial marketplace. It answered the financial queries and generated reports at a broad portfolio level, which included total earnings, debt situation, interest income, cost, fee income, and profits," said Sedjwick John Joseph, Head-Business Intelligence Unit, SCB.

The bank realized that it needed to go a step further and deploy a solution which it can use to analyze the huge volumes of data captured by its OLTP systems. The idea was to search for crucial nuggets of information from the vast amounts of transactional data at its disposal to get the right information, to the right executive and at the right time. This information can help a bank take critical business decisions in the dog-eat-dog financial world.

The bank's IT team looked at the business requirement in detail and deduced that the organization needed a data warehousing and analytical solution that would help analyze customer data to enable fact-based decision making in areas ranging from acquisition and risk management to cross-selling and portfolio management. After evaluating a number of vendor offerings, SCB decided to use a suite of products from SAS. It went for the SAS Customizable CRM Solutions (See box: The solution up close).

In a nutshell

The company

Standard Chartered Bank has over 2.2 million retail customers and over 1.3 million credit card customers nationwide. Its products and services include cash management, custody, lending, foreign exchange, interest rate management, and debt capital markets.

The need

The bank needed to manage and analyze the huge volumes of data captured by its OLTP systems. It had to get the right information, to the right people, at the right time, in order to carry out a number of critical business activities and provide excellent customer service.

The solution

SCB decided to go for SAS Customizable CRM Solutions to address its business needs.

The benefits

The bank can now exploit changing and widening markets; implement a customer-centric approach; concentrate on financial budgeting, cost control, and risk management; and figure out new ways to minimize costs, while increasing profitability and shareholder value.

Varied services

A better way to understand the bank's need would be to understand its customer base and the varied services it provides.

SCB has over 2.2 million retail customers and over 1.3 million credit card customers nationwide. It claims to be the first to launch initiatives like a Global Credit Card and a Photocard in India. Its products and services include cash management, custody, lending, foreign exchange, interest rate management, and debt capital markets for corporates. And credit cards, personal loans, mortgages, deposit taking activity, wealth management services to individuals and medium-sized businesses, and mutual funds to retail customers.

"Our customer base has grown three-fold in the last three years. Such a fervent pace needed to be supported by efficient management of the huge volumes of data generated and captured at each touch-point. After all it is absolutely essential to keep up the bank's unchallenged reputation of efficiency," said Sedjwick.

Defining benefits

The bank's vision was to champion fact-based strategic business decisions using best-in-class analytics. The objective was to enhance the organization's competitive advantage and boost profits. The bank was looking forward to the following broad benefits:

The ability to exploit changing and widening markets.

The ability to implement a customer-centric approach focused on optimizing the lifetime value of the customer.

The ability to concentrate on financial budgeting, cost control, and risk management.

To look for new ways to minimize costs, while increasing profitability and shareholder value by effectively managing consumer relationships.

Solution needs

It was clear that in order to achieve the desired benefits, the bank had to implement a data warehouse and analytical solution. Sedjwick said, "We wanted a solution that can perform analytics on the valuable customer data to answer queries across divisions. The answers would then enable us to proactively service customers and thereby ensure customer loyalty and retention. This exercise is a must for survival in a fiercely competitive environment."

He continues, "Any bank today cannot ignore the risk:reward equation. Calculating it is a complex and challenging task that all bankers have to accomplish. It's the process of applying a variety of scoring techniques across product lines to arrive at the probable risk associated with each product sale and the possible rewards. Examples of products are credit cards, auto loans, and personal loans. We wanted the solution to leverage information on customer profiles and segments and enable us to spread our risks based on empirical data analysis."

"We also wanted the solution to be scalable. This was crucial as the solutions would be very critical to our business, and the volumes of data kept increasing exponentially."

Evaluation

The bank created a team of 25 people in Bangalore and called it a Business Intelligence Unit. This unit was responsible for deriving and implementing strategies to analyze and exploit customer data.

"The company evaluated a number of solutions from Brio, Cognos, Business Objects, and SAS. SAS was chosen as the preferred solution partner and SCB today relies on SAS solutions across Asia for its customer analytics," said Sedjwick.

The SAS solutions reside on an IBM RS/6000 server running the AIX operating system. The SAS software accesses and integrates data from multiple sources and disparate systems across the enterprise. This data is then used for a variety of analyses by the Business Intelligence Unit and is disseminated to all information consumers across the bank. The information consumers include sales managers, finance resources, credit resources, product heads and managers, and the head of consumer banking via the SCB Intranet. "As a result, analytics provide a key competitive edge and are used seamlessly for empowering business manager in their goals," said Sedjwick.

Analytics' benefit

The solution has helped the bank effectively manage and optimize profitability of all the products that constitute its retail portfolio.

Sedjwick said, "SAS's solutions forms a central part of the bank's CRM strategy. It is easier for us to run targeted campaigns and elicit substantially higher returns since we perform profit modelling for each account. This also enables micro-segmentation. Using analytics, and a test and learn culture we know the likelihood of customers to take a new product. We now know which card member is more likely to take an auto loan. This has resulted in more focused marketing campaigns and reduced costs with improved customer satisfaction."

The organization's marketing team is now empowered with information to increase cross holding, and can target its most valuable customers (not accounts within a product line) and also help in the next best product strategy for a customer.

New products

With the help of the Business Intelligence (BI) solutions, SCB was able to successfully launch DIVA. DIVA is a specially designed women's international credit card targeted at the Indian woman and bundled with several features. It includes discounts and zero interest rates on categories like jewellery, cosmetics, apparel, consumer durables, leather products, and mobile phones.

"This was possible due to an in-depth analysis of our customer data provided by the BI solutions. We realized that a significant proportion of our business came from the upwardly mobile Indian woman and was likely to grow substantially from this section in the coming months. This gave us an impetus to launch a product which catered to the needs of this segment and consolidate our position in the mind of the customer," said Sedjwick.

The bank also launched the aXcess plus savings account. Customers who have this account can access cash at over 1800 ATMs worldwide through the Visa network. Besides, they can use this account to shop for goods and services at over 25,000 outlets in India and at 10 million outlets worldwide. "This strategy was validated and facilitated by the information provided to us by the BI unit. We realized that by using this technique we could provide more value to our savings account customers and help increase customer loyalty," declared Sedjwick.

Other benefits

"We are successfully able to calculate our risk:reward equation," said Sedjwick. SCB uses SAS for scoring virtually all its products in the asset portfolio ranging from its 1.3 million credit card holders to its loan portfolio in excess of $ 860 million. "Information on customer profiles and segments forms the backbone of product strategy for us. It allows us to tailor our products across a diversified consumer base, enabling us to spread the risk across a much wider spectrum," explained Sedjwick.

SAS solutions are also used to carry out simulations that help the bank assess its overall profitability and balance its exposures across portfolios. The bank can carry out stress tests on its portfolios and learn about the best case and worst case scenarios. The working of the SAS library of advanced statistical techniques helps in achieving the results and arriving at an optimized risk-adjusted capital.

"The solution can scale to handle different sizes of data and takes much less time to analyze SAS data sets than it takes to analyze a standard relational database," said Sedjwick.

Future plans

In future SCB plans to embark on SAS' data mining technologies for various predictive modelling and advanced scoring initiatives to strengthen its risk management framework in the area of retail lending.

"Now that we know our customer well enough to provide effective customer service and maximize shareholder value, we will keep using information strategically so that it contributes in providing a cutting edge to our organization," said Sedjwick.

The solution up close

Standard Chartered Bank uses SAS Customizable CRM Solution.

SAS feels that a company has to adopt a truly customer-centric approach to manage its business. It means that fundamental decisions on strategy and resource allocation must be based on a detailed and accurate understanding of customers and the overall market. It feels that customized CRM solutions can provide access to the information you need to come out on top.

The customizable CRM solution can:

Integrate information from multiple sources, eliminate data errors and redundancies, tailor data for efficient access and analysis, and reduce the complexity of data management.

Anticipate customer expectations and predict customer behaviour like, propensity to purchase, lifetime profitability, and credit risk.

Allow to cross-sell and up-sell. It can help identify the best candidates for purchasing particular combinations of products and services, and focus the marketing efforts on a more receptive audience.

Combine business rules and analytic models to accurately segment and profile customers, and construct a personalized strategy for each group.

Deliver customer intelligence into front office systems to enable smarter customer interactions through various channels.

Combine behavioural insights derived from analytics with attitudinal data obtained from online and offline customer surveys.

Source: www.sas.com

Adapted: Networkmagazine.

Case discussion:

1. Discuss the Standard Chartered Bank's Customer-centric design.
2. Explain the challenges involved in the Standard Chartered Bank's Customer-centric design.

6.8 SUMMARY

The customer-centricity is an approach to doing business in which a company focuses on creating a positive consumer experience at the point of sale and post-sale.

Customers are an extension of the organization and act as raving fans, having a stake in the organization's success. Both the rational and emotional needs of the customers are considered and met.

Organizations often promote at the level of customer-centric but deliver at Customer focus, resulting in disappointment and unmet expectations. Customer-centric design is design centered on what the customer wants (as opposed to what the company wants). To do this, the organization always keep in mind why the customer came to the organization's site and make it as easy as possible for them to accomplish their goals. The customer focus is the essence of the organization. The organization changes the dynamics of the relationship between the organization and the customer. The customer is more empowered, more in control. To keep in touch with the customers the organization should have a customer-centric website.

Customer focus is about hard-edged business. Customers are hugely impatient on the Web. They don't need to hang around a website that is not directly focused on them. Customer focus is the beginning, middle and end of a successful web strategy.

6.9 SELF ASSESSMENT QUESTIONS

Part – A

1. What is customer-centricity?
2. Define Customer-centric design.
3. What is Customer Interaction Management (CIM) solution?
4. What is the need for Customer focus?
5. What are the organizational capabilities?

Part – B

1. Discuss the methods to be carried out by the organization while executing good strategy.
2. Explain the Components of Building a Capable Organization towards customer-centricity.
3. Explain the steps involved in the customer focused action plan.

OBJECTIVE TYPE QUESTIONS

1. The customer-centricity is an approach to doing business in which a company focuses on creating a positive consumer experience
   (a) at the point of sale and post-sale.
   (b) at the point of sale and pre-sale
   (c) at the point of resale and post-sale
   (d) at the point of resale and pre-sale
2. Customer-centric design is design-centered on
   (a) what the customer wants
   (b) What the customer reject
   (c) What the customer needs
   (d) What the customer prefer
3. Customer-centric design is the creation of new methodologies and technologies to support customers and companies in the design and development of
   (a) massively customizable new products
   (b) massively customizable old products
   (c) massively customizable new services
   (d) massively customizable old services
4. Customer preferences shift from
   (a) standardized to customized products
   (b) standardized to customized services
   (c) standardized to customized markets
   (d) standardized to customized approach

□□□

Chapter 7

CUSTOMER-CENTRIC ORGANISATIONAL MODEL

Objectives

After going through this chapter, you will be able to understand:

- To identify about the customer experience and profitability
- To familiarize about the customer-centric business model
- To identify the implications of customer-centric organizational model
- To know about the approaches to customer-centric organizational model
- To learn about the customer mapping

Structure:

7.1 Customer Experience

7.2 Customer Profitability

7.3 Customer-centric Business Model

7.4 Implications of Customer-Centric Organizational Model

7.5 A customer-Focused Approach Leads to Customer Mapping

7.6 The Customer-centric Organization: From Pushing Products to Winning Customers

7.7 Approaches to Customer-centric Organizational Model

7.8 Summary

7.9 Self Assessment Questions

7.1 CUSTOMER EXPERIENCE

The Customer experience is the sum of all experiences a customer has with a supplier of goods or services, over the duration of their relationship with that supplier. It can also be used to mean an individual experience over one transaction; the distinction is usually clear in context.

The concept of customer experience was first introduced by Pine and Gilmore in their 1998 *Harvard Business Review* article. They believe that successful businesses influence people through engaging, authentic experiences that render personal value (Pine and Gilmore 1998).

According to **Harvard Management Update**, Vol. 10, No. 10, October 2005, "Financial software powerhouse Intuit briefly fell into this trap, despite a history of excellent customer service. In 2001, its Turbo Tax programme commanded 70 per cent of the retail market for tax-preparation software and 83 per cent of the online market. But then it began doing things that annoyed customers, such as upping the price of tech-support calls and limiting software licenses to one computer. Store-based retail growth flattened, and as Web-based tax preparation sites sprang up, online buyers started jumping ship. In 2003, Turbo Tax's share of the online market plummeted.''

A recent Bain & Company survey reveals just how commonly companies misread the market. They surveyed 362 firms and found that 80 per cent believed they delivered a "superior experience" to their customers. But when they asked customers about their own perceptions, they found that they rated only 8 per cent of companies as truly delivering a superior experience. Clearly, it's easy for leading companies to assume they're keeping customers happy; it's quite another thing to achieve that kind of customer devotion.

According to Ron Rogowski, Emotional Experience Design (EED) focuses on the following

Address customers' real goals, develop a coherent personality, and engage a mix of senses.

Customer experience is the value that we add to the customer so that he is emotionally touched. Most of the times the effort required to enhance customer experience is nothing to do with the core product but about:

- how we delight the customer when he receives the product
- what kind of personalized service we provide to solve their issues.
- how we remember their preferences them when they come back for second purchase
- how we can surprise them on their important occasions like Birthday with a simple wish and some goody from our organization.
- how simple we keep the process of ordering and collecting feedback.
- how flexible we are in changing our process or offering to suit someone's specific need.

The organization should have employees who are capable of personally delivering lots of customized products to customers and the response received from them need to be truly amazing. Each of the customers should point out the personalized service they received from the organization and the flexibility the organization offered in getting a product closely suited to their needs as the primary reason they had a great experience with the organization itself.

As per the Delta Air Lines, the world's largest carrier, has stopped using India-based call centres to handle sales and reservations. The company has decided the cost savings of directing calls offshore are outweighed by the backlash from customers.

Delta had said previously that moving calls to India saved $25 million a year. However, they hadn't anticipated all the complaints by American customers who say they sometimes have tremendous difficulty understanding the foreign telephone workers.

"Customer acceptance of call centres in foreign countries is low and our customers are not shy about letting us have that feedback," said Richard Anderson, Delta's chief executive.

While Delta has closed centres in India, it will maintain its centres in Jamaica and South Africa which haven't generated such turbulent feedback.

The move makes Delta the second big U.S. carrier in 2009 to return customer service work back to America. In February, United Airlines announced they would also be moving some India-based phone work back to Chicago and Honolulu.

This is a classical example of customer service provided by the employees of call centre in India. Customers experience the brand in numerous ways: products, packaging, price, marketing, sales personnel, etc. Each of these contacts or touchpoints molds the customer's impression of the brand. Some of these touchpoints are obvious, like product performance and one-on-one customer interactions. Other touch points, like the product manual, monthly statements, or post-sale support, may be subtler in their brand effects.

According to Scott Glatstein, the following are the five easy steps to building a strong brand and an optimized customer experience:

1. Identify the Organization's Reasons to Believe

The brand promise is irrelevant if the customers do not believe it. Therefore, the organization promise must be supported by reasons to believe. This will automatically add substance to the promise and define specific expectations for the customer.

For example, an automobile manufacturer promises potential customers that car XYZ is an "intelligent choice for serious drivers." What makes it an intelligent choice? Why should the customer believe this promise?

To address this question effectively, the manufacturer could frame its promise with two reasons to believe: sporty performance and safety. These two reasons, in essence, define "intelligent choice" and clearly set up customer expectations. They also give the company specific direction for designing the customer experience through tangible customer touch points like vehicle design features, advertising campaigns, dealer sales approaches, and customer service activities.

2. Identify Customer Touch points

Each individual step in the business process contains a number of touch points where the customer comes in contact with your brand. The ultimate goal is to have each touch point reinforce and fulfil your marketplace promise.

Walk through the commercial processes. How do we generate customer demand? How are products sold? How do our customers use our products? How do we provide after-sale support?

This comprehensive tracing of the marketing, selling, and servicing processes allows the organization to create a simple touch point map that defines the customers' experiences with the brand.

3. Determine the Most Influential Touchpoints

All touchpoints are not created equal. Some will naturally play a larger role in determining the company's overall customer experience. For example, if the product is ice cream, taste is typically more important than package design. Both are touchpoints, but each has a different effect on our customer's experience as a whole.

To determine the touchpoints driving our customer's overall experience, our organization can use a wide array of techniques ranging from quantitative research to institutional knowledge. The methods we use will depend on the complexity of the products, commercial processes, and our existing knowledge base.

4. Design the Optimal Experience

Once we have completed the above three steps to building a strong brand, we should be able to design our optimal customer experience. Here's how:

Determine how to express each reason to believe at each key touchpoint. For example, how can we reinforce sporty performance (a reason to believe) in product design, at the dealership, and in marketing campaigns (the influential touchpoints)?

5. Align the Organization to Consistently Deliver the Optimal Experience

A holistic approach to aligning the organization to consistently deliver the optimal experience is essential. Identify the people, processes, and tools that drive each key touch point.

Look beyond employees who have direct contact with the customers. The impacts of behind-the-scenes employees are less obvious but no less important. Similarly, the impact of workflow processes and tools (i.e., technology systems) on the customer experience may be less intuitive but crucial to consistent delivery.

Identify which activities don't align with your envisioned customer experience. Determine how to address them so that these components can be brought into alignment.

The Final Word

Every product or service you bring to market yields a customer experience. Is it the experience you intend? Does that experience fulfil the promise you've made to the marketplace?

By identifying the people, processes, and tools that drive your customer experience, you can actively design and control your own unique, optimized experience. The brand promise we make to the marketplace will be kept day in and day out across every key customer touch point.

Customer experience can be defined as "the quality of the experience as apprehended by a customer resulting from direct or indirect contact with any touch point of a company".

In other words, the customer experience is the impression created on the customer as the results of contact with a company through any touch point, whether through marketing, branding, customer service, support, in-store experience, usage of a product, service or Website, etc. Customer experience in this broader sense also includes "User Experience", which as the name suggests, is concerned with, and limited to, direct usage of a product.

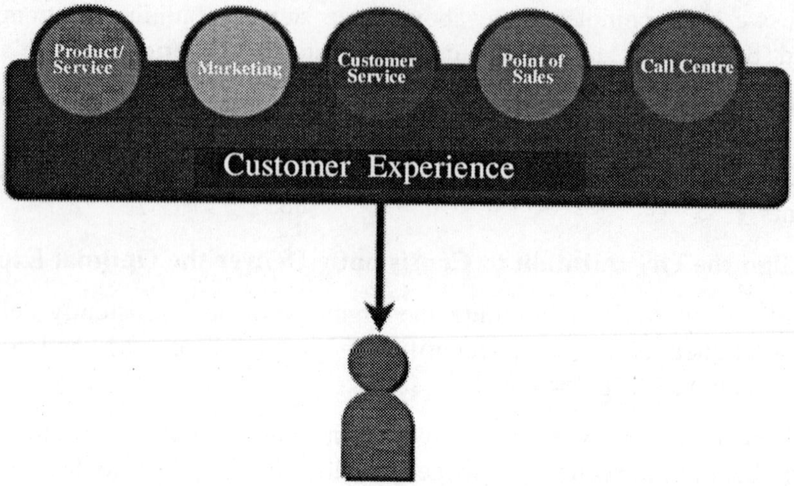

Customer Experience	Customer Service
Customer experience is the sum of all experiences a customer has with a supplier of goods or services, over the duration of their relationship with that supplier. It can also be used to mean an individual experience over one transaction; the distinction is usually clear in context.	Is the provision of service to customers before, during and after a purchase. Customer service is a series of activities designed to enhance the level of customer satisfaction – that is, the feeling that a product or service has met the customer expectation.

The above diagram shows the difference between the customer experience and customer service. Customer service is one of the touch points that contribute to the overall customer experience. Here are few interpretations on Customer Experience & Customer Service.

The Customer Experience Management solution that complements the business operation with increased customer loyalty, retention, improved service quality and profitability.

To deliver superior customer experience does not require mere change in administration and business process. The organization need a customer focused management concept called Customer Experience Management. Customer Experience Management (CEM) is a process of strategically managing a customer's entire experience with a product or a company (Schmitt, 2003). CEM is an integrated approach of managing customer experience while interacting with your environment, products, services, and employees.

The below given diagram shows the steps to be followed in the customer experience management.

Step-1	Step-2	Step-3	Step- 4	Step -5
The first is to step the analyze experiential world of the customers that prvides customer insight	Building experiential platform for Yourfor Your compny and brands, This Platform helps to developed positioning strategy for a company product or brand. It is strategic connection between analysis and implementation	Designing the Brand Experience, once the experiential platfrom is decided It must be implemented in the brand experience this includes all the static elements that customer come across- the product, logo and signage, packaging, brochures, and advertising.	In step- 4 experiential platfrom is implemented in customer interface. customer interface is dynamic exchanges and contact points with the customer	The final step is to engage customer in continuous innovations. These innovations must be planned, properly managed, and marketed to improve customer experience

7.2 CUSTOMER PROFITABILITY

Customer profitability (CP) is the difference between the revenues earned from and the costs associated with the customer relationship in a specified period.

According to Philip Kotler, "a profitable customer is a person, household or a company that overtime, yields a revenue stream that exceeds by an acceptable amount the company's cost stream of attracting, selling and servicing the customer".

Mitch Rosenbleeth, a vice president in Booz Allen's Dallas office and co-author of a recent report titled "Capturing Value Through Customer Strategy," says the process of identifying unprofitable customers is challenging for companies to embrace because the value is not obvious and it is painstaking.

"We just finished a project for a client where, when we looked at customer profitability, 30% of the customers created 200% of the client's profits," Rosenbleeth says. "About 50% of the customers weren't very profitable and the remaining 20% destroyed profits. So should the client have cut those 20% loose? That wasn't the answer."

Therefore the customer profitability involves the analysis of an organization, through which they identify the profitable customer segment and non-profitable customer segment.

Example:

Capital One became one of the world's largest — and most profitable — credit-card issuers in a few short years during the late 1980s and 1990s. The company, a pioneer in customer segmentation, achieved its robust growth by exploiting an innovative approach to targeted marketing, based on customer profitability analysis.

Capital One attributes its success to efforts in applying information technology tools to customer acquisition and retention. Specifically, the company has relied on what it calls its Information-Based Strategy (IBS), a proprietary set of analytical tools, to tailor its products to the appropriate customers and ensure that each customer is serviced efficiently.

7.3 CUSTOMER-CENTRIC BUSINESS MODEL

The customer-centric approach of Indian Companies. The US $6.3 billion Mahindra Group is among the top 10 industrial houses in India. Mahindra is the market leader in multi-utility vehicles in India. It made a milestone entry into the passenger car segment with the Logan. Mahindra & Mahindra is the only Indian company among the top tractor brands in the world. Mahindra & Mahindra is the only Indian company among the top three tractor manufacturers in the world and is the market leader in multi-utility vehicles in India. The Group has a leading presence in key sectors of the Indian economy, including trade and financial services (Mahindra Intertrade, Mahindra & Mahindra Financial Services Ltd.), automotive components, information technology & telecom (Tech Mahindra, Bristlecone), and infrastructure development (Mahindra GESCO, Mahindra Holidays & Resorts India Ltd., Mahindra World City). With over 60 years of manufacturing experience, the Mahindra Group has built a strong base in technology, engineering, marketing and distribution which are key in its evolution as a customer-centric organization. The Group employs over 40,000 people and has several state-of-the-art facilities in India and overseas. The Mahindra Group has ambitious global aspirations and has a presence in five continents. Mahindra products are today available in every continent except Antarctica. M&M has one tractor manufacturing plant in China and three assembly plants in the United States. It has made strategic acquisitions across the globe including Stokes Forgings (UK), Jeco Holding AG (Germany) and Schoneweiss & Co GmbH (Germany). Its global subsidiaries include Mahindra Europe Srl. based in Italy, Mahindra USA Inc. and Mahindra South Africa. M&M has entered into partnerships with international companies like Renault SA, France, and International Truck and Engine Corporation, USA. The Group recently made a milestone entry into the passenger car segment with Logan, a product of its JV with Renault SA. Forbes has ranked the Mahindra Group in its Top 200 list of the World's Most Reputable Companies and in the Top 10 list of Most Reputable Indian companies.

Mahindra Tractors gifts farmers a freedom week

In 2007, to commemorate India's 60th year of independence, Mahindra Tractors offered a bonanza of benefits to the Indian farmers

- A week-long programme that presents new expressions of freedom for the Indian Farmer
- Freedom from:
    - Interest on loans, with 0% interest scheme
    - Service cost on tractors, with labour-free service
    - Traditional ways of farming, through exchange scheme
    - Travelling distances to get his own and his tractor's health checked, with the unique Swasth Tractor, Swasth Chalak scheme
- A special offer for soldiers from Indian Armed Forces under the Mahindra Jai Jawan se Jai Kisan scheme

Celebrating the spirit of freedom, Mahindra & Mahindra Limited, the No. 1 tractor manufacturer in the country, flagged off the Mahindra Swatantrata Mahotsav - a week-long programme that presents the farmer with a host of benefits, such as 0% interest scheme on loans, exchange of old tractors, labour free service and health check-up camps for farmers. The benefits offered between 13th and 19th August, 2007 at Mahindra Tractor dealerships across the country.

Over the past six decades, Mahindra has been able to build a huge customer base of over 12 lakh customers by focusing on customer-centric initiatives and designing its products, services and offerings, in consonance with the farmer's needs. Swatantrata Mahotsav is another customer-centric initiative that will bring smiles on the faces of the farmers. This is part of Mahindra Tractors innovative and customer-centric approach, which has enabled it to sustain its leadership position for more than two decades.

On the 60th anniversary of the country's independence, Mahindra & Mahindra Limited extends its unique 'Jai Jawaan se Jai Kisaan' rehabilitation scheme for the brave soldiers of the country. Under this scheme, Mahindra Tractors will be made available at attractive prices across Mahindra Tractor dealerships to soldiers of the Indian Armed Forces.

Mahindra has made an entry in the two-wheeler segment which will see the company emerge as a full-range player with a presence in almost every segment of the automobile industry.

Mahindra is also one of the few Indian companies to receive an A+ GRI checked rating for its first Sustainability Report for the year 2007-08.

Mahindra Group's foray into the two-wheeler segment with the acquisition of the Pune-based Kinetic Motor Company Ltd. (KMCL) resulted in the creation of a new company, Mahindra Two Wheelers Ltd. extending Mahindra's heritage and pedigree into the two-wheeler space. Mahindra Two Wheelers will design and market a range of scooters and motorcycles for the Indian and global markets, helping it establish a robust, end-to-end two-wheeler business in every segment of the industry. The Company has a state-of-the-art manufacturing facility at Pithampur, near Indore in Madhya Pradesh. The plant, products and processes are ISO 9001 certified from DNV.

Mahindra & Mahindra's stringent quality standards, which are a part of its customer-centric approach, will be reflected in all its products. The company will also use the design and engineering services of its affiliates including the Italy based Engines Engineering in all its product development work to deliver technologically superior products to consumers. Engines Engineering based in Castenaso near Bologna offers services in the area of two-wheeler design and development of motorcycle prototype.

Engines Engineering carries out a full range of activities (starting from a basic idea on a blank sheet, culminating to a finished product on the road) to deliver a product in line with the latest styling trends and incorporates the most advanced technology in terms of mechanics. It thus provides a 'One Stop Solution': conception, design, styling, online assembly, industrialization and marketing. Some of the most prestigious names associated with Engines Engineering include Ferrari, Ducati, Honda, and Yahama. Apart from these, the company has also developed several products for a wide array of manufacturers in various geographies, ranging from Spain to the Far East.

Mahindra Two Wheelers also has a partnership with Taiwan's Sanyang Industry Company Limited (SYM). A US $ 1 billion automobile giant, SYM is a leading manufacturer of two-wheelers, including scooters, motorcycles and ATVs in a variety of designs and specifications. SYM has a complete, advanced research and design facility that develops products from concept upto production. It also has tie-ups with the world's leading international companies including International Truck, Bombardier Recreational Products and Hyundai. The association with SYM is going to translate into cutting edge technology and best products from Mahindra.

ITC INITIATIVES

ITC won the top UNIDO award at the International Conference on Sharing Innovative Agribusiness Solutions 2008 at Cairo in recognition for its exemplary initiatives in agri business.The ITC initiatives is an example for the customer-centric approach of the organization.

ITC's agri business was adjudged the winner, out of 120 solutions presented by 65 countries, for providing innovative solutions including updated information on crops in remote Indian villages. ITC's e-Choupal, the largest rural digital infrastructure in the world, today covers over 40,000 villages and benefits over 4 million farmers. This rural distribution network, comprising of digital and human infrastructure, not only empowers farmers with information but has also helped transform rural communities into vibrant economic organizations by co-creating thriving markets. The e-Choupal network is an efficient two-way channel, facilitating the flow of goods and services to and from largely inaccessible rural markets.

ITC's initiative was presented the top award among the fifteen shortlisted for their innovative character and their potential to help developing countries attract agribusiness-related investments. Agribusiness stakeholders, representatives of public and private technical and financial institutions, international organizations, donors, NGOs and academia from various countries presented over 120 new solutions at the UNIDO International Conference.

ITC was the only winner from India, others being the UK's COLEACP-PIP (to enable compliance solutions for the export of fruits and vegetables), Passive Refrigeration from Italy (to maintain the cold chain from farms to markets) and Sri Lanka's Cargills (Ceylon) Ltd. (to link small farmers directly to markets). Special awards were given to the SEKEM farm (for ecologically responsible development in Egypt), the Songhai Centre in Benin (for holistic agricultural development) and UNIDO's ETRACE programme (to establish an effective traceability system for Egyptian producers).

Demag India is a whole owned subsidiary of Demag Cranes & Components, GmbH Germany, one of the world's leading providers of material handling technology, a group which has its legacy rooted in a 180-year-old culture of excellence in the field of material handling. A visionary and industrious group which started its operation way back in 1819 in Germany, witnessed three centuries of industrial growth all across the world, today operating in 48 countries across five continents and its range of cranes installed in almost every habited region of the world.

Demag provides solutions for material flow and logistics requirements and drive applications with the most comprehensive range of products and services for companies of all sizes – from small workshops to the trade sector and major industrial enterprises. Worldwide, Demag has a business volume of over Euro 1 Billion with over 7,000 employees and a network of offices, factories and subsidiaries. It has subsidiary companies in 21 countries across the world and its operations currently extend to 48 countries.

In India, Demag has had a very reputable presence since its first sale in 1913 to TISCO. Represented by an agent from 1958, in 1997 Demag decided to incorporate its own subsidiary in India to be closer to its customers and provide them with superior solutions, products and service support.

Demag India offers the complete range of products and services available under the Demag AG umbrella in India. Its business is broadly divided under Industrial Cranes and Services Division and Port/ Mobile Cranes Division.

With its headquarters and manufacturing facility in Pune, Maharashtra, the company has sales and service offices in Mumbai, Delhi, Kolkata, Bangalore and Chennai.

Demag India is soon going to complete 10 successful years of operations in India and can proudly claim that it knows the Indian market, and understands the need of Indian customers far better than any competitor. Demag's decade long presence in India has helped establish the company and brand Demag as a reliable and trustworthy partner in the chosen field of EOT Cranes, Handling technology and harbour cranes. Demag is today one of the top five companies in the business in India.

Staying close to the customer, articulating their needs precisely and offering right kind of solution that exactly matches the customer's need has been the core of Demag's DNA right from its inception. Through continued and sustained product innovation, Demag is emerging as a leader in its line of business in India too. In view of this, recently the company has taken a strategic decision to proliferate its presence more in the Indian market. And the move couldn't have been better than to appoint competent, financially sound and exclusive channel partners of Demag. As a strategy of depth domination, Demag is appointing dealers all over India in order to enable them to stay close to the customers, serving them better and giving proactive support for every customer's business requirement. The channel partners will act as an extended arm of Demag's sales organization and will exhibit the same customer-centric approach as Demag.

Customer-Centric Materials Management-A Case Study of ECIL

ECIL – An Overview

Electronics Corporation of India Ltd.(ECIL) is a Public Enterprise under the Department of Atomic Energy established with the purpose of supporting India's Nuclear Power Programme and help the country achieve self-reliance in professional electronics. Over the years the company evolved itself into a multi-product and multi-disciplinary organisation with focus on Computers, Control Systems and Communications. In the post-liberalisation scenario, the compulsions of global competition on local soil guided its Vision, Mission and Objectives as follows:

Vision

To help the country achieve self-reliance in Strategic Electronics.

Mission

To strengthen the status as a valued national asset in the area of Strategic Electronics meeting the requirements of Atomic Energy, Defence, Space, Civil Aviation, Security and such other sectors of strategic importance.

Objectives

- To strengthen the technology base and thereby the capability to combat technology denials
- To promote creativity and innovation and realise higher levels of operational efficiency through actionable learning
- To attain and maintain world-class competitiveness by pursuing global benchmarks
- To lay down plans and programmes for effective succession at senior management level

- To consistently ensure a customer-centric organisational culture
- To achieve steady growth in business performance and generate reasonable internal resources

The operations are therefore focussed towards meeting the requirements of Strategic Electronics in the Nuclear, Defence, Security and such other sectors of National Importance.

The Crisis

The post-liberalisation period of 90s was characterised by intense competition from both the MNCs and private sector. The impact of the globalisation process and the sanctions in the wake of Pokhran-11 experiments have brought the company to the brink of sickness in 1998-99. ECIL suffered a loss of Rs.10 crore in 1997-98 and a substantial loss of Rs.60 crore in 1998-99. The networth of the company was badly eroded and ECIL had to be reported to BIFR.

The Initiatives in Materials Management

The company had to initiate a number of innovative measurers to tide over the crisis. Material costs constituting around 55-60% of the total cost, it became imperative for the company to introduce a host of innovative practices in the area of materials management. These initiatives need to be in consonance with the nature of global electronics business characterised by high rate of obsolescence, falling prices, high quality inputs and global sourcing. More over the business environment of ECIL is different even from other PSUs as there is no assured market, customer-driven requirements and threat of denials. It is against this background that the entire supply chain is addressed and briefed below are the salient aspects of this process.

Supplier Communication

It was ensured that the requirements of the customers of ECIL are clearly communicated to the suppliers, thus making the latter jointly responsible for ensuring customer satisfaction. This is done through constant touch with the suppliers to indicate the priorities through written and verbal means and by hosting vendor meets Vendor Development and Quality Assurance.

The suppliers were continuously provided all the support during product development and engineering, prototype testing, evaluation, qualification and guidance in the implementation of ISO 9000 Quality Management system and other industry standards and practices. Emphasis was on prevention rather than detection and correction. Suppliers are encouraged to imbibe the culture of 'Ownership of Quality' as?

Inventory Control

The scheduling of placement of orders and receipt of materials was streamlined to ensure efficient inventory management covering such requirements as timely availability of material, minimisation of waste and surplus due to obsolescence etc.

Negotiations and Payments

Suppliers are involved right from the tender stage to offer the most competitive terms to the customers in terms of quality, cost and delivery. Mutually beneficial payment terms are negotiated and strictly adhered to.

Implementation of IT

All the processes involved in Integrated Materials Management are fully computerised for speedy disposal of material requisitions, resulting in substantial reductions in lead times across various operations.

The Results

These simple intiatives were implemented effectively resulting in incredible results that culminated in the historic turnaround of the company that brought wide recognition and national awards like SCOPE award for Outstanding Performance and Contribution to Public Sector Management. Specifically the following achievements were realised.

Between 1998-99 and 2002-03

- Turnover shot up from Rs. 250 crore to Rs. 1000 crore
- Profitability reversed from a loss of Rs. 60 crore to a profit of 130 crore
- Networth increased from Rs. 7 crore to Rs. 309 crore
- Loans Outstanding and Statutory Outstandings became nil
- Inventory levels and Sundry Debtors demonstrated efficient Working Capital Management
- Substantial cost Reductions were realised through negotiations and improved quality levels across various processes
- Procurement lead-times reduced substantially from about 60 days to 30 days Customer Satisfaction Index improved phenominally from 66% to 95%
- MoU rating of 'Excellent' has been achieved and is maintained and
- Image of the company enhanced remarkably.

Future Plans

The multi-disciplinary competencies and capabilities of ECIL coupled with the Strategic Sectors it has chosen, is bound to give the company a competitive advantage to succeed in the national market but explore avenues in the international market. Many of its products have been identified for export promotion and the brilliant performance of the Electronic Voting Machines in the recent general elections established its export worthiness with many countries evincing interest in the product. While all the processes under materials management are fully computerised, plans are underway to instal a fully IT enabled Supply Chain Management including e-procurement. The company is fully aware of the competitive global environment surrounding it in the high technology electronics and is focussing continuously on enhancing its technology base and enrichning its skill base to strengthen its status as a valued national asset.

Case discussion:

Discuss the ECIL customer-centric model.

One of the business ideologies that have gained the maximum currency in the recent past is the customer-centric business operations. With the immense power bestowed upon customers by the Internet, companies were forced to sit up and think about their business models. Companies modified their businesses from company-centric models to customer-centric models, where customers were the focal points in all matters. They enjoyed the power of information and speed.

But today, customer-centricism has been taken to a new different level– customer driven models. In this new scenario, companies explicitly solicit customers' opinions and ideas to further enhance the products and services. The simple objective is to bring the brand closer to customers and in line with their needs and wants.

A case in point is Procter & Gamble' Vocalpoint. Vocalpoint is a new initiative of Procter & Gamble to enhance their brand with influential moms. The interactive website allows mothers to register and offer opinions on Procter & Gamble' products in exchange for special discounts, coupons, inside information about new products and samples of products in pipeline. This way, Procter & Gamble ensures that its customers are involved in the product development process from an early stage.

This initiative not only helps Procter & Gamble to constantly feel the pulse on the market in the specific segments but also facilitates an emotional bonding between the customers and the brand. The result is a very focused and cost-efficient approach to research and development that helps Procter & Gamble to drive brand innovation across new boundaries.

7.4 IMPLICATIONS OF CUSTOMER-CENTRIC ORGANIZATIONAL MODEL

The following are the implications of customer-centric organization model:

1. Improving the Basic performance: The top level management pays attention to personal and organizational performance measurement, process mindedness, personal integrity, and knowledge and talent management. Performance measurement is confined to the organization's financial statements, deciding on pay raises for employees, and transactional process improvements. Further attention is given to the performance implications of personal integrity. As a consequence, there is mutual trust and increase of talent in the organization.
2. Although organizations have recognized the value of a customer focus for several decades, fewer than 20% of marketing organizations among Global 1000 enterprises report that they have evolved enough to leverage customer-centric, value-added processes and capabilities successfully. The first step in the migration from a product-centric to a customer-centric organization is the informal coordination of customer-connecting activities, such as sales calls across product silos (i.e., implementing a customer-focused sales campaign).
3. The customer-focused sales campaigns are theoretically expected to increase profits and improve return on investment (ROI).
4. A customer-focused sales campaign also improved the relationship quality between the customer and the firm.
5. Customer-facing activities, such as sales calls, can be realized by (1) understanding each customer's needs, (2) by customizing the firm's offerings to customer needs, and (3) by coordinating sales calls across product silos to deliver a consistent and single message to the customer.
6. Determine the value of customers. The customer value led to the customer profitability of an organization.
7. Helps in Correlate customer acquisition and retention costs to customer profitability.
8. Understand the profitability implications of customer transactions through multiple channels.

9. The organization know how much they should invest in building their brand to maximize customer profitability.
10. Identify whether the most profitable customers are also the best customers in providing the maximum referral.
11. Determine the strength of individual customer relationships.
12. Know when or whether to intervene to prevent customer attrition. This part is considered as most important one.
13. Offer the right product to the right customer at the right time.
14. Manage the merchandise return process for maximum profitability.
15. Employ the best strategies for cross-selling/up-selling.
16. Develop the right strategic orientation to implement a customer-focused strategy.
17. Find out how to link their branding investment to Customer Lifetime Value.
18. Developing customer retention strategies.
19. Developing a core service around which to build a customer relationship. Customizing the relationship to the individual customer, augmenting the core service with extra benefits.
20. Pricing services to encourage customer loyalty, marketing to employees so that they will perform well for customers.

7.5 A CUSTOMER-FOCUSED APPROACH LEADS TO CUSTOMER MAPPING

The successful customer focused approach leads to customer mapping. The customer mapping may be defined as graphical representation of a procedure, process, structure, or system that depicts arrangement of customer in an organization's focus point and relationships of these customers among its different components, and traces flows of energy, goods, information, materials, money, etc.

The customer mapping provides complete information about a customer of an organization. The following is the customer information mapping which shows the complete information about a customer.

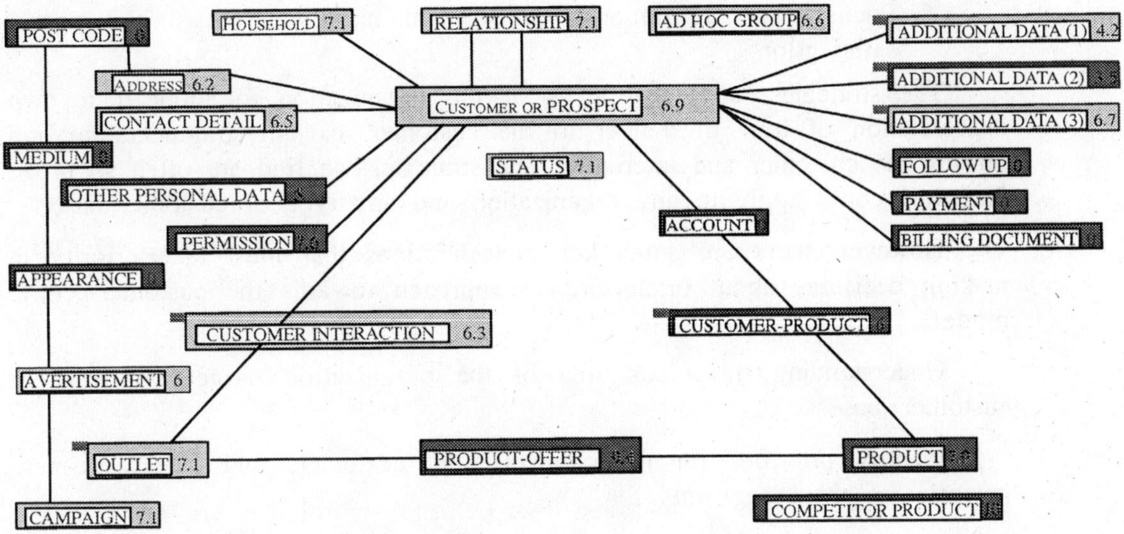

Adapted from http://thecustomerframework.com/

The customer information mapping focuses on the following

1. status of the customer
2. the relationship of the organization with the customer
3. personal data of the customer
4. address of the customer
6. customer's interaction with the organization
7. customer-product relationship etc.

7.6 THE CUSTOMER-CENTRIC ORGANIZATION: FROM PUSHING PRODUCTS TO WINNING CUSTOMERS

From a selling function perspective, a customer-centric culture includes, but is not limited to, the following major components (Chally Group 1998):

1. Adoption of a relationship or partnership business model, with mutually shared rewards and risk management.
2. Defining the selling role in terms of the provision of customer business consultation and solutions.
3. Increased formalization of customer analysis processes and agreements.
4. Taking a proactive leadership role in educating customers about value chain and cost reduction opportunities.

5. Focusing on continuous improvement principles stressing customer satisfaction.

The strategies, allow all areas of the organization to adopt their own interpretation of how to deliver to the customer, causing fragmentation and serving the customer and internally. The strategies we find are often so broad that they could apply to any organization and any type of customer base.

However, there are some key considerations that must take priority in making decisions about organizational approach towards the customer-centric model.

Understanding the focus area of the organization /target segments or customer bases.

Identify priorities for the company and customers and assess business potential of these segments.

Ensure cross functional teams are wrapped around these segments as far as possible, either virtually or physically.

Ensure that targets and measures are reviewed – clashing measures need to be removed or changed and new ones implemented – to motivate and reward these teams for delivering to these segments.

Understand skills, competencies, knowledge bases and attitudes – and build a plan to encourage the development require delivering customer-centric business success.

Encourage internal and customer input to your organizational structure through feedback and involvement mechanisms.

7.7 APPROACHES TO CUSTOMER-CENTRIC ORGANIZATIONAL MODEL

The above diagram shows the customer-centric model of an organization.

The following are the areas concentrated by the customer-centric organization

Professional service foundation

Services segments

Services benefits

Services objectives

Services goal

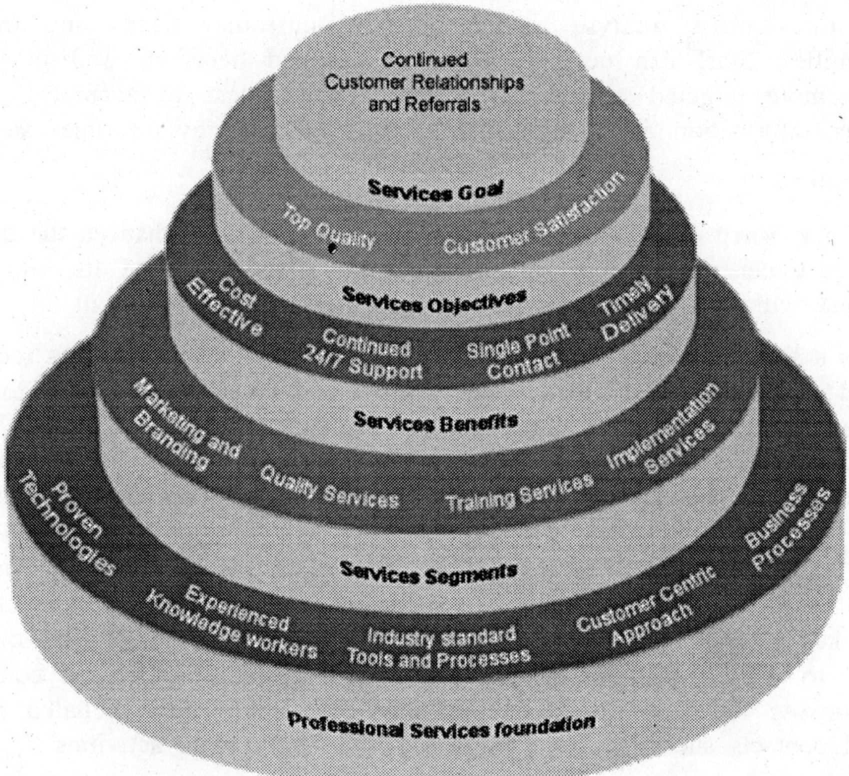

Continued customer relationships and referrals.

Example:

Merck Sharp & Dohme New Zealand (MSD NZ) is a subsidiary of international pharmaceutical, Merck & Co. Based in Auckland, MSD NZ employs over 95 people in roles ranging from sales and marketing through to clinical research, customer services and administration.

Challenge: To transition from a reach-and-frequency contact model to a customer-centric model that delivers new ways to capture, analyse and use customer and market intelligence to support sales and marketing objectives and enable strategic forward-planning.

Solution: Replace MSD NZ's tracking based electronic territory management system with a customer-centric solution comprised of StayinFront CRM with StayinFront Survey, StayinFront Workflow, StayinFront Campaign Management and StayinFront Analytics.

Result: MSD NZ has reduced its costs while significantly improving its ability to identify, analyse and respond to customer needs and market opportunities. Staff can now make more informed decisions and plan and execute more targeted campaigns through ready access to accurate, robust customer information and market intelligence, validated by customer surveys.

Example:

Merck Sharp & Dohme New Zealand (MSD NZ) has enhanced the quality of its customer relationships and boosted the effectiveness of its sales and marketing with a customer-centric CRM solution from StayinFront.

As a sales-focused pharmaceutical company, MSD NZ has always required its field representatives to make regular visits and calls to customers, logging outcomes in a traditional electronic territory management system (ETMS). While the old application documented information about its sales representatives' activities, MSD NZ wanted more tangible information about its customers.

Putting Customers First

MSD NZ identified the need for a more customer-centric sales model, based around key account management. Since MSD NZ 's 15-year- old ETMS did not allow it to analyse customer information in any meaningful way, the company went looking for a new customer information solution that included multi-channel contacts such as direct marketing and direct sales activities.

The following are the benefits of customer-centric approaches of the organization;

The organization uses a unique framework and measure business processes to find out exactly which ones benefit the customer or citizen

- Has clearly demonstrated cost reductions for client. Is built around clear goals and measurable objectives
- Leads to increased customer loyalty and drives customer profitability
- Will provide tools and approaches required to deal with future change and to address customer wants and needs
- Will make the organisation more agile and able to respond quickly, effectively and appropriately to the challenges posed by the customers.

According to Woodruff 'Woody' Driggs, "A survey across Australia, Brazil, Canada, China, France, Germany, India, the United States and the United Kingdom, we saw that customer services have become increasingly important and consumers are no longer driven by price. Expectations in China, Brazil and

India, are rising faster than any other developed economy. But eventually companies across the globe are failing to keep up the expectations. The gap is because the companies cannot deliver what customer expectations are. We saw 67% of the respondents say that they switched their major service providers as a result of poor service and, over 50% switched their service provider two times in the last one year. The service provider category includes wireless service providers, banks, retail firms and airlines. The gap is getting wider and therefore companies need to take it up as a concern."

Expectations are rising fast in the emerging markets as new technologies and services are being provided. One-third of our global sample and 67% of those in India described their expectations as higher now than one year ago; 52% globally and 85% in India described their expectations as higher now than five years ago.

In mature markets for customers in general, the bar has been raised across industries and have emerged into different service levels. So the customers are driven by knowledge of customer service representative, technical service availability and then price.

Indian respondents were least satisfied with their ability to resolve questions or issues on their own without speaking to a service agent. They are most frustrated with having to contact a customer service multiple times for the same reason and being placed on hold for a long time. Indian respondents along with those in Brazil and China were far more likely than those in other countries to expect much better service when they spend more or purchase more often.

Indians were most likely to consider customer service as the main factor for choosing a new provider after switching from an established one (cited by 79%), while convenience was the second-most popular factor (named by 69%). And for the largest percentage of Indians (about 79%), their preference would be to receive faster service. Indian consumers were the most likely (about 49% in our survey) to strongly agree that the use of technology in customer service has significantly improved service levels.

In India, calling for assistance is by far the preferred method for accessing customer service, cited by 85% of consumers.

The second-most popular method, sending an e-mail, was named by 68%, followed by getting information from the company's website (47%) and going to the company's place of business (31%). When they have a bad customer service experience, Indian consumers are among the most likely of those surveyed to say they will ask to speak to a supervisor (37%) and the most likely to send a formal complaint to the company (21%).

Source: Financial Express, 16th March, 2009.

Whirlpool case study

Whirlpool, right from its inception in 1911 as first commercial manufacturer of motorized washers to the current market position of being world's number one manufacturer and marketer of major home appliances, has always set industry milestones and benchmarks. The parent company is headquartered at Benton Harbour, Michigan, USA with a global presence in over 170 countries and manufacturing operation in 13 countries with 11 major brand names such as Whirlpool, KitchenAid, Roper, Estate, Bauknecht, Laden and Ignis. The company boasts of resources and capabilities beyond achievable feat of any other in the industry.

Whirlpool initiated its international expansion in 1958 by entering Brazil. However, it emerged as truly global leader in the 1980s. This encouraging trend brought the company to India in the late 1980s. It forayed into the market under a joint venture with TVS group and established the first Whirlpool manufacturing facility in Pondicherry.

Soon Whirlpool acquired Kelvinator India Limited in 1995 and marked an entry into Indian refrigerator market as well. The same year also saw acquisition of major share in TVS joint venture and later in 1996, Kelvinator and TVS acquisitions were merged to create Indian home appliance leader of the future, Whirlpool India. This expanded the company's portfolio in the Indian subcontinent to washing machines, refrigerator, microwave ovens and air-conditioners.

Today, Whirlpool is the most recognized brand in home appliances in India and holds a market share of over 25%. The company owns three state-of-the-art manufacturing facilities at Faridabad, Pondicherry and Pune. Each of these manufacturing set-ups features an infrastructure that is witness of Whirlpool's commitment to consumer interests and advanced technology.

In the year ending in March '09, the annual turnover of the company for its Indian enterprise was Rs.1,719 Crores.

The company's brand and image speaks of its commitment to the homemaker from every aspect of its functioning. It has derived its functioning principles out of an undaunted partnership with the homemakers and thus a slogan of "You and whirlpool, the world's best homemaker" dots its promotional campaigns. The products are engineered to suit the requirements of 'smart, confident and in-control' homemaker who knows what she wants. The product range is designed in a way that it employs unique technology and offers consumer relevant solutions.

Innovation: Unique and compelling solutions valued by our customers and aligned to our brands create competitive advantage and differentiated shareholder value.

Operational Excellence (OPEX): A methodology for solving problems and continuous improvement of products and processes through pursuit, acquisition, and utilization of knowledge using critical thought and planned experimentation helps us achieve operational excellence.

Customer Excellence: Excelling the customer expectation from the company, its brands, products and services are a three-step process. The three steps are: Know a customer, Be a customer, Serve a customer.

Knowing a customer helps us know who our customers are, how to treat them, how we add value, and what the drivers of brand loyalty are. This information is gathered from the customer's data base history. This way we are better able to customize products for them and recommend the right product to solve problems. Being a customer is important to share customer knowledge and insights, drive actions based on customer insights, be passionate about our brands and customer loyalty and provide a positive voice for our brands. We show empathy for customers and seek to resolve their problems by creating consistent customer touch-points, with our endeavour always being to provide unique solutions for the customer.

Supply chain management was not always a competitive advantage for Whirlpool. Penske initially partnered with Whirlpool as its single logistics provider for the quality express network. Penske was responsible for the logistics of the entire network, including managing the relationship of the two regions it subcontracted to Kenco. This Penske-Whirlpool partnership replaced Whirlpool's previous logistics solution, comprised of two incumbent third-party logistics providers. The partnership accomplished Whirlpool's early logistics objectives, most notably, to establish effective processes and procedures, allow for more visibility of the company's distribution network and reduce supply chain costs.

Recently, Whirlpool's management took a more customer-centric approach to analyzing its supply chain and began benchmarking its supply chain against other companies to identify "best in class" practices. This exercise prompted Whirlpool to question whether having a single logistics provider was the best structure to exceed customer expectations and maximize cost savings.

Case discussion:

1. Explain the customer-centric approach of Whirlpool India.

Case study -2

Tata Steel, the flagship of India's $22 billion Tata Group, is Asia's first and India's largest private-sector steel company. One of the lowest cost producers of steel in the world, it was ranked fifth in the Asian BusinessWeek 50 performers in 2005, and has twice topped the "World-Class Steelmakers" list issued by World Steel Dynamics, a leading steel information service. Tata recently purchased Thailand's Millennium Steel and Singapore's NatSteel Asia, and in January 2007 announced the acquisition of Anglo-Dutch Corus Group in a $12 billion transaction.

"Before we started looking at supply chain optimization, we suffered from all of the typical problems manufacturers face: non-optimized asset utilization, long cycle times, disparate IT systems and lack of visibility into demand, orders and shipments," says Anand Sen, vice president of Tata's Flat Product Division. "We knew that we simply couldn't meet our strategic objectives by maintaining the status quo."

Customer satisfaction

Customer satisfaction was a real issue at Tata Steel. When orders were placed, customers were promised a due date that was not based on hard data, plant capacity or raw material availability. Orders were delivered when promised only about 50 per cent of the time. To make matters worse, customers would generally not receive advance notice if their order would not be ready as promised, and this lack of communication burdened customer resources down the line, in the finishing and distribution channels.

The plant would often scramble to address the needs of high-priority customers, further alienating customers whose orders may have been just as important but less urgent. Without any method to analyze forecast versus actual performance, it was impossible to design improvements in the overall delivery system.

Realizing that its industry-leading position was hanging in the balance, Tata started the improvement process by articulating its strategic drivers: improved customer satisfaction and higher asset utilization. To address customer needs, the company conducted an exhaustive survey to establish detailed customer requirements. The survey yielded three imperatives. First, provide an accurate promise as to when the order would be delivered. Second, in the event that the order due date would be missed, notify the customer early in the process—not at the point of the missed delivery. And third, accurately project a revised delivery date so that the customer could modify its schedules accordingly.

Business process reengineering

After mapping the entire supply chain process in great detail, Tata engaged in an extensive business process reengineering effort. The objectives were to evaluate the gaps in current supply chain processes with respect to industry demands, to redesign the processes to achieve a dominant service position and to identify the IT enablers that could make this happen. "We saw the relationship with i2 as a critical partnership," says Biswajit Roychowdhury, chief of planning for Tata's Flat Steel Division. "Our final decision to go with i2 Sales and Operations Planning, i2 Factory Planner and i2 Material Allocator was the culmination of a long process of due diligence and included all members of executive management."

The business issues Tata wanted its process reengineering and IT implementation to address included:

Optimizing inventory investment, including raw materials, work-in-process and finished inventories

Maximizing the value of supplier relationships

Improving the accuracy of price and volume forecasts

Determining the best product mix

Making reliable customer delivery promises

Utilizing key assets optimally

Prioritizing orders for key customers

Improving quality and product yields through better scheduling decisions

Improving transportation efficiency

Tata Steel completed its technology implementation earlier this year and has seen significant improvements already in critical areas. Most importantly, 85 per cent of orders are promised within the desired delivery week and do not require any manual intervention or adjustment—up from 50 per cent. "Sometimes it's even as high as 92 per cent," asserts Roychowdhury. "Now, when we understand that an order is in jeopardy, we have the tools in place to troubleshoot the order and can often take corrective action to fix the problem before we even have to notify the customer." In addition, late orders running in the production line have been reduced to less than 10 per cent, and order booking efficiency has risen to above 80 per cent.

Forecasting capability

Tata's forecasting ability has also improved dramatically. Prior to implementing supply chain software, the company had no systematic insight into how to evaluate the accuracy of its forecasts for demand as well as for raw materials. Now, it has the tools to analyze its forecast predictions against actual results, enabling root-cause analysis capabilities to identify what has caused the differences. "Improving our ability to forecast allows us to use due-date-based planning, which helps us to meet demand with higher utilization of assets," says Roychowdhury. "Also, instead of manually balancing resources as before, we can now automatically identify bottlenecks deep in our processes, and take corrective action to increase our overall production efficiency, thus realizing the benefits of continuous improvement. In support of our strategic objectives, our supply chain data are fully integrated with the rest of Tata Steel's business infrastructure, so we're able to scale effectively as we grow."

The new generation software from i2 has given Tata planners several capabilities they lacked prior to implementation. Planners can now project business over a year's time and monitor performance against those projections. They can also make product-mix decisions based on profit optimization goals and take orders as late as possible with postponement strategies. Tata's planners can also refresh the expected time of arrival with up-to-the-minute information.

Prognosis

The rapid pace of change in the steel industry—and, for that matter, in heavy industrial manufacturing in general—is not expected to slow down. Stoked by these results, Tata executives are optimistic. "We're shifting from being order-takers in a relatively controlled pricing environment 20 years ago to being sophisticated marketers adroitly negotiating the profitable space between supply and demand across multiple markets on an almost daily basis," says Sen. "Someday, we'll be able to predict not just the delivery date, but the actual hour that our truck will be pulling up to a customer's warehouse. It opens up a whole world of possibilities."

1. Discuss the customer-centric model adopted by the Tata Steel.

Emerging issues in customer-centric approach

The master data management (MDM) market is predicted to grow to $10.4 billion by 2009, with a compound annual growth rate of 13.8 per cent, according to industry analyst firm IDC. Other analyst firms, such as Gartner and Forrester, claim that MDM provides significant business benefits and is a critical foundation for managing enterprise information assets. Not surprisingly, the market hype from the mega-vendor triad (IBM, Oracle, and SAP) has been deafening as each one attempts to position its platform as a single enterprisewide solution for an organization's MDM strategy.

Companies generally recognize that customer-centric master data management solutions help achieve critical cross-functional business imperatives to bolster customer profitability, reduce operational costs, and adhere to regulatory compliance. However, many IT departments are finding it difficult to persuade business to take the MDM plunge. Often they don't know how to begin building a compelling business case, or their choice of architecture limits the return on investment and makes it difficult to deliver on the business case.

The final principal dictates that, wherever possible, organizations need to explain how the customer-centric MDM initiative will help in addressing strategic top-of-mind issues. Instead of competing for attention and funding, position the MDM business case as part of a larger business solution without devaluing the initiative. For example, there are several top-of-mind issues which customer-centric MDM can help address, including:

For high technology: return-on-marketing-investment and marketing-analytics measurement demand accurate and unified customer views.

In the financial services sector: Basel II has created the need for effective counterparty management, and increased competition requires improvements to the customer experience.

For pharmaceutical companies: current mandates include the newly established physician "gift law" and the need to create unified customer views in the face of increased competition, government regulations, and corporate consolidation.

At insurance companies: acquisitions are driving the requirement for improved visibility across the organization.

In the manufacturing sector: pressure is mounting to correct perceived failures of prior CRM and data warehouse efforts.

Implementing a customer-centric solution

Understanding the customers must be the first step in achieving improved service delivery.

Creating a consolidated, holistic view of each customer, whether across a single council or a consortium, and capturing information from all touch-points and across all functions, allows the organization to better understand the customer and their needs. Furthermore, the organization internal communication is also improved through the sharing and transfer of knowledge.

Streamlining the organization's business processes means all customers are managed in a consistent, professional manner, whilst ensuring the appropriate level of information is captured to resolve or progress the enquiry to the appropriate specialist.

The introduction of scheduled follow up courtesy calls allows the organisation to take a more proactive approach to customer service delivery leading to increased customer satisfaction.

Defining and executing notification and escalation processes, based on internal targets or external service level agreements, prevent enquiries from slipping through the net and ensure all enquiries are followed up in a timely manner.

Provide a single, unified face to the internal customer Shared Services for the internal customer can encompass all of the back-office teams including the HR, Payroll and Finance functions.

7.8 SUMMARY

The customer experience is the sum of all experiences a customer has with a supplier of goods or services, over the duration of their relationship with that supplier. It can also be used to mean an individual experience over one transaction; the distinction is usually clear in context.The concept of customer experience was first introduced by Pine and Gilmore in their 1998 *Harvard Business Review* article. A recent Bain & Company survey reveals just how commonly companies misread the market. They surveyed 362 firms and found that 80 per cent believed they delivered a "superior experience" to their customers. But when they asked customers about their own perceptions, they found that they rated only 8 per cent of companies as truly delivering a superior experience. Clearly, it's easy for leading companies to assume they're keeping customers happy; it's quite another thing to achieve that kind of customer devotion. customer-facing activities, such as sales calls, can be realized by (1) understanding each customer's needs, (2) by customizing the firm's offerings to customer needs, and (3) by coordinating sales calls across product silos to deliver a consistent and single message to the customer. The emerging trend in customer-centric approach is the master data management (MDM) market is predicted to grow to $10.4 billion by 2009, with a compound annual growth rate of 13.8 per cent, according to industry analyst firm IDC. Other analyst firms, such as Gartner and Forrester, claim that MDM provides significant business benefits and is a critical foundation for managing enterprise information assets.

7.9 SELF ASSESSMENT QUESTIONS

Part – A

1. Define customer experience
2. Distinguish between customer experience and superior customer experience.
3. What is customer profitability?
4. What is master data management?
5. What is the need for customer experience management?

Part – B

1. Explain the implications of customer-centric organizational model
2. Define Emotional Experience Design (EED).What are the implications of Emotional Experience Design (EED)? Discuss.
3. Discuss steps involved in building a strong brand and an optimized customer experience.

Objective type questions

1. The concept of customer experience was first introduced by
   (a) Pine and Gilmore
   (b) Pine and Bain
   (c) Gilmore and Drucker
   (d) Peter Drucker and Pine
2. The emerging trend in customer-centric approach is the
   (a) Master data management
   (b) Master file management
   (c) Master focus management
   (d) Master customer management

3. Customer profitability (CP) is the difference between the
   (a) Revenues earned from and the costs associated with the customer relationship in a specified period.
   (b) Expenses incurred and the costs associated with the customer relationship in a specified period.
   (c) Revenues earned from and the expenses associated with the customer relationship in a specified period.
   (d) Revenues earned from and the capital associated with the customer relationship in a specified period.

□□□

NOTES

NOTES